Developing Web Applications with Haskell and Yesod

Michael Snoyman

Beijing · Cambridge · Farnham · Köln · Sebastopol · Tokyo

Developing Web Applications with Haskell and Yesod

by Michael Snoyman

Copyright © 2012 Michael Snoyman. All rights reserved.
Printed in the United States of America.

Published by O'Reilly Media, Inc., 1005 Gravenstein Highway North, Sebastopol, CA 95472.

O'Reilly books may be purchased for educational, business, or sales promotional use. Online editions are also available for most titles (*http://my.safaribooksonline.com*). For more information, contact our corporate/institutional sales department: 800-998-9938 or *corporate@oreilly.com*.

Editor: Simon St. Laurent	**Cover Designer:** Karen Montgomery
Production Editor: Iris Febres	**Interior Designer:** David Futato
Proofreader: Iris Febres	**Illustrator:** Robert Romano

Revision History for the First Edition:
  2012-04-20   First release
See *http://oreilly.com/catalog/errata.csp?isbn=9781449316976* for release details.

Nutshell Handbook, the Nutshell Handbook logo, and the O'Reilly logo are registered trademarks of O'Reilly Media, Inc. *Developing Web Applications with Haskell and Yesod*, the rhinoceros beetle, the mountain apollo butterfly, and related trade dress are trademarks of O'Reilly Media, Inc.

Many of the designations used by manufacturers and sellers to distinguish their products are claimed as trademarks. Where those designations appear in this book, and O'Reilly Media, Inc., was aware of a trademark claim, the designations have been printed in caps or initial caps.

While every precaution has been taken in the preparation of this book, the publisher and authors assume no responsibility for errors or omissions, or for damages resulting from the use of the information contained herein.

ISBN: 978-1-449-31697-6

[LSI]

1334936558

Table of Contents

Preface ix

Part I. Basics

1. Introduction 3
    Type Safety   3
    Concise   4
    Performance   4
    Modular   4
    A Solid Foundation   5
    Introduction to Haskell   5

2. Haskell 7
    Terminology   7
    Tools   8
    Language Pragmas   9
    Overloaded Strings   10
    Type Families   11
    Template Haskell   12
    QuasiQuotes   13
    Summary   13

3. Basics 15
    Hello World   15
    Routing   16
    Handler Function   17
    The Foundation   18
    Running   18
    Resources and Type-Safe URLs   19
    The Scaffolded Site   20

iii

	Development Server	20
	Summary	21

4. Shakespearean Templates 23
Synopsis	23
Hamlet (HTML)	23
Cassius (CSS)	24
Lucius (CSS)	24
Julius (JavaScript)	24
Types	24
Type-Safe URLs	26
Syntax	27
Hamlet Syntax	27
Cassius Syntax	32
Lucius Syntax	32
Julius Syntax	33
Calling Shakespeare	33
Alternate Hamlet Types	35
Other Shakespeare	37
General Recommendations	37

5. Widgets 39
Synopsis	39
What's in a Widget?	40
Constructing Widgets	41
Combining Widgets	42
Generate IDs	42
whamlet	43
Types	44
Using Widgets	45
Summary	46

6. Yesod Typeclass 49
Rendering and Parsing URLs	49
joinPath	50
cleanPath	51
defaultLayout	52
getMessage	53
Custom Error Pages	54
External CSS and JavaScript	54
Smarter Static Files	55
Authentication/Authorization	56
Some Simple Settings	57

Summary	57

7. Routing and Handlers 59
Route Syntax	59
Pieces	60
Resource Name	61
Handler Specification	62
Dispatch	63
Return Type	63
Arguments	64
The Handler Monad	64
Application Information	65
Request Information	65
Short Circuiting	66
Response Headers	66
Summary	67

8. Forms 69
Synopsis	69
Kinds of Forms	71
Types	72
Converting	74
Create AForms	74
Optional Fields	75
Validation	76
More Sophisticated Fields	77
Running Forms	78
i18n	79
Monadic Forms	80
Input Forms	82
Custom Fields	83
Summary	84

9. Sessions 85
Clientsession	85
Controlling Sessions	86
Session Operations	87
Messages	87
Ultimate Destination	89
Summary	91

10. Persistent 93
Synopsis	94

Solving the Boundary Issue	94
Types	95
Code Generation	96
PersistStore	98
Migrations	99
Uniqueness	101
Queries	102
Fetching by ID	102
Fetching by Unique Constraint	103
Select Functions	103
Manipulation	105
Insert	105
Update	106
Delete	107
Attributes	108
Relations	110
Closer Look at Types	111
Custom Fields	113
Persistent: Raw SQL	113
Integration with Yesod	114
Summary	116

11. Deploying Your Webapp 117

Compiling	117
Warp	117
Configuration	118
Server Process	120
FastCGI	120
Desktop	121
CGI on Apache	121
FastCGI on lighttpd	122
CGI on lighttpd	123

Part II. Advanced

12. RESTful Content 127

Request Methods	127
Representations	128
RepHtmlJson	129
News Feeds	131
Other Request Headers	131
Stateless	132

Summary   132

13. Yesod's Monads 135
Monad Transformers   135
The Three Transformers   136
Example: Database-Driven Navbar   137
Example: Request Information   139
Summary   140

14. Authentication and Authorization 141
Overview   141
Authenticate Me   142
Email   145
Authorization   149
Conclusion   151

15. Scaffolding and the Site Template 153
How to Scaffold   153
File Structure   154
    Cabal File   154
    Routes and Entities   155
    Foundation and Application Modules   155
    Import   156
    Handler Modules   157
widgetFile   157
defaultLayout   158
Static Files   158
Conclusion   159

16. Internationalization 161
Synopsis   161
Overview   163
Message Files   164
    Specifying Types   165
RenderMessage Typeclass   165
Interpolation   166
Phrases, Not Words   167

17. Creating a Subsite 169
Hello World   169

Part III. Examples

18. Blog: i18n, Authentication, Authorization, and Database 175

19. Wiki: Markdown, Chat Subsite, Event Source 185

20. JSON Web Service 193
    Server   193
    Client   194

21. Case Study: Sphinx-Based Search 197
    Sphinx Setup   197
    Basic Yesod Setup   198
    Searching   200
    Streaming xmlpipe Output   203
    Full Code   206

Part IV. Appendices

A. monad-control 213

B. Conduit 223

C. Web Application Interface 255

D. Settings Types 259

E. http-conduit 261

F. xml-conduit 267

Preface

It's fair to say that dynamic languages currently dominate the web development scene. Ruby, Python, and PHP are common choices for quickly creating a powerful web application. They give a much faster and more comfortable development setting than standard static languages in the C family, like Java.

But some of us are looking for something more in our development toolbox. We want a language that gives us guarantees that our code is doing what it should. Instead of writing up a unit test to cover every bit of functionality in our application, wouldn't it be wonderful if the compiler could *automatically* ensure that our code is correct? And as an added bonus, wouldn't it be nice if our code ran quickly too?

These are the goals of Yesod. Yesod is a web framework bringing the strengths of the Haskell programming language to the web development world. Yesod not only uses a pure language to interact with an impure world, it allows safe interactions with the outside world by automatically sanitizing incoming and outgoing data. Not only do we avoid basic mistakes such as mixing up integers and strings, it even allows us to statically prevent many cases of security holes like cross-site scripting (XSS) attacks.

Who This Book Is For

In general, there are two groups of people coming to Yesod. The first group is long time Haskell users—already convinced of the advantages of Haskell—who are looking for a powerful framework for creating web applications. The second is web developers who are either dissatisfied with their existing tools, or are looking to expand their horizons into the functional world.

This book assumes a basic familiarity with both web development and Haskell. We don't use many complicated Haskell concepts, and those we do use are introduced separately. For the most part, understanding the basics of the syntax of the language should be sufficient.

If you want to come up to speed on Haskell, I recommend another wonderful O'Reilly book: *Real World Haskell* (http://shop.oreilly.com/product/9780596514983.do).

Conventions Used in This Book

The following typographical conventions are used in this book:

Italic
: Indicates new terms, URLs, email addresses, filenames, and file extensions.

`Constant width`
: Used for program listings, as well as within paragraphs to refer to program elements such as variable or function names, databases, data types, environment variables, statements, and keywords.

`Constant width bold`
: Shows commands or other text that should be typed literally by the user.

`Constant width italic`
: Shows text that should be replaced with user-supplied values or by values determined by context.

 This icon signifies a tip, suggestion, or general note.

 This icon indicates a warning or caution.

Using Code Examples

This book is here to help you get your job done. In general, you may use the code in this book in your programs and documentation. You do not need to contact us for permission unless you're reproducing a significant portion of the code. For example, writing a program that uses several chunks of code from this book does not require permission. Selling or distributing a CD-ROM of examples from O'Reilly books does require permission. Answering a question by citing this book and quoting example code does not require permission. Incorporating a significant amount of example code from this book into your product's documentation does require permission.

We appreciate, but do not require, attribution. An attribution usually includes the title, author, publisher, and ISBN. For example: "*Developing Web Applications with Haskell and Yesod* by Michael Snoyman (O'Reilly). Copyright 2012 Michael Snoyman, 978-1-449-31697-6."

If you feel your use of code examples falls outside fair use or the permission given above, feel free to contact us at *permissions@oreilly.com*.

Safari® Books Online

Safari Books Online (*www.safaribooksonline.com*) is an on-demand digital library that delivers expert content in both book and video form from the world's leading authors in technology and business.

Technology professionals, software developers, web designers, and business and creative professionals use Safari Books Online as their primary resource for research, problem solving, learning, and certification training.

Safari Books Online offers a range of product mixes and pricing programs for organizations, government agencies, and individuals. Subscribers have access to thousands of books, training videos, and prepublication manuscripts in one fully searchable database from publishers like O'Reilly Media, Prentice Hall Professional, Addison-Wesley Professional, Microsoft Press, Sams, Que, Peachpit Press, Focal Press, Cisco Press, John Wiley & Sons, Syngress, Morgan Kaufmann, IBM Redbooks, Packt, Adobe Press, FT Press, Apress, Manning, New Riders, McGraw-Hill, Jones & Bartlett, Course Technology, and dozens more. For more information about Safari Books Online, please visit us online.

How to Contact Us

Please address comments and questions concerning this book to the publisher:

O'Reilly Media, Inc.
1005 Gravenstein Highway North
Sebastopol, CA 95472
800-998-9938 (in the United States or Canada)
707-829-0515 (international or local)
707-829-0104 (fax)

We have a web page for this book, where we list errata, examples, and any additional information. You can access this page at:

http://shop.oreilly.com/product/0636920023142.do

To comment or ask technical questions about this book, send email to:

bookquestions@oreilly.com

For more information about our books, courses, conferences, and news, see our website at *http://www.oreilly.com*.

Find us on Facebook: *http://facebook.com/oreilly*

Follow us on Twitter: *http://twitter.com/oreillymedia*

Watch us on YouTube: *http://www.youtube.com/oreillymedia*

Acknowledgements

Yesod has been created by an entire community of developers, all of whom have put in significant effort to make sure that the final product is as polished and user-friendly as possible. Everyone from the core development team to the person making an API request on the mailing list has had an impact on bringing Yesod to where it is today.

In particular, I'd like to thank Greg Weber, who has shared the maintenance burden of the project; Kazu Yamamoto and Matt Brown, who transformed Warp from a simple testing server to one of the fastest application servers available today; and Felipe Lessa, Patrick Brisbin, and Luite Stegeman for their numerous contributions across the board.

A big thank you to my editor, Simon St. Laurent, for all of his guidance and support. Mark Lentczner, Johan Tibell, and Adam Turoff provided incredibly thorough reviews of this book, cleaning up many of my mistakes. Additionally, there have been dozens of readers who have looked over the content of this book online, and provided feedback on where either the prose or the message was not coming through clearly—not to mention numerous spelling errors.

But finally, and most importantly, I'd like to thank my wife, Miriam, for enduring all of the time spent on both this book and Yesod in general. She has been my editor and sounding-board, though I'm sure the intricacies of Template Haskell sometimes worked more as a sedative than any meaningful conversation. Without her support, neither the Yesod project nor this book would have been able to happen.

Also, you'll notice that I use my kids' names (Eliezer and Gavriella) in some examples throughout the book. They deserve special mention in a Haskell text, since I think they're the youngest people to ever use the word "monad" in a sentence with their "Transformers: Monads in Disguise."

PART I
Basics

CHAPTER 1
Introduction

Since web programming began, people have been trying to make the development process a more pleasant one. As a community, we have continually pushed new techniques to try and solve some of the lingering difficulties of security threats, the stateless nature of HTTP, the multiple languages (HTML, CSS, JavaScript) necessary to create a powerful web application, and more.

Yesod attempts to ease the web development process by playing to the strengths of the Haskell programming language. Haskell's strong compile-time guarantees of correctness not only encompass types; referential transparency ensures that we don't have any unintended side effects. Pattern matching on algebraic data types can help guarantee we've accounted for every possible case. By building upon Haskell, entire classes of bugs disappear.

Unfortunately, using Haskell isn't enough. The Web, by its very nature, is *not* type safe. Even the simplest case of distinguishing between an integer and string is impossible: all data on the Web is transferred as raw bytes, evading our best efforts at type safety. Every app writer is left with the task of validating all input. I call this problem *the boundary issue*: as much as your application is type safe on the inside, every boundary with the outside world still needs to be sanitized.

Type Safety

This is where Yesod comes in. By using high-level declarative techniques, you can specify the exact input types you are expecting. And the process works the other way as well: using a process of type-safe URLs, you can make sure that the data you send out is also guaranteed to be well formed.

The boundary issue is not just a problem when dealing with the client: the same problem exists when persisting and loading data. Once again, Yesod saves you on the boundary by performing the marshaling of data for you. You can specify your entities in a high-level definition and remain blissfully ignorant of the details.

Concise

We all know that there is a lot of boilerplate coding involved in web applications. Wherever possible, Yesod tries to use Haskell's features to save your fingers the work:

- The forms library reduces the amount of code used for common cases by leveraging the Applicative type class.
- Routes are declared in a very terse format, without sacrificing type safety.
- Serializing your data to and from a database is handled automatically via code generation.

In Yesod, we have two kinds of code generation. To get your project started, we provide a scaffolding tool to set up your file and folder structure. However, most code generation is done at compile time via meta programming. This means your generated code will never get stale, as a simple library upgrade will bring all your generated code up-to-date.

But for those who like to stay in control, and know exactly what their code is doing, you can always run closer to the compiler and write all your code yourself.

Performance

Haskell's main compiler, the GHC, has amazing performance characteristics, and is improving all the time. This choice of language by itself gives Yesod a large performance advantage over other offerings. But that's not enough: we need an architecture designed for performance.

Our approach to templates is one example: by allowing HTML, CSS, and JavaScript to be analyzed at compile time, Yesod both avoids costly disk I/O at runtime and can optimize the rendering of this code. But the architectural decisions go deeper: we use advanced techniques such as conduits and builders in the underlying libraries to make sure our code runs in constant memory, without exhausting precious file handles and other resources. By offering high-level abstractions, you can get highly compressed and properly cached CSS and JavaScript.

Yesod's flagship web server, Warp, is the fastest Haskell web server around. When these two pieces of technology are combined, it produces one of the fastest web application deployment solutions available.

Modular

Yesod has spawned the creation of dozens of packages, most of which are usable in a context outside of Yesod itself. One of the goals of the project is to contribute back to the community as much as possible; as such, even if you are not planning on using

Yesod in your next project, a large portion of this book may still be relevant for your needs.

Of course, these libraries have all been designed to integrate well together. Using the Yesod Framework should give you a strong feeling of consistency throughout the >various APIs.

A Solid Foundation

I remember once seeing a PHP framework advertising support for UTF-8. This struck me as surprising: you mean having UTF-8 support isn't automatic? In the Haskell world, issues like character encoding are already well addressed and fully supported. In fact, we usually have the opposite problem: there are a number of packages providing powerful and well-designed support for the problem. The Haskell community is constantly pushing the boundaries finding the cleanest, most efficient solutions for each challenge.

The downside of such a powerful ecosystem is the complexity of choice. By using Yesod, you will already have most of the tools chosen for you, and you can be guaranteed they work together. Of course, you always have the option of pulling in your own solution.

As a real-life example, Yesod and Hamlet (the default templating language) use `blaze-builder` for textual content generation. This choice was made because blaze provides the fastest interface for generating UTF-8 data. Anyone who wants to use one of the other great libraries out there, such as `text`, should have no problem dropping it in.

Introduction to Haskell

Haskell is a powerful, fast, type-safe, functional programming language. This book takes as an assumption that you are already familiar with most of the basics of Haskell. There are two wonderful books for learning Haskell, both of which are available for reading online:

- Learn You a Haskell for Great Good! (*http://learnyouahaskell.com*)
- Real World Haskell (*http://book.realworldhaskell.org/read*)

Yesod relies on a few features in Haskell that most introductory tutorials do not cover. Though you will rarely need to understand how these work, it's always best to start off with a good appreciation for what your tools are doing. These are covered in the next chapter.

CHAPTER 2
Haskell

In order to use Yesod, you're going to have to know at least the basics of Haskell. Additionally, Yesod uses some features of Haskell that aren't covered in most introductory texts. While this book assumes the reader has a basic familiarity with Haskell, this chapter is intended to fill in the gaps.

If you are already fluent in Haskell, feel free to completely skip this chapter. Also, if you would prefer to start off by getting your feet wet with Yesod, you can always come back to this chapter later as a reference.

If you are looking for a more thorough introduction to Haskell, I would recommend either *Real World Haskell* or *Learn You a Haskell*.

Terminology

Even for those familiar with Haskell as a language, there can sometimes be some confusion about terminology. Let's establish some base terms that we can use throughout this book.

Data type
> This is one of the core building blocks for a strongly typed language like Haskell. Some data types, like Int, can be treated as primitive values, while other data types will build on top of these to create more complicated values. For example, you might represent a person with:
>
> ```
> data Person = Person Text Int
> ```

Here, the Text would give the person's name, and the Int would give the person's age. Due to its simplicity, this specific example type will recur throughout the book. There are essentially three ways you can create a new data type:

- A type declaration such as type GearCount = Int merely creates a synonym for an existing type. The type system will do nothing to prevent you from using an Int where you asked for a GearCount. Using this can make your code more self-documenting.

- A newtype declaration such as `newtype Make = Make Text`. In this case, you cannot accidentally use a `Text` in place of a `Make`; the compiler will stop you. The newtype wrapper always disappears during compilation, and will introduce no overhead.
- A data declaration, such as `Person` above. You can also create Algebraic Data Types (ADTs), such as `data Vehicle = Bicycle GearCount | Car Make Model`.

Data constructor
   In our examples above, `Person`, `Make`, `Bicycle`, and `Car` are all data constructors.

Type constructor
   In our examples above, `Person`, `Make`, and `Vehicle` are all type constructors.

Type variables
   Consider the data type `data Maybe a = Just a | Nothing`. In this case, a is a type variable.

Tools

There are two main tools you'll need to develop in Haskell. The Glasgow Haskell Compiler (GHC) is the standard Haskell compiler, and the only one officially supported by Yesod. You'll also need Cabal, which is the standard Haskell build tool. Not only do we use Cabal for building our local code, but it can automatically download and install dependencies from Hackage, the Haskell package repository.

If you're on Windows or Mac, it is strongly recommended that you download the Haskell Platform (*http://hackage.haskell.org/platform/*). On Linux, many distributions include the Haskell Platform in their repositories. On Debian-based systems, for example, you can get started by running `sudo apt-get install haskell-platform`. If your distribution does not include the Haskell Platform, you can install it manually by following the instructions on the Haskell Platform page.

One important tool you'll need to update is *alex*. The Haskell Platform includes version 2, while the JavaScript minifier Yesod uses, `hjsmin`, requires version three. Be sure to *cabal install alex* after getting set up with the Haskell Platform, or you'll run into error messages about the `language-javascript` package.

Some people like to live on the bleeding edge and install the latest version of GHC before it is available in the Haskell Platform. We try to keep Yesod up-to-date with all current versions of GHC, but we only officially support the Haskell Platform. If you do go the route of manually installing GHC, here are a few notes:

- You'll need to install some additional build tools, *alex* and *happy* in particular.
- Make sure to install all of the required C libraries (*http://www.vex .net/%7Etrebla/haskell/haskell-platform.xhtml*). On Debian-based systems, you would need to run:

```
sudo apt-get install libedit-dev libbsd-dev libgmp3-dev zlib1g-dev freeglut3-dev
```

Regardless of how you've installed your tools, you should be sure to put `cabal`'s bin folder in your `PATH` variable. On Mac and Linux, this will be `$HOME/.cabal/bin` and on Windows it will be `%APPDATA%\cabal\bin`.

`cabal` has lots of different options available, but for now, just try out two commands:

- *cabal update* will download the most recent list of packages from Hackage.
- *cabal install yesod* will install Yesod and all its dependencies.

Many people in the community prefer to perform sandboxed builds of their Haskell packages, which prevents your install of Yesod from breaking existing packages, or packages you install in the future, from breaking your Yesod install. I won't go into detail on how to use these in this book, but the two most commonly used tools are cabal-dev (*http://hackage.haskell.org/package/cabal-dev*) and virthualenv (*http://hackage.haskell.org/package/virthualenv*).

Language Pragmas

GHC will run by default in something very close to Haskell98 mode. It also ships with a large number of language extensions, allowing more powerful type classes, syntax changes, and more. There are multiple ways to tell GHC to turn on these extensions. For most of the code snippets in this book, you'll see *language pragmas*, which look like this:

```
{-# LANGUAGE MyLanguageExtension #-}
```

These should always appear at the top of your source file. Additionally, there are two other common approaches:

- On the GHC command line, pass an extra argument **-XMyLanguageExtension**.
- In your `cabal` file, add an `extensions` block.

I personally never use the GHC command line argument approach. It's a personal preference, but I like to have my settings clearly stated in a file. In general it's recommended to avoid putting extensions in your cabal file; however, in the Yesod scaffolded site we specifically use this approach to avoid the boilerplate of specifying the same language pragmas in every source file.

We'll end up using quite a few language extensions in this book (the scaffolding uses 11). We will not cover the meaning of all of them. Instead, please see the GHC documentation (*http://www.haskell.org/ghc/docs/latest/html/users_guide/ghc-language -features.html*).

Overloaded Strings

What's the type of "hello"? Traditionally, it's String, which is defined as type String = [Char]. Unfortunately, there are a number of limitations with this:

- It's a very inefficient implementation of textual data. We need to allocate extra memory for each cons cell, plus the characters themselves each take up a full machine word.
- Sometimes we have string-like data that's not actually text, such as ByteStrings and HTML.

To work around these limitations, GHC has a language extension called Overloaded Strings. When enabled, literal strings no longer have the monomorphic type String; instead, they have the type IsString a => a, where IsString is defined as:

```
class IsString a where
    fromString :: String -> a
```

There are IsString instances available for a number of types in Haskell, such as Text (a much more efficient packed String type), ByteString, and Html. Virtually every example in this book will assume that this language extension is turned on.

Unfortunately, there is one drawback to this extension: it can sometimes confuse GHC's type checker. Imagine we have:

```
{-# LANGUAGE OverloadedStrings, TypeSynonymInstances, FlexibleInstances #-}
import Data.Text (Text)

class DoSomething a where
    something :: a -> IO ()

instance DoSomething String where
    something _ = putStrLn "String"

instance DoSomething Text where
    something _ = putStrLn "Text"

myFunc :: IO ()
myFunc = something "hello"
```

Will the program print out String or Text? It's not clear. So instead, you'll need to give an explicit type annotation to specify whether "hello" should be treated as a String or Text.

Type Families

The basic idea of a type family is to state some association between two different types. Suppose we want to write a function that will safely take the first element of a list. But we don't want it to work just on lists; we'd like it to treat a ByteString like a list of Word8s. To do so, we need to introduce some *associated type* to specify what the contents of a certain type are.

```
{-# LANGUAGE TypeFamilies, OverloadedStrings #-}
import Data.Word (Word8)
import qualified Data.ByteString as S
import Data.ByteString.Char8 () -- get an orphan IsString instance

class SafeHead a where
    type Content a
    safeHead :: a -> Maybe (Content a)

instance SafeHead [a] where
    type Content [a] = a
    safeHead [] = Nothing
    safeHead (x:_) = Just x

instance SafeHead S.ByteString where
    type Content S.ByteString = Word8
    safeHead bs
        | S.null bs = Nothing
        | otherwise = Just $ S.head bs

main :: IO ()
main = do
    print $ safeHead ("" :: String)
    print $ safeHead ("hello" :: String)

    print $ safeHead ("" :: S.ByteString)
    print $ safeHead ("hello" :: S.ByteString)
```

The new syntax is the ability to place a type inside of a class and instance. We can also use data instead, which will create a new data type instead of reference an existing one.

There are other ways to use associated types outside the context of a typeclass. However, in Yesod, all of our associated types are in fact part of a type class. For more information on type families, see the Haskell wiki page (*http://www.haskell.org/haskellwiki/GHC/Type_families*).

Template Haskell

Template Haskell (TH) is an approach to *code generation*. We use it in Yesod in a number of places to reduce boilerplate, and to ensure that the generated code is correct. Template Haskell is essentially Haskell that generates a Haskell Abstract Syntax Tree (AST).

 There's actually more power in TH than that, as it can actually introspect code. We don't use these facilities in Yesod, however.

Writing TH code can be tricky, and unfortunately there isn't very much type safety involved. You can easily write TH that will generate code that won't compile. This is only an issue for the developers of Yesod, not for its users. During development, we use a large collection of unit tests to ensure that the generated code is correct. As a user, all you need to do is call these already existing functions. For example, to include an externally defined Hamlet template, you can write:

```
$(hamletFile "myfile.hamlet")
```

(Hamlet is discussed in the Shakespeare chapter.) The dollar sign immediately followed by parantheses tell GHC that what follows is a Template Haskell function. The code inside is then run by the compiler and generates a Haskell AST, which is then compiled. And yes, it's even possible to go meta with this (*http://www.yesodweb.com/blog/2010/09/yo-dawg-template-haskell*).

A nice trick is that TH code is allowed to perform arbitrary IO actions, and therefore we can place some input in external files and have it parsed at compile time. One example usage is to have compile-time checked HTML, CSS, and JavaScript templates.

If your Template Haskell code is being used to generate declarations, and is being placed at the top level of our file, we can leave off the dollar sign and parentheses. In other words:

```
{-# LANGUAGE TemplateHaskell #-}

-- Normal function declaration, nothing special
myFunction = ...

-- Include some TH code
$(myThCode)

-- Or equivalently
myThCode
```

It can be useful to see what code is being generated by Template Haskell for you. To do so, you should use the -ddump-splices GHC option.

 There are many other features of Template Haskell not covered here. For more information, see the Haskell wiki page (*http://www.haskell.org/haskellwiki/Template_Haskell*).

QuasiQuotes

QuasiQuotes (QQ) are a minor extension of Template Haskell that let us embed arbitrary content within our Haskell source files. For example, we mentioned previously the `hamletFile` TH function, which reads the template contents from an external file. We also have a quasi-quoter named `hamlet` that takes the content inline:

```
{-# LANGUAGE QuasiQuotes #-}

[hamlet|<p>This is quasi-quoted Hamlet.|]
```

The syntax is set off using square brackets and pipes. The name of the quasi-quoter is given between the opening bracket and the first pipe, and the content is given between the pipes.

Throughout the book, we will often use the QQ approach over a TH-powered external file since the former is simpler to copy and paste. However, in production, external files are recommended for all but the shortest of inputs as it gives a nice separation of the non-Haskell syntax from your Haskell code.

Summary

You don't need to be an expert in Haskell to use Yesod, a basic familiarity will suffice. This chapter hopefully gave you just enough extra information to feel more comfortable following the rest of the book.

CHAPTER 3
Basics

The first step with any new technology is getting it to run. The goal of this chapter is to get you started with a simple Yesod application, and cover some of the basic concepts and terminology.

Hello World

Let's get this book started properly: a simple web page that says Hello World:

```
{-# LANGUAGE TypeFamilies, QuasiQuotes, MultiParamTypeClasses,
             TemplateHaskell, OverloadedStrings #-}
import Yesod

data HelloWorld = HelloWorld

mkYesod "HelloWorld" [parseRoutes|
/ HomeR GET
|]

instance Yesod HelloWorld

getHomeR :: Handler RepHtml
getHomeR = defaultLayout [whamlet|Hello World!|]

main :: IO ()
main = warpDebug 3000 HelloWorld
```

If you save that code in **helloworld.hs** and run it with **runhaskell helloworld.hs**, you'll get a web server running on port 3000. If you point your browser to *http://localhost:3000*, you'll get the following HTML:

```
<!DOCTYPE html>
<html><head><title></title></head><body>Hello World!</body></html>
```

We'll refer back to this example through the rest of the chapter.

Routing

Like most modern web frameworks, Yesod follows a front controller pattern (*http://en.wikipedia.org/wiki/Front_Controller_pattern*). This means that every request to a Yesod application enters at the same point and is routed from there. As a contrast, in systems like PHP and ASP you usually create a number of different files, and the web server automatically directs requests to the relevant file.

In addition, Yesod uses a declarative style for specifying routes. In our example above, this looked like:

```
mkYesod "HelloWorld" [parseRoutes|
/ HomeR GET
|]
```

mkYesod is a Template Haskell function, and parseRoutes is a Quasi-Quoter.

In English, all this means is: "In the HelloWorld application, create one route. I'd like to call it HomeR, it should listen for requests to / (the root of the application), and should answer GET requests." We call HomeR a *resource*, which is where the "R" suffix comes from.

The R suffix on resource names is simply convention, but it's a fairly universally followed convention. It makes it just a bit easier to read and understand code.

The mkYesod TH function generates quite a bit of code here: a route data type, a dispatch function, and a render function. We'll look at this in more detail in the routing chapter. But by using the -ddump-splices GHC option, we can get an immediate look at the generated code. A much cleaned up version of it is:

```
instance RenderRoute HelloWorld where
  data Route HelloWorld = HomeR
    deriving (Show, Eq, Read)
  renderRoute HomeR = ([], [])

instance YesodDispatch HelloWorld HelloWorld where
  yesodDispatch master sub toMaster app404 app405 method pieces =
    case dispatch pieces of
      Just f -> f
        master
        sub
        toMaster
        app404
        app405
```

16 | Chapter 3: Basics

```
                    method
            Nothing -> app404
      where
        dispatch = Yesod.Routes.Dispatch.toDispatch
            [ Yesod.Routes.Dispatch.Route [] False onHome
            ]
        onHome [] = Just $ \master sub toMaster _app404 app405 method ->
            case method of
                "GET" -> yesodRunner
                    (fmap chooseRep getHomeR)
                    master
                    sub
                    (Just HomeR)
                    toMaster
                _ -> app405 HomeR
```

Some of that will likely not make sense yet. In particular, the implementation of `yesod Dispatch` is a bit hairy to accomodate different dispatch approaches and fit the model necessary for our high-performance routing structures. However, the `RenderRoute` implementation with its associated data type should already give you a good feel for what's going on under the surface.

Handler Function

So we have a route named `HomeR`, and it responds to `GET` requests. How do you define your response? You write a *handler function*. Yesod follows a standard naming scheme for these functions: it's the lower case method name (e.g., `GET` becomes `get`) followed by the route name. In this case, the function name would be `getHomeR`.

Most of the code you write in Yesod lives in handler functions. This is where you process user input, perform database queries, and create responses. In our simple example, we create a response using the `defaultLayout` function. This function wraps up the content it's given in your site's template. By default, it produces an HTML file with a doctype and `html`, `head`, and `body` tags. As we'll see in the Yesod typeclass chapter, this function can be overridden to do much more.

In our example, we pass `[whamlet|Hello World!|]` to `defaultLayout`. `whamlet` is another quasi-quoter. In this case, it converts Hamlet syntax into a Widget. Hamlet is the default HTML templating engine in Yesod. Together with its siblings Cassius, Lucius, and Julius, you can create HTML, CSS, and JavaScript in a fully type-safe and compile-time-checked manner. We'll see much more about this in the Shakespeare chapter.

Widgets are another cornerstone of Yesod. They allow you to create modular components of a site consisting of HTML, CSS, and JavaScript and reuse them throughout your site. We'll get into more detail on them in the widgets chapter.

The Foundation

The word "HelloWorld" shows up a number of times in our example. Every Yesod application has a *foundation* data type. This data type must be an instance of the Yesod typeclass, which provides a central place for declaring a number of different settings controlling the execution of our application.

In our case, this data type is pretty boring: it doesn't contain any information. Nonetheless, the foundation is central to how our example runs: it ties together the routes with the instance declaration and lets it all be run. We'll see throughout this book that the foundation pops up in a whole bunch of places.

But foundations don't have to be boring: they can be used to store lots of useful information, usually stuff that needs to be initialized at program launch and used throughout. Some very common examples are:

- A database connection pool
- Settings loaded from a config file
- An HTTP connection manager

 By the way, the word Yesod (יסוד) means *foundation* in Hebrew.

Running

Once again we mention `HelloWorld` in our main function. Our foundation contains all the information we need to route and respond to requests in our application; now we just need to convert it into something that can run. A useful function for this in Yesod is `warpDebug`, which runs the Warp web server with debug output enabled on the specified port (here, it's 3000).

One of the features of Yesod is that you aren't tied down to a single deployment strategy. Yesod is built on top of the Web Application Interface (WAI), allowing it to run on FastCGI, SCGI, Warp, or even as a desktop application using the Webkit library. We'll discuss some of these options in the deployment chapter. And at the end of this chapter, we will explain the development server.

Warp is the premiere deployment option for Yesod. It is a lightweight, highly efficient web server developed specifically for hosting Yesod. It is also used outside of Yesod for other Haskell development (both framework and non-framework applications), as well as a standard file server in a number of production environments.

Resources and Type-Safe URLs

In our hello world, we defined just a single resource (HomeR). A web application is usually much more exciting with more than one page on it. Let's take a look:

```
{-# LANGUAGE TypeFamilies, QuasiQuotes, MultiParamTypeClasses,
             TemplateHaskell, OverloadedStrings #-}
import Yesod

data Links = Links

mkYesod "Links" [parseRoutes|
/ HomeR GET
/page1 Page1R GET
/page2 Page2R GET
|]

instance Yesod Links

getHomeR  = defaultLayout [whamlet|<a href=@{Page1R}>Go to page 1!|]
getPage1R = defaultLayout [whamlet|<a href=@{Page2R}>Go to page 2!|]
getPage2R = defaultLayout [whamlet|<a href=@{HomeR}>Go home!|]

main = warpDebug 3000 Links
```

Overall, this is very similar to Hello World. Our foundation is now `Links` instead of `HelloWorld`, and in addition to the `HomeR` resource, we've added `Page1R` and `Page2R`. As such, we've also added two more handler functions: `getPage1R` and `getPage2R`.

The only truly new feature is inside the `whamlet` quasi-quotation. We'll delve into syntax in the Shakespeare chapter, but we can see that:

```
<a href=@{Page1R}>Go to page 1!
```

creates a link to the `Page1R` resource. The important thing to note here is that `Page1R` is a data constructor. By making each resource a data constructor, we have a feature called *type-safe URLs*. Instead of splicing together strings to create URLs, we simply create a plain old Haskell value. By using at-sign interpolation (@{...}), Yesod automatically renders those values to textual URLs before sending things off to the user. We can see how this is implemented by looking again at the *-ddump-splices* output:

```
instance RenderRoute Links where
    data Route Links = HomeR | Page1R | Page2R
      deriving (Show, Eq, Read)

    renderRoute HomeR  = ([], [])
    renderRoute Page1R = (["page1"], [])
    renderRoute Page2R = (["page2"], [])
```

In the `Route` associated type for `Links`, we have additional constructors for `Page1R` and `Page2R`. We also now have a better glimpse of the return values for `returnRoute`. The first part of the tuple gives the *path pieces* for the given route. The second part gives the query string parameters; for almost all use cases, this will be an empty list.

It's hard to over-estimate the value of type-safe URLs. They give you a huge amount of flexibility and robustness when developing your application. You can move URLs around at will without ever breaking links. In the routing chapter, we'll see that routes can take parameters, such as a blog entry URL taking the blog post ID.

Let's say you want to switch from routing on the numerical post ID to a year/month/slug setup. In a traditional web framework, you would need to go through every single reference to your blog post route and update appropriately. If you miss one, you'll have 404s at runtime. In Yesod, all you do is update your route and compile: GHC will pinpoint every single line of code that needs to be corrected.

The Scaffolded Site

Installing Yesod will give you both the Yesod library, as well as a `yesod` executable. This executable accepts a few commands, but the first one you'll want to be acquainted with is `yesod init`. It will ask you some questions, and then generate a folder containing the default *scaffolded site*. Inside that folder, you can run `cabal install --only-dependencies` to build any extra dependencies (such as your database backends), and then `yesod devel` to run your site.

The scaffolded site gives you a lot of best practices out of the box, setting up files and dependencies in a time-tested approach used by most production Yesod sites. However, all this convenience can get in the way of actually learning Yesod. Therefore, most of this book will avoid the scaffolding tool, and instead deal directly with Yesod as a library.

We will cover the structure of the scaffolded site in more detail later.

Development Server

One of the advantages interpreted languages have over compiled languages is fast prototyping: you save changes to a file and hit refresh. If we want to make any changes to our Yesod apps above, we'll need to call *runhaskell* from scratch, which can be a bit tedious.

Fortunately, there's a solution to this: `yesod devel` automatically rebuilds and reloads your code for you. This can be a great way to develop your Yesod projects, and when you're ready to move to production, you still get to compile down to incredibly efficient code. The Yesod scaffolding automatically sets things up for you. This gives you the best of both worlds: rapid prototyping **and** fast production code.

It's a little bit more involved to set up your code to be used by *yesod devel*, so our examples will just use `warpDebug`. But when you're ready to make your real world information, *yesod devel* will be waiting for you.

Summary

Every Yesod application is built around a foundation data type. We associate some resources with that data type and define some handler functions, and Yesod handles all of the routing. These resources are also data constructors, which lets us have type-safe URLs.

By being built on top of WAI, Yesod applications can run with a number of different backends. `warpDebug` is an easy way to get started, as it's included with Yesod. For rapid development, you can use `yesod devel`. And when you're ready to move to production, you have Warp as a high-performance option.

When developing in Yesod, we get a number of choices for coding style: quasi-quotation or external files, `warpDebug` or `yesod devel`, and so on. The examples in this book will tend toward using the choices that are easiest to copy and paste, but the more powerful options will be available when you start building real Yesod applications.

CHAPTER 4
Shakespearean Templates

Yesod uses the Shakespearean family of template languages as its standard approach to HTML, CSS, and JavaScript creation. This language family shares some common syntax, as well as overarching principles:

- As little interference to the underlying language as possible, while providing conveniences where unobtrusive
- Compile-time guarantees on well-formed content
- Static type safety, greatly helping the prevention of XSS (cross-site scripting) (*http://en.wikipedia.org/wiki/Cross-site_scripting*) attacks
- Automated checking of valid URLs, whenever possible, through *type-safe URLs*

There is nothing inherently tying Yesod to these languages, or the other way around: each can be used independently of the other. This chapter will address these template languages on their own, while the remainder of the book will use them to enhance Yesod application development.

Synopsis

There are four main languages at play: Hamlet is an HTML templating language, Julius is for JavaScript, and Cassius and Lucius are both for CSS. Hamlet and Cassius are both whitespace-sensitive formats, using indentation to denote nesting. By contrast, Lucius is a superset of CSS, keeping CSS's braces for denoting nesting. Julius is a simple pass-through language for producing JavaScript; the only added feature is variable interpolation.

Hamlet (HTML)

```
$doctype 5
<html>
    <head>
        <title>#{pageTitle} - My Site
```

```
    <link rel=stylesheet href=@{Stylesheet}>
<body>
    <h1 .page-title>#{pageTitle}
    <p>Here is a list of your friends:
    $if null friends
        <p>Sorry, I lied, you don't have any friends.
    $else
        <ul>
            $forall Friend name age <- friends
                <li>#{name} (#{age} years old)
    <footer>^{copyright}
```

Cassius (CSS)

```
#myid
    color: #{red}
    font-size: #{bodyFontSize}
foo bar baz
    background-image: url(@{MyBackgroundR})
```

Lucius (CSS)

```
section.blog {
    padding: 1em;
    border: 1px solid #000;
    h1 {
        color: #{headingColor};
    }
}
```

Julius (JavaScript)

```
$(function(){
    $("section.#{sectionClass}").hide();
    $("#mybutton").click(function(){document.location = "@{SomeRouteR}";});
    ^{addBling}
});
```

Types

Before we jump into syntax, let's take a look at the various types involved. We mentioned in the introduction that types help protect us from XSS attacks. For example, let's say that we have an HTML template that should display someone's name; it might look like this:

```
<p>Hello, my name is #{name}
```

> `#{...}` is how we do variable interpolation in Shakespeare.

What should happen to `name`, and what should its data type be? A naive approach would be to use a `Text` value, and insert it verbatim. But that would give us quite a problem when `name="<script src='http://nefarious.com/evil.js'></script>"`. What we want is to be able to entity-encode the name, so that `<` becomes `&lt;`.

An equally naive approach is to simply entity-encode **every** piece of text that gets embedded. What happens when you have some preexisting HTML generated from another process? For example, on the Yesod website, all Haskell code snippets are run through a colorizing function that wraps up words in appropriate `span` tags. If we entity escaped everything, code snippets would be completely unreadable!

Instead, we have an `Html` data type. In order to generate an `Html` value, we have two options for APIs: the `ToHtml` typeclass provides a way to convert `String` and `Text` values into `Html`, via its `toHtml` function, automatically escaping entities along the way. This would be the approach we'd want for the name above. For the code snippet example, we would use the preEscaped family of functions.

When you use variable interpolation in Hamlet (the HTML Shakespeare language), it automatically applies a `toHtml` call to the value inside. So if you interpolate a `String`, it will be entity-escaped. But if you provide an `Html` value, it will appear unmodified. In the code snippet example, we might interpolate with something like `#{preEscapedText myHaskellHtml}`.

> The `Html` data type, as well as the functions mentioned, are all provided by the `blaze-html` package. This allows Hamlet to interact with all other blaze-html packages, and lets Hamlet provide a general solution for producing blaze-html values. Also, we get to take advantage of blaze-html's amazing performance.

Similarly, we have `Css/ToCss`, as well as `Javascript/ToJavascript`. These provide some compile-time sanity checks that we haven't accidentally stuck some HTML in our CSS.

> One other advantage on the CSS side is some helper data types for colors and units. For example: `.red { color: #{colorRed} }` Please see the Haddock documentation for more details.

Type-Safe URLs

Possibly the most unique feature in Yesod is type-safe URLs, and the ability to use them conveniently is provided directly by Shakespeare. Usage is nearly identical to variable interpolation, we just use the at-sign (@) instead of the hash (#). We'll cover the syntax later; first, let's clarify the intuition.

Suppose we have an application with two routes: *http://example.com/profile/home* is the homepage, and *http://example.com/display/time* displays the current time. And let's say we want to link from the homepage to the time. I can think of three different ways of constructing the URL:

1. As a relative link: *../display/time*
2. As an absolute link, without a domain: */display/time*
3. As an absolute link, with a domain: *http://example.com/display/time*

There are problems with each approach: the first will break if either URL changes. Also, it's not suitable for all use cases; RSS and Atom feeds, for instance, require absolute URLs. The second is more resilient to change than the first, but still won't be acceptable for RSS and Atom. And while the third works fine for all use cases, you'll need to update every single URL in your application whenever your domain name changes. You think that doesn't happen often? Just wait till you move from your development to staging and finally production server.

But more importantly, there is one huge problem with all approaches: if you change your routes at all, the compiler won't warn you about the broken links. Not to mention that typos can wreak havoc as well.

The goal of type-safe URLs is to let the compiler check things for us as much as possible. In order to facilitate this, our first step must be to move away from plain old text, which the compiler doesn't understand, to some well defined data types. For our simple application, let's model our routes with a sum type:

```
data MyRoute = Home | Time
```

Instead of placing a link like /display/time in our template, we can use the `Time` constructor. But at the end of the day, HTML is made up of text, not data types, so we need some way to convert these values to text. We call this a *URL rendering function*, and a simple one is:

```
renderMyRoute :: MyRoute -> Text
renderMyRoute Home = "http://example.com/profile/home"
renderMyRoute Time = "http://example.com/display/time"
```

> URL rendering functions are actually a bit more complicated than this. They need to address query string parameters, handle records within the constructor, and more intelligently handle the domain name. But in practice, you don't need to worry about this, since Yesod will automatically create your render functions. The one thing to point out is that the type signature is actually a little more complicated when handling query strings:

```
type Query = [(Text, Text)]
type Render url = url -> Query -> Text
renderMyRoute :: Render MyRoute
renderMyRoute Home _ = ...
renderMyRoute Time _ = ...
```

OK, we have our render function, and we have type-safe URLs embedded in the templates. How does this fit together exactly? Instead of generating an `Html` (or `Css` or `Javascript`) value directly, Shakespearean templates actually produce a function, which takes this render function and produces HTML. To see this better, let's have a quick (fake) peek at how Hamlet would work under the surface. Supposing we had a template:

```
<a href=@{Time}>The time
```

this would translate roughly into the Haskell code:

```
\render -> mconcat ["<a href='", render Time, "'>The time</a>"]
```

Syntax

All Shakespearean languages share the same interpolation syntax, and are able to utilize type-safe URLs. They differ in the syntax specific for their target language (HTML, CSS, or JavaScript).

Hamlet Syntax

Hamlet is the most sophisticated of the languages. Not only does it provide syntax for generating HTML, it also allows for basic control structures: conditionals, looping, and maybes.

Tags

Obviously tags will play an important part of any HTML template language. In Hamlet, we try to stick very close to existing HTML syntax to make the language more comfortable. However, instead of using closing tags to denote nesting, we use indentation. So something like this in HTML:

```
<body>
<p>Some paragraph.</p>
<ul>
<li>Item 1</li>
```

```
        <li>Item 2</li>
    </ul>
</body>
```

would be

```
<body>
    <p>Some paragraph.
    <ul>
        <li>Item 1
        <li>Item 2
```

In general, we find this to be easier to follow than HTML once you get accustomed to it. The only tricky part comes with dealing with whitespace before and after tags. For example, let's say you want to create the HTML

```
<p>Paragraph <i>italic</i> end.</p>
```

We want to make sure that there is a whitespace preserved after the word "Paragraph" and before the word "end". To do so, we use two simple escape characters:

```
<p>
    Paragraph #
    <i>italic
    \ end.
```

The whitespace escape rules are actually very simple:

1. If the first non-space character in a line is a backslash, the backslash is ignored.
2. If the last character in a line is a hash, it is ignored.

One other thing. Hamlet does **not** escape entities within its content. This is done on purpose to allow existing HTML to be more easily copied in. So the example above could also be written as:

```
<p>Paragraph <i>italic</i> end.
```

Notice that the first tag will be automatically closed by Hamlet, while the inner "i" tag will not. You are free to use whichever approach you want, there is no penalty for either choice. Be aware, however, that the **only** time you use closing tags in Hamlet is for such inline tags; normal tags are not closed.

Interpolation

What we have so far is a nice, simplified HTML, but it doesn't let us interact with our Haskell code at all. How do we pass in variables? Simple: with interpolation:

```
<head>
    <title>#{title}
```

The hash followed by a pair of braces denotes **variable interpolation**. In the case above, the title variable from the scope in which the template was called will be used. Let me state that again: Hamlet automatically has access to the variables in scope when it's called. There is no need to specifically pass variables in.

You can apply functions within an interpolation. You can use string and numeric literals in an interpolation. You can use qualified modules. Both parentheses and the dollar sign can be used to group statements together. And at the end, the `toHtml` function is applied to the result, meaning *any* instance of `ToHtml` can be interpolated. Take, for instance, the following code.

```haskell
-- Just ignore the quasiquote stuff for now, and that shamlet thing.
-- It will be explained later.
{-# LANGUAGE QuasiQuotes #-}
import Text.Hamlet (shamlet)
import Text.Blaze.Renderer.String (renderHtml)
import Data.Char (toLower)
import Data.List (sort)

data Person = Person
    { name :: String
    , age  :: Int
    }

main :: IO ()
main = putStrLn $ renderHtml [shamlet|
<p>Hello, my name is #{name person} and I am #{show $ age person}.
<p>
    Let's do some funny stuff with my name: #
    <b>#{sort $ map toLower (name person)}
<p>Oh, and in 5 years I'll be #{show (5 + (age person))} years old.
|]
  where
    person = Person "Michael" 26
```

What about our much-touted type-safe URLs? They are almost identical to variable interpolation in every way, except they start with an at-sign (@) instead. In addition, there is embedding via a caret (^) which allows you to embed another template of the same type. The next code sample demonstrates both of these.

```haskell
{-# LANGUAGE QuasiQuotes #-}
{-# LANGUAGE OverloadedStrings #-}
import Text.Hamlet (HtmlUrl, hamlet)
import Text.Blaze.Renderer.String (renderHtml)
import Data.Text (Text)

data MyRoute = Home

render :: MyRoute -> [(Text, Text)] -> Text
render Home _ = "/home"

footer :: HtmlUrl MyRoute
footer = [hamlet|
<footer>
    Return to #
    <a href=@{Home}>Homepage
    .
|]
```

```
main :: IO ()
main = putStrLn $ renderHtml $ [hamlet|
<body>
    <p>This is my page.
    ^{footer}
|] render
```

Attributes

In that last example, we put an href attribute on the "a" tag. Let's elaborate on the syntax:

- You can have interpolations within the attribute value.
- The equals sign and value for an attribute are optional, just like in HTML. So `<input type=checkbox checked>` is perfectly valid.
- There are two convenience attributes: for id, you can use the hash, and for classes, the period. In other words, `<p #paragraphid .class1 .class2>`.
- While quotes around the attribute value are optional, they are required if you want to embed spaces.
- You can add an attribute optionally by using colons. To make a checkbox only checked if the variable isChecked is True, you would write `<input type=check box :isChecked:checked>`. To have a paragraph be optionally red, you could use `<p :isRed:style="color:red">`.

Conditionals

Eventually, you'll want to put some logic in your page. The goal of Hamlet is to make the logic as minimalistic as possible, pushing the heavy lifting into Haskell. As such, our logical statements are very basic...so basic, that it's `if`, `elseif`, and `else`.

```
$if isAdmin
    <p>Welcome to the admin section.
$elseif isLoggedIn
    <p>You are not the administrator.
$else
    <p>I don't know who you are. Please log in so I can decide if you get access.
```

All the same rules of normal interpolation apply to the content of the conditionals.

Maybe

Similarly, we have a special construct for dealing with Maybe values. This could technically be dealt with using `if`, `isJust`, and `fromJust`, but this is more convenient and avoids partial functions.

```
$maybe name <- maybeName
    <p>Your name is #{name}
$nothing
    <p>I don't know your name.
```

In addition to simple identifiers, you can use a few other, more complicated values on the left-hand side, such as constructors and tuples.

```
$maybe Person firstName lastName <- maybePerson
    <p>Your name is #{firstName} #{lastName}
```

The right-hand side follows the same rules as interpolations, allow variables, function application, and so on.

Forall

And what about looping over lists? We have you covered there too:

```
$if null people
    <p>No people.
$else
    <ul>
        $forall person <- people
            <li>#{person}
```

Case

Pattern matching is one of the great strengths of Haskell. Sum types let you cleanly model many real-world types, and `case` statements let you safely match, letting the compiler warn you if you missed a case. Hamlet gives you the same power.

```
$case foo
    $of Left bar
        <p>It was left: #{bar}
    $of Right baz
        <p>It was right: #{baz}
```

With

Rounding out our statements, we have `with`. It's basically just a convenience for declaring a synonym for a long expression.

```
$with foo <- some very (long ugly) expression that $ should only $ happen once
    <p>But I'm going to use #{foo} multiple times. #{foo}
```

Doctype

Last bit of syntactic sugar: the doctype statement. We have support for a number of different versions of a `doctype`, though we recommend $doctype 5 for modern web applications, which generates `<!DOCTYPE html>`.

```
$doctype 5
<html>
    <head>
        <title>Hamlet is Awesome
    <body>
        <p>All done.
```

There is an older and still supported syntax: three exclamation points (!!!). You may still see this in code out there. We have no plans to remove support for this, but in general find the $doctype approach easier to read.

Cassius Syntax

Cassius is the original CSS template language. It uses simple whitespace rules to delimit blocks, making braces and semicolons unnecessary. It supports both variable and URL interpolation, but not embedding. The syntax is very straightforward:

```
#banner
    border: 1px solid #{bannerColor}
    background-image: url(@{BannerImageR})
```

Lucius Syntax

While Cassius uses a modified, whitespace-sensitive syntax for CSS, Lucius is true to the original. You can take any CSS file out there and it will be a valid Lucius file. There are, however, a few additions to Lucius:

- Like Cassius, we allow both variable and URL interpolation.
- CSS blocks are allowed to nest.
- You can declare variables in your templates.

Starting with the second point: let's say you want to have some special styling for some tags within your `article`. In plain ol' CSS, you'd have to write:

```
article code { background-color: grey; }
article p { text-indent: 2em; }
article a { text-decoration: none; }
```

In this case, there aren't that many clauses, but having to type out article each time is still a bit of a nuisance. Imagine if you had a dozen or so of these. Not the worst thing in the world, but a bit of an annoyance. Lucius helps you out here:

```
article {
    code { background-color: grey; }
    p { text-indent: 2em; }
    a { text-decoration: none; }
}
```

Having Lucius variables allows you to avoid repeating yourself. A simple example would be to define a commonly used color:

```
@textcolor: #ccc; /* just because we hate our users */
body { color: #{textcolor} }
a:link, a:visited { color: #{textcolor} }
```

Other than that, Lucius is identical to CSS.

Julius Syntax

Julius is the simplest of the languages discussed here. In fact, some might even say it's really just JavaScript. Julius allows the three forms of interpolation we've mentioned so far, and otherwise applies no transformations to your content.

> If you use Julius with the scaffolded Yesod site, you may notice that your JavaScript is automatically minified. This is not a feature of Julius; instead, Yesod uses the `hjsmin` package to minify Julius output.

Calling Shakespeare

The question of course arises at some point: how do I actually use this stuff? There are three different ways to call out to Shakespeare from your Haskell code:

Quasiquotes
    Quasiquotes allow you to embed arbitrary content within your Haskell, and for it to be converted into Haskell code at compile time.

External file
    In this case, the template code is in a separate file which is referenced via Template Haskell.

Reload mode
    Both of the above modes require a full recompile to see any changes. In reload mode, your template is kept in a separate file and referenced via Template Haskell. But at runtime, the external file is reparsed from scratch each time.

> Reload mode is not available for Hamlet, only for Cassius, Lucius, and Julius. There are too many sophisticated features in Hamlet that rely directly on the Haskell compiler and could not feasibly be reimplemented at runtime.

One of the first two approaches should be used in production. They both embed the entirety of the template in the final executable, simplifying deployment and increasing performance. The advantage of the quasiquoter is the simplicity: everything stays in a single file. For short templates, this can be a very good fit. However, in general, the external file approach is recommended because:

- It follows nicely in the tradition of separate logic from presentation.
- You can easily switch between external file and debug mode with some simple CPP macros, meaning you can keep rapid development and still achieve high performance in production.

Since these are special QuasiQuoters and Template Haskell functions, you need to be sure to enable the appropriate language extensions and use correct syntax. You can see a simple example of each in the examples.

Example 4-1. Quasiquoter

```haskell
{-# LANGUAGE OverloadedStrings #-} -- we're using Text below
{-# LANGUAGE QuasiQuotes #-}
import Text.Hamlet (HtmlUrl, hamlet)
import Data.Text (Text)
import Text.Blaze.Renderer.String (renderHtml)

data MyRoute = Home | Time | Stylesheet

render :: MyRoute -> [(Text, Text)] -> Text
render Home       _ = "/home"
render Time       _ = "/time"
render Stylesheet _ = "/style.css"

template :: Text -> HtmlUrl MyRoute
template title = [hamlet|
$doctype 5
<html>
    <head>
        <title>#{title}
        <link rel=stylesheet href=@{Stylesheet}>
    <body>
        <h1>#{title}
|]

main :: IO ()
main = putStrLn $ renderHtml $ template "My Title" render
```

Example 4-2. External file

```haskell
{-# LANGUAGE OverloadedStrings #-} -- we're using Text below
{-# LANGUAGE TemplateHaskell #-}
{-# LANGUAGE CPP #-} -- to control production versus debug
import Text.Lucius (CssUrl, luciusFile, luciusFileDebug, renderCss)
import Data.Text (Text)
import qualified Data.Text.Lazy.IO as TLIO

data MyRoute = Home | Time | Stylesheet

render :: MyRoute -> [(Text, Text)] -> Text
render Home       _ = "/home"
render Time       _ = "/time"
render Stylesheet _ = "/style.css"

template :: CssUrl MyRoute
#if PRODUCTION
template = $(luciusFile "template.lucius")
#else
template = $(luciusFileDebug "template.lucius")
#endif
```

```
main :: IO ()
main = TLIO.putStrLn $ renderCss $ template render

-- @template.lucius
foo { bar: baz }
```

The naming scheme for the functions is very consistent.

Language	Quasiquoter	External file	Reload
Hamlet	hamlet	hamletFile	N/A
Cassius	cassius	cassiusFile	cassiusFileReload
Lucius	lucius	luciusFile	luciusFileReload
Julius	julius	juliusFile	juliusFileReload

Alternate Hamlet Types

So far, we've seen how to generate an `HtmlUrl` value from Hamlet, which is a piece of HTML with embedded type-safe URLs. There are currently three other values we can generate using Hamlet: plain HTML, HTML with URLs **and** internationalized messages, and widgets. That last one will be covered in the widgets chapter.

To generate plain HTML without any embedded URLs, we use "simplified Hamlet". There are a few changes:

- We use a different set of functions, prefixed with an "s". So the quasiquoter is `shamlet` and the external file function is `shamletFile`. How we pronounce those is still up for debate.
- No URL interpolation is allowed. Doing so will result in a compile-time error.
- Embedding (the caret-interpolator) no longer allows arbitrary `HtmlUrl` values. The rule is that the embedded value must have the same type as the template itself, so in this case it must be `Html`. That means that for `shamlet`, embedding can be completely replaced with normal variable interpolation (with a hash).

Dealing with internationalization (i18n) in Hamlet is a bit complicated. Hamlet supports i18n via a message data type, very similar in concept and implementation to a type-safe URL. As a motivating example, let's say we want to have an application that tells you hello and how many apples you have eaten. We could represent those messages with a data type.

```
data Msg = Hello | Apples Int
```

Next, we would want to be able to convert that into something human-readable, so we define some render functions:

```
renderEnglish :: Msg -> Text
renderEnglish Hello = "Hello"
renderEnglish (Apples 0) = "You did not buy any apples."
```

```
renderEnglish (Apples 1) = "You bought 1 apple."
renderEnglish (Apples i) = T.concat ["You bought ", T.pack $ show i, " apples."]
```

Now we want to interpolate those Msg values directly in the template. For that, we use underscore interpolation.

```
$doctype 5
<html>
    <head>
        <title>i18n
    <body>
        <h1>_{Hello}
        <p>_{Apples count}
```

This kind of a template now needs some way to turn those values into HTML. So just like type-safe URLs, we pass in a render function. To represent this, we define a new type synonym:

```
type Render url = url -> [(Text, Text)] -> Text
type Translate msg = msg -> Html
type HtmlUrlI18n msg url = Translate msg -> Render url -> Html
```

At this point, you can pass renderEnglish, renderSpanish, or renderKlingon to this template, and it will generate nicely translated output (depending, of course, on the quality of your translators). The complete program is:

```
{-# LANGUAGE QuasiQuotes #-}
{-# LANGUAGE OverloadedStrings #-}
import Data.Text (Text)
import qualified Data.Text as T
import Text.Hamlet (HtmlUrlI18n, ihamlet)
import Text.Blaze (toHtml)
import Text.Blaze.Renderer.String (renderHtml)

data MyRoute = Home | Time | Stylesheet

renderUrl :: MyRoute -> [(Text, Text)] -> Text
renderUrl Home       _ = "/home"
renderUrl Time       _ = "/time"
renderUrl Stylesheet _ = "/style.css"

data Msg = Hello | Apples Int

renderEnglish :: Msg -> Text
renderEnglish Hello = "Hello"
renderEnglish (Apples 0) = "You did not buy any apples."
renderEnglish (Apples 1) = "You bought 1 apple."
renderEnglish (Apples i) = T.concat ["You bought ", T.pack $ show i, " apples."]

template :: Int -> HtmlUrlI18n Msg MyRoute
template count = [ihamlet|
$doctype 5
<html>
    <head>
        <title>i18n
    <body>
```

Chapter 4: Shakespearean Templates

```
        <h1>_{Hello}
        <p>_{Apples count}
|]

main :: IO ()
main = putStrLn $ renderHtml
    $ (template 5) (toHtml . renderEnglish) renderUrl
```

Other Shakespeare

In addition to HTML, CSS, and JavaScript helpers, there is also some more general-purpose Shakespeare available. shakespeare-text provides a simple way to create interpolated strings, much like people are accustomed to in scripting languages like Ruby and Python. This package's utility is definitely not limited to Yesod.

```
{-# LANGUAGE QuasiQuotes, OverloadedStrings #-}
import Text.Shakespeare.Text
import qualified Data.Text.Lazy.IO as TLIO
import Data.Text (Text)
import Control.Monad (forM_)

data Item = Item
    { itemName :: Text
    , itemQty :: Int
    }

items :: [Item]
items =
    [ Item "apples" 5
    , Item "bananas" 10
    ]

main :: IO ()
main = forM_ items $ \item -> TLIO.putStrLn
    [lt|You have #{show $ itemQty item} #{itemName item}.|]
```

Some quick points about this simple example:

- Notice that we have three different textual data types involved (String, strict Text and lazy Text). They all play together well.
- We use a quasiquoter named lt, which generates lazy text. There is also st.
- Also, there are longer names for these quasiquoters (ltext and stext).

General Recommendations

Here are some general hints from the Yesod community on how to get the most out of Shakespeare.

- For actual sites, use external files. For libraries, it's OK to use quasiquoters, assuming they aren't too long.

- Patrick Brisbin has put together a Vim code highlighter (*https://github.com/pbrisbin/html-template-syntax*) that can help out immensely.
- You should almost always start Hamlet tags on their own line instead of embedding start/end tags after an existing tag. The only exception to this is the occasional `<i>` or `<b>` tag inside a large block of text.

CHAPTER 5
Widgets

One of the challenges in web development is that we have to coordinate three different client-side technologies: HTML, CSS, and JavaScript. Worse still, we have to place these components in different locations on the page: CSS in a style tag in the head, JavaScript in a script tag in the head, and HTML in the body. And never mind if you want to put your CSS and JavaScript in separate files!

In practice, this works out fairly nicely when building a single page, because we can separate our structure (HTML), style (CSS), and logic (JavaScript). But when we want to build modular pieces of code that can be easily composed, it can be a headache to coordinate all three pieces separately. Widgets are Yesod's solution to the problem. They also help with the issue of including libraries, such as jQuery, one time only.

Our four template languages—Hamlet, Cassius, Lucius and Julius—provide the raw tools for constructing your output. Widgets provide the glue that allows them to work together seamlessly.

Synopsis

```
getRootR = defaultLayout $ do
    setTitle "My Page Title"
    toWidget [lucius| h1 { color: green; } |]
    addScriptRemote "https://ajax.googleapis.com/ajax/libs/jquery/1.6.2/jquery.min.js"
    toWidget [julius|
$(function() {
    $("h1").click(function(){ alert("You clicked on the heading!"); });
});
|]
    toWidgetHead [hamlet| <meta name=keywords content="some sample keywords">|]
    toWidget [hamlet| <h1>Here's one way of including content |]
    [whamlet| <h2>Here's another |]
    toWidgetBody [julius| alert("This is included in the body itself"); |]
```

This produces the following HTML (indentation added):

```
<!DOCTYPE html>
<html>
```

```
        <head>
            <title>My Page Title</title>
            <style>h1 { color : green }</style>
            <script src="https://ajax.googleapis.com/ajax/libs/jquery/1.6.2/
jquery.min.js"></script>
            <script>
$(function() {
        $("h1").click(function(){ alert("You clicked on the heading!"); });
});
</script>
            <meta name="keywords" content="some sample keywords">
        </head>
        <body>
            <h1>Here's one way of including content </h1>
            <h2>Here's another </h2>
            <script> alert("This is included in the body itself"); </script>
        </body>
</html>
```

What's in a Widget?

At a very superficial level, an HTML document is just a bunch of nested tags. This is the approach most HTML generation tools take: you simply define hierarchies of tags and are done with it. But let's imagine that I want to write a component of a page for displaying the navbar. I want this to be "plug and play": I simply call the function at the right time, and the navbar is inserted at the correct point in the hierarchy.

This is where our superficial HTML generation breaks down. Our navbar likely consists of some CSS and JavaScript in addition to HTML. By the time we call the navbar function, we have already rendered the `<head>` tag, so it is too late to add a new `<style>` tag for our CSS declarations. Under normal strategies, we would need to break up our navbar function into three parts: HTML, CSS, and JavaScript, and make sure that we always call all three pieces.

Widgets take a different approach. Instead of viewing an HTML document as a monolithic tree of tags, widgets see a number of distinct components in the page. In particular:

- The title
- External stylesheets
- External JavaScript
- CSS declarations
- JavaScript code
- Arbitrary `<head>` content
- Arbitrary `<body>` content

Different components have different semantics. For example, there can only be one title, but there can be multiple external scripts and stylesheets. However, those external scripts and stylesheets should only be included once. Arbitrary head and body content, on the other hand, has no limitation (someone may want to have five lorem ipsum blocks after all).

The job of a widget is to hold onto these disparate components and apply proper logic for combining different widgets together. This consists of things like taking the first title set and ignoring others, filtering duplicates from the list of external scripts and stylesheets, and concatenating head and body content.

Constructing Widgets

In order to use widgets, you'll obviously need to be able to get your hands on them. The most common way will be via the `ToWidget` typeclass, and its `toWidget` method. This allows you to convert your Shakespearean templates directly to a `Widget`: Hamlet code will appear in the body, Julius scripts inside a `<script>` tag in the head, and Cassius and Lucius in a `<style>` tag.

> You can actually override the default behavior and have the script and style code appear in a separate file. The scaffolded site provides this for you automatically. Additionally, we'll see in the Yesod typeclass chapter how to turn on asynchronous script loading, which will place your script content at the end of the body.

But what if you want to add some `<meta>` tags, which need to appear in the head? Or if you want some JavaScript to appear in the body instead of the head? For these purposes, Yesod provides two additional type classes: `ToWidgetHead` and `ToWidgetBody`. These work exactly as they seem they should.

In addition, there are a number of other functions for creating specific kinds of Widgets:

setTitle
: Turns some HTML into the page title.

addCassiusMedia, addLuciusMedia
: Works the same as toWidget, but takes an additional parameter to indicate what kind of media this applies to. Useful for creating print stylesheets, for instance.

addStylesheet
: Adds a reference, via a `<link>` tag, to an external stylesheet. Takes a type-safe URL.

addStylesheetRemote
: Same as `addStylesheet`, but takes a normal URL. Useful for referring to files hosted on a CDN, like Google's jQuery UI CSS files.

addScript
: Adds a reference, via a `<script>` tag, to an external script. Takes a type-safe URL.

addScriptRemote
> Same as `addScript`, but takes a normal URL. Useful for referring to files hosted on a CDN, like Google's jQuery.

Combining Widgets

The whole idea of widgets is to increase composability. You can take these individual pieces of HTML, CSS, and JavaScript, combine them together into something more complicated, and then combine these larger entities into complete pages. This all works naturally through the `Monad` instance of `Widget`, meaning you can use do-notation to compose pieces together.

Example 5-1. Combining Widgets

```
myWidget1 = do
    toWidget [hamlet|<h1>My Title|]
    toWidget [lucius|h1 { color: green } |]

myWidget2 = do
    setTitle "My Page Title"
    addScriptRemote "http://www.example.com/script.js"

myWidget = do
    myWidget1
    myWidget2

-- or, if you want
myWidget' = myWidget1 >> myWidget2
```

> If you're so inclined, there's also a `Monoid` instance of `Widget`, meaning you can use `mconcat` or a `Writer` monad to build things up. In my experience, it's easiest and most natural to just use do-notation.

Generate IDs

If we're really going for true code reuse here, we're eventually going to run into name conflicts. Let's say that there are two helper libraries that both use the class name "foo" to affect styling. We want to avoid such a possibility. Therefore, we have the `newIdent` function. This function automatically generates a word that is unique for this handler.

Example 5-2. Using newIdent

```
getRootR = defaultLayout $ do
    headerClass <- lift newIdent
    toWidget [hamlet|<h1 .#{headerClass}>My Header|]
    toWidget [lucius| .#{headerClass} { color: green; } |]
```

> You might be wondering: what does lift mean? A `Widget` is a monad transformer, sitting on top of a `Handler`. `newIdent` is a function of a `Handler`, so we need to "lift" the function from the `Handler` layer to the `Widget` layer to use it. We can actually use this same approach to perform complex actions, like database queries, from within a widget. We'll cover that when we discuss Yesod's monads.

whamlet

Let's say you've got a fairly standard Hamlet template that embeds another Hamlet template to represent the footer:

```
page = [hamlet|
<p>This is my page. I hope you enjoyed it.
^{footer}
|]

footer = [hamlet|
<footer>
    <p>That's all folks!
|]
```

That works fine if the footer is plain old HTML, but what if we want to add some style? Well, we can easily spice up the footer by turning it into a Widget:

```
footer = do
    toWidget [lucius| footer { font-weight: bold; text-align: center } |]
    toWidget [hamlet|
<footer>
    <p>That's all folks!
|]
```

But now we've got a problem: a Hamlet template can only embed another Hamlet template; it knows nothing about a Widget. This is where `whamlet` comes in. It takes exactly the same syntax as normal Hamlet, and variable (#{...}) and URL (@{...}) interpolation are unchanged. But embedding (^{...}) takes a `Widget`, and the final result is a `Widget`. To use it, we can just do:

```
page = [whamlet|
<p>This is my page. I hope you enjoyed it.
^{footer}
|]
```

There is also `whamletFile`, if you would prefer to keep your template in a separate file.

> The scaffolded site has an even more convenient function, `widgetFile`, which will also include your Lucius, Cassius, and Julius files automatically. We'll cover that in the scaffolding chapter.

Types

You may have noticed that I've been avoiding type signatures so far. That's because there's a little bit of a complication involved here. At the most basic level, all you need to know is that there's a type synonym called `Widget` which you will almost always use. The technical details follow, but don't worry if it's a little hazy.

There isn't actually a `Widget` type defined in the Yesod libraries, since the exact meaning of it changes between sites. Instead, we have a more general type `GWidget sub master a`. The first two parameters give the sub and master foundation types, respectively. The final parameter is the contained value, just like any `Monad` has.

So what's the deal with that sub/master stuff? Well, when you're writing some reusable code, such as a CRUD application, you can write it as a subsite that can be embedded within any other Yesod application. In such a case, we need to keep track of information for both the sub and master sites. The simplest example is for the type-safe URLs: Yesod needs to know how to take a route for your CRUD subsite and turn it into a route for the master site so that it can be properly rendered.

However, that sub/master distinction only ever matters when you're interacting with subsites. When you're writing your standard response code, you're dealing with just your application, and so the sub and master sites will be the same. Since this is the most common case, the scaffolded site declares a type synonym to help you out. Let's say your foundation type is MyCoolApp, it will define `type Widget = GWidget MyCoolApp MyCoolApp ()`. Therefore, we can get some very user-friendly type signatures on our widgets:

```
footer :: Widget
footer = do
    toWidget [lucius| footer { font-weight: bold; text-align: center } |]
    toWidget [hamlet|
<footer>
    <p>That's all folks!
|]

page :: Widget
page = [whamlet|
<p>This is my page. I hope you enjoyed it.
^{footer}
|]
```

If you've been paying close attention, you might be confused. We used `lift` on `Widget` in the ID generation example above, but `GWidget` isn't actually a monad transformer. What's going on here? Well, in older versions of Yesod, it *was* a transformer around the `Handler` type. Unfortunately, this led to difficult-to-parse error messages. As a result, `GWidget` is now a `newtype` wrapper that hides away its monad-transformer essence. But we still want to be able to `lift` functions from the inner `Handler` monad.

To solve this, Yesod provides an alternate, more general `lift` function that works for both standard `MonadTrans` instances, and special `newtype` wrappers like `GWidget`. As a result, you can pretend like `GWidget` is a standard transformer, while still getting to keep your nice error message.

One last point: just like we have the breakdown between `Widget` and `GWidget`, we have a similar breakdown between `Handler` and `GHandler`.

Using Widgets

It's all well and good that we have these beautiful Widget data types, but how exactly do we turn them into something the user can interact with? The most commonly used function is `defaultLayout`, which essentially has the type signature `Widget -> Handler RepHtml`. (I say "essentially" because of the whole `GHandler` issue.) `RepHtml` is a data type containing some raw HTML output ready to be sent over the wire.

`defaultLayout` is actually a typeclass method, which can be overridden for each application. This is how Yesod apps are themed. So we're still left with the question: when we're inside `defaultLayout`, how do we unwrap a `Widget`? The answer is `widgetToPageContent`. Let's look at some (simplified) types:

```
widgetToPageContent :: Widget -> Handler (PageContent url)
data PageContent url = PageContent
    { pageTitle :: Html
    , pageHead :: HtmlUrl url
    , pageBody :: HtmlUrl url
    }
```

This is getting closer to what we need. We now have direct access to the HTML making up the head and body, as well as the title. At this point, we can use Hamlet to combine them all together into a single document, along with our site layout, and we use `hamletToRepHtml` to render that Hamlet result into actual HTML that's ready to be shown to the user. The next figure demonstrates this process.

Example 5-3. Using widgetToPageContent

```
myLayout :: GWidget s MyApp () -> GHandler s MyApp RepHtml
myLayout widget = do
    pc <- widgetToPageContent widget
    hamletToRepHtml [hamlet|
$doctype 5
<html>
    <head>
        <title>#{pageTitle pc}
        <meta charset=utf-8>
        <style>body { font-family: verdana }
        ^{pageHead pc}
    <body>
        <article>
            ^{pageBody pc}
|]
```

```
instance Yesod MyApp where
    defaultLayout = myLayout
```

> You may have noticed that we used `GWidget` and `GHandler` instead of `Widget` and `Handler`. That's because `defaultLayout` is a method that can be called by subsites to ensure that they get the same styling as the master site. Therefore, we need to keep our types flexible here.

This is all well and good, but there's one thing that bothers me: that `style` tag. There are a few problems with it:

- Unlike Lucius or Cassius, it doesn't get compile-time checked for correctness.
- Granted that the current example is very simple, but in something more complicated we could get into character escaping issues.
- We'll now have two style tags instead of one: the one produced by `myLayout`, and the one generated in the `pageHead` based on the styles set in the widget.

We have one more trick in our bag to address this: we apply some last-minute adjustments to the widget itself before calling `widgetToPageContent`. It's actually very easy to do: we just use do-notation again, as in Example 5-4.

Example 5-4. Last-Minute Widget Adjustment

```
myLayout :: GWidget s MyApp () -> GHandler s MyApp RepHtml
myLayout widget = do
    pc <- widgetToPageContent $ do
        widget
        toWidget [lucius| body { font-family: verdana } |]
    hamletToRepHtml [hamlet|
$doctype 5
<html>
    <head>
        <title>#{pageTitle pc}
        <meta charset=utf-8>
        ^{pageHead pc}
    <body>
        <article>
            ^{pageBody pc}
|]
```

Summary

The basic building block of each page is a widget. Individual snippets of HTML, CSS, and JavaScript can be turned into widgets via the polymorphic `toWidget` function. Using do-notation, you can combine these individual widgets into larger widgets, eventually containing all the content of your page.

Unwrapping these widgets is usually performed within the `defaultLayout` function, which can be used to apply a unified look-and-feel to all your pages.

CHAPTER 6
Yesod Typeclass

Every one of our Yesod applications requires an instance of the `Yesod` typeclass. So far, we've only seen `defaultLayout`. In this chapter, we'll explore the meaning of many of the methods of the `Yesod` typeclass.

The `Yesod` typeclass gives us a central place for defining settings for our application. Everything else has a default definition that is usually the right thing. But in order to build a powerful, customized application, you'll usually end up wanting to override at least a few of these methods.

Rendering and Parsing URLs

We've already mentioned how Yesod is able to automatically render type-safe URLs into a textual URL that can be inserted into an HTML page. Let's say we have a route definition that looks like:

```
mkYesod "MyApp" [parseRoutes|
/some/path SomePathR GET
]
```

If we place `SomePathR` into a hamlet template, how does Yesod render it? Yesod always tries to construct *absolute* URLs. This is especially useful once we start creating XML sitemaps and Atom feeds, or sending emails. But in order to construct an absolute URL, we need to know the domain name of the application.

You might think we could get that information from the user's request, but we still need to deal with ports. And even if we get the port number from the request, are we using HTTP or HTTPS? And even if you know *that*, such an approach would mean that different URLs would be generated depending on how the user submitted a request. For example, we would generate different URLs depending on whether the user connected to "example.com" or "www.example.com". For Search Engine Optimization, we want to be able to consolidate on a single canonical URL.

And finally, Yesod doesn't make any assumption about *where* you host your application. For example, I may have a mostly static site (http://static.example.com/), but I'd like to stick a Yesod-powered Wiki at /wiki/. There is no reliable way for an application to determine what subpath it is being hosted from. So instead of doing all of this guesswork, Yesod needs you to tell it the *application root*.

Using the wiki example, you would write your `Yesod` instance as:

```
instance Yesod MyWiki where
    approot = ApprootStatic "http://static.example.com/wiki"
```

Notice that there is no trailing slash there. Next, when Yesod wants to construct a URL for `SomePathR`, it determines that the relative path for `SomePathR` is /some/path, appends that to your approot, and creates http://static.example.com/wiki/some/path.

> We've used the `ApprootStatic` constructor here, which allows you to hardcode an approot value in your Haskell code. We also have an `ApprootMaster` constructor, which allows you to grab the approot from the foundation value. In the scaffolded site, you can configure the approot via a YAML settings file, and the approot is automatically parsed and loaded from it at runtime.

And by the way, the scaffolded site can load different settings for developing, testing, staging, and production builds, so you can easily test on one domain—like localhost —and serve from a different domain.

> To reiterate: even though for the simple cases in this book, the first argument to approot is usually ignored; in real life code it usually isn't. We also need to keep that argument so that Haskell's type system can determine which instance of Yesod to use in grabbing the approot.

joinPath

In order to convert a type-safe URL into a text value, Yesod uses two helper functions. The first is the `renderRoute` method of the `RenderRoute` typeclass. Every type-safe URL is an instance of this typeclass. `renderRoute` converts a value into a list of path pieces. For example, our `SomePathR` from above would be converted into ["some", "path"].

> Actually, `renderRoute` produces both the path pieces and a list of query-string parameters. The default instances of `renderRoute` always provide an empty list of query string parameters. However, it is possible to override this. One notable case is the static subsite, which puts a hash of the file contents in the query string for caching purposes.

The other function is the `joinPath` method of the Yesod typeclass. This function takes four arguments: the foundation value, the application root, a list of path segments, and a list of query string parameters, and returns a textual URL. The default implementation does the "right thing": it separates the path pieces by forward slashes, prepends the application root and appends the query string.

If you are happy with default URL rendering, you should not need to modify it. However, if you want to modify URL rendering to do things like append a trailing slash, this would be the place to do it.

cleanPath

The flip side to `joinPath` is `cleanPath`. Let's look at how it gets used in the dispatch process:

1. The path info requested by the user is split into a series of path pieces.
2. We pass the path pieces to the `cleanPath` function.
3. If `cleanPath` indicates a redirect (a `Left` response), then a 301 response is sent to the client. This is used to force canonical URLs (e.g., remove extra slashes).
4. Otherwise, we try to dispatch using the response from `cleanPath` (a `Right`). If this works, we return a response. Otherwise, we return a 404.

This combination allows subsites to retain full control of how their URLs appear, yet allows master sites to have modified URLs. As a simple example, let's see how we could modify Yesod to always produce trailing slashes on URLs:

```
{-# LANGUAGE TypeFamilies, QuasiQuotes, MultiParamTypeClasses, TemplateHaskell,
OverloadedStrings #-}
import Yesod
import Network.HTTP.Types (encodePath)
import Blaze.ByteString.Builder.Char.Utf8 (fromText)
import qualified Data.Text as T
import qualified Data.Text.Encoding as TE
import Control.Arrow ((***))
import Data.Monoid (mappend)

data Slash = Slash

mkYesod "Slash" [parseRoutes|
/ RootR GET
/foo FooR GET
|]

instance Yesod Slash where
    joinPath _ ar pieces' qs' =
        fromText ar `mappend` encodePath pieces qs
      where
        qs = map (TE.encodeUtf8 *** go) qs'
        go "" = Nothing
        go x = Just $ TE.encodeUtf8 x
        pieces = pieces' ++ [""]

    -- We want to keep canonical URLs. Therefore, if the URL is missing a
    -- trailing slash, redirect. But the empty set of pieces always stays the
```

```
           -- same.
        cleanPath _ [] = Right []
        cleanPath _ s
            | dropWhile (not . T.null) s == [""] = -- the only empty string is the last one
                Right $ init s
            -- Since joinPath will append the missing trailing slash, we simply
            -- remove empty pieces.
            | otherwise = Left $ filter (not . T.null) s

    getRootR = defaultLayout [whamlet|
<p>
    <a href=@{RootR}>RootR
<p>
    <a href=@{FooR}>FooR
|]

    getFooR = getRootR

main = warpDebug 3000 Slash
```

First, let's look at our `joinPath` implementation. This is copied almost verbatim from the default Yesod implementation, with one difference: we append an extra empty string to the end. When dealing with path pieces, an empty string will append another slash. So adding an extra empty string will force a trailing slash.

`cleanPath` is a little bit trickier. First, we check for the empty path like before, and if so pass it through as-is. We use Right to indicate that a redirect is not necessary. The next clause is actually checking for two different possible URL issues:

- There is a double slash, which would show up as an empty string in the middle of our paths.
- There is a missing trailing slash, which would show up as the last piece not being an empty string.

Assuming neither of those conditions hold, then only the last piece is empty, and we should dispatch based on all but the last piece. However, if this is not the case, we want to redirect to a canonical URL. In this case, we strip out all empty pieces and do not bother appending a trailing slash, since `joinPath` will do that for us.

defaultLayout

Most websites like to apply some general template to all of their pages. `defaultLayout` is the recommended approach for this. While you could just as easily define your own function and call that instead, when you override `defaultLayout` all of the Yesod-generated pages (error pages, authentication pages) automatically get this style.

Overriding is very straightforward: we use `widgetToPageContent` to convert a `Widget` to a title, head tags, and body tags, and then use `hamletToRepHtml` to convert a Hamlet template into a `RepHtml`. We can even add extra widget components, like a Lucius template, from within `defaultLayout`. An example should make this all clear:

```
        defaultLayout contents = do
            PageContent title headTags bodyTags <- widgetToPageContent $ do
                addCassius [cassius|
#body
    font-family: sans-serif
#wrapper
    width: 760px
    margin: 0 auto
|]
                addWidget contents
            hamletToRepHtml [hamlet|
$doctype 5

<html>
    <head>
        <title>#{title}
        ^{headTags}
    <body>
        <div id="wrapper">
            ^{bodyTags}
|]
```

getMessage

Even though we haven't covered sessions yet, I'd like to mention `getMessage` here. A common pattern in web development is setting a message in one handler and displaying it in another. For example, if a user `POST`s a form, you may want to redirect him/her to another page along with a "Form submission complete" message.

> This is commonly known as Post/Redirect/Get (*http://en.wikipedia.org/wiki/Post/Redirect/Get*).

To facilitate this, Yesod comes built in with a pair of functions: `setMessage` sets a message in the user session, and `getMessage` retrieves the message (and clears it, so it doesn't appear a second time). It's recommended that you put the result of `getMessage` into your `defaultLayout`. For example:

```
        defaultLayout contents = do
            PageContent title headTags bodyTags <- widgetToPageContent contents
            mmsg <- getMessage
            hamletToRepHtml [hamlet|
$doctype 5

<html>
    <head>
        <title>#{title}
        ^{headTags}
    <body>
        $maybe msg <- mmsg
```

```
        <div #message>#{msg}
    ^{bodyTags}
|]
```

We'll cover `getMessage`/`setMessage` in more detail when we discuss sessions.

Custom Error Pages

One of the marks of a professional website is a properly designed error page. Yesod gets you a long way there by automatically using your `defaultLayout` for displaying error pages. But sometimes, you'll want to go even further. For this, you'll want to override the `errorHandler` method:

```
    errorHandler NotFound = fmap chooseRep $ defaultLayout $ do
        setTitle "Request page not located"
        toWidget [hamlet|
<h1>Not Found
<p>We apologize for the inconvenience, but the requested page could not be located.
|]
    errorHandler other = defaultErrorHandler other
```

Here we specify a custom 404 error page. We can also use the `defaultErrorHandler` when we don't want to write a custom handler for each error type. Due to type constraints, we need to start off our methods with `fmap chooseRep`, but otherwise you can write a typical handler function.

In fact, you could even use special responses like redirects:

```
    errorHandler NotFound = redirect RootR
    errorHandler other = defaultErrorHandler other
```

> Even though you *can* do this, I don't actually recommend such practices. A 404 should be a 404.

External CSS and JavaScript

> The functionality described here is automatically included in the scaffolded site, so you don't need to worry about implementing this yourself.

One of the most powerful, and most intimidating, methods in the Yesod typeclass is `addStaticContent`. Remember that a Widget consists of multiple components, including CSS and JavaScript. How exactly does that CSS/JS arrive in the user's browser? By default, they are served in the `<head>` of the page, inside `<style>` and `<script>` tags, respectively.

That might be simple, but it's far from efficient. Every page load will now require loading up the CSS/JS from scratch, even if nothing changed! What we really want is to store this content in an external file and then refer to it from the HTML.

This is where `addStaticContent` comes in. It takes three arguments: the filename extension of the content (`css` or `js`), the mime-type of the content (`text/css` or `text/javascript`) and the content itself. It will then return one of three possible results:

Nothing
: No static file saving occurred; embed this content directly in the HTML. This is the default behavior.

Just (Left Text)
: This content was saved in an external file, and use the given textual link to refer to it.

Just (Right (Route a, Query))
: Same, but now use a type-safe URL along with some query string parameters.

The `Left` result is useful if you want to store your static files on an external server, such as a CDN or memory-backed server. The `Right` result is more commonly used, and ties in very well with the static subsite. This is the recommended approach for most applications, and is provided by the scaffolded site by default.

> You might be wondering: if this is the recommended approach, why isn't it the default? The problem is that it makes a number of assumptions that don't universally hold: your application has a static subsite, and the location of your static files.

The scaffolded `addStaticContent` does a number of intelligent things to help you out:

- It automatically minifies your JavaScript using the `hjsmin` package.
- It names the output files based on a hash of the file contents. This means you can set your cache headers to far in the future without fears of stale content.
- Also, since filenames are based on hashes, you can be guaranteed that a file doesn't need to be written if a file with the same name already exists. The scaffold code automatically checks for the existence of that file, and avoids the costly disk I/O of a write if it's not necessary.

Smarter Static Files

Google recommends an important optimization: serve static files from a separate domain (*http://code.google.com/speed/page-speed/docs/request.html#ServeFromCookielessDomain*). The advantage to this approach is that cookies set on your main domain are not sent when retrieving static files, thus saving on a bit of bandwidth.

To facilitate this, we have the `urlRenderOverride` method. This method intercepts the normal URL rendering and sets a special value for some routes. For example, the scaffolding defines this method as:

```
urlRenderOverride y (StaticR s) =
    Just $ uncurry (joinPath y (Settings.staticRoot $ settings y)) $ renderRoute s
urlRenderOverride _ _ = Nothing
```

This means that static routes are served from a special static root, which you can configure to be a different domain. This is a great example of the power and flexibility of type-safe URLs: with a single line of code you're able to change the rendering of static routes throughout all of your handlers.

Authentication/Authorization

For simple applications, checking permissions inside each handler function can be a simple, convenient approach. However, it doesn't scale well. Eventually, you're going to want to have a more declarative approach. Many systems out there define ACLs, special config files, and a lot of other hocus-pocus. In Yesod, it's just plain old Haskell. There are three methods involved:

isWriteRequest
> Determine if the current request is a "read" or "write" operations. By default, Yesod follows RESTful principles, and assumes `GET`, `HEAD`, `OPTIONS`, and `TRACE` requests are read-only, while all others are can write.

isAuthorized
> Takes a route (i.e., type-safe URL) and a boolean indicating whether or not the request is a write request. It returns an `AuthResult`, which can have one of three values:
> - `Authorized`
> - `AuthenticationRequired`
> - `Unauthorized`
>
> By default, it returns `Authorized` for all requests.

authRoute
> If `isAuthorized` returns `AuthenticationRequired`, then redirect to the given route. If no route is provided (the default), return a 403 "Permission Denied" message.

These methods tie in nicely with the `yesod-auth` package, which is used by the scaffolded site to provide a number of authentication options, such as OpenID, BrowserID, email, username, and Twitter. We'll cover more concrete examples in the auth chapter.

Some Simple Settings

Not everything in the Yesod typeclass is complicated. Some methods are simple functions. Let's just go through the list:

encryptKey
> Yesod uses client-side sessions, which are stored in encrypted, cryptographically-hashed cookies. Well, as long as you provide an encryption key. If this function returns Nothing, then sessions are disabled. This can be a useful optimization on sites that don't need session facilities, as it avoids an encrypt/decrypt pair on each request.

> The combination of encryption and hashing guarantees two properties: the session payload is tamper-proof, and is opaque. Encryption without hashing would allow a user to randomly change the cookie data and still have it accepted by the server, while hashing without encryption would allow inspection of the data.

clientSessionDuration
> How long a session should last for. By default, this is two hours.

sessionIpAddress
> By default, sessions are tied to an individual IP address. If your users are sitting behind a proxy server, this can cause trouble when their IP suddenly changes. This setting lets you disable this security feature.

cookiePath
> What paths within your current domain to set cookies for. The default is "/", and will almost always be correct. One exception might be when you're serving from a subpath within a domain (like our wiki example above).

maximumContentLength
> To prevent Denial of Server (DoS) attacks, Yesod will limit the size of request bodies. Some of the time, you'll want to bump that limit for some routes (e.g., a file upload page). This is where you'd do that.

yepnopeJs
> You can specify the location of the yepnope (*http://yepnopejs.com/*) JavaScript library. If this is given, then yepnope will be used to asynchronously load all of the JavaScript on your page.

Summary

The Yesod typeclass has a number of overrideable methods that allow you to configure your application. They are all optional, and provide sensible defaults. By using built-in Yesod constructs like `defaultLayout` and `getMessage`, you'll get a consistent look-

and-feel throughout your site, including pages automatically generated by Yesod such as error pages and authentication.

We haven't covered all the methods in the Yesod typeclass in this chapter. For a full listing of methods available, you should consult the Haddock documentation.

CHAPTER 7
Routing and Handlers

If we look at Yesod as a Model-View-Controller framework, routing and handlers make up the controller. For contrast, let's describe two other routing approaches used in other web development environments:

- Dispatch based on file name. This is how PHP and ASP work, for example.
- Have a centralized routing function that parses routes based on regular expressions. Django and Rails follow this approach.

Yesod is closer in principle to the latter technique. Even so, there are significant differences. Instead of using regular expressions, Yesod matches on pieces of a route. Instead of having a one-way route-to-handler mapping, Yesod has an intermediate data type (called the route data type, or a type-safe URL) and creates two-way conversion functions.

Coding this more advanced system manually is tedious and error prone. Therefore, Yesod defines a Domain Specific Language (DSL) for specifying routes, and provides Template Haskell functions to convert this DSL to Haskell code. This chapter will explain the syntax of the routing declarations, give you a glimpse of what code is generated for you, and explain the interaction between routing and handler functions.

Route Syntax

Instead of trying to shoe-horn route declarations into an existing syntax, Yesod's approach is to use a simplified syntax designed just for routes. This has the advantage of making the code not only easy to write, but simple enough for someone with no Yesod experience to read and understand the sitemap of your application.

A basic example of this syntax is:

```
/              RootR      GET
/blog          BlogR      GET POST
/blog/#BlogId  BlogPostR  GET POST

/static        StaticR    Static getStatic
```

The next few sections will explain the full details of what goes on in the route declaration.

Pieces

One of the first thing Yesod does when it gets a request is to split up the requested path into pieces. The pieces are tokenized at all forward slashes. For example:

```
toPieces "/" = []
toPieces "/foo/bar/baz/" = ["foo", "bar", "baz", ""]
```

You may notice that there are some funny things going on with trailing slashes, or double slashes ("/foo//bar//"), or a few other things. Yesod believes in having *canonical URLs*; if someone requests a URL with a trailing slash, or with a double slash, they automatically get a redirect to the canonical version. This ensures you have one URL for one resource, and can help with your search rankings.

What this means for you is that you needn't concern yourself with the exact structure of your URLs: you can safely think about pieces of a path, and Yesod automatically handles intercalating the slashes and escaping problematic characters.

If, by the way, you want more fine-tuned control of how paths are split into pieces and joined together again, you'll want to look at the `cleanPath` and `joinPath` methods in the Yesod typeclass chapter.

Types of Pieces

When you are declaring your routes, you have three types of pieces at your disposal:

Static
   This is a plain string that must be matched against precisely in the URL.

Dynamic single
   This is a single piece (i.e., between two forward slashes), but can be a user-submitted value. This is the primary method of receiving extra user input on a page request. These pieces begin with a hash (#) and are followed by a data type. The data type must be an instance of `PathPiece`.

Dynamic multi
   The same as before, but can receive multiple pieces of the URL. This must always be the last piece in a resource pattern. It is specified by an asterisk (*) followed by a data type, which must be an instance of `PathMultiPiece`. Multi pieces are not as common as the other two, though they are very important for implementing features like static trees representing file structure or wikis with arbitrary hierarchies.

Let us take a look at some standard kinds of resource patterns you may want to write. Starting simply, the root of an application will just be /. Similarly, you may want to place your FAQ at /page/faq.

Now let's say you are going to write a Fibonacci website. You may construct your URLs like `/fib/#Int`. But there's a slight problem with this: we do not want to allow negative numbers or zero to be passed into our application. Fortunately, the type system can protect us:

```
newtype Natural = Natural Int
instance PathPiece Natural where
    toPathPiece (Natural i) = T.pack $ show i
    fromPathPiece s =
        case reads $ T.unpack s of
            (i, ""):_
                | i < 1 -> Nothing
                | otherwise -> Just $ Natural i
            [] -> Nothing
```

On line 1 we define a simple newtype wrapper around Int to protect ourselves from invalid input. We can see that `PathPiece` is a typeclass with two methods. `toPath Piece` does nothing more than convert to a `Text`. `fromPathPiece` *attempts* to convert a `Text` to our data type, returning `Nothing` when this conversion is impossible. By using this data type, we can ensure that our handler function is only ever given natural numbers, allowing us to once again use the type system to battle the boundary issue.

> In a real life application, we would also want to ensure we never accidentally constructed an invalid `Natural` value internally to our app. To do so, we could use an approach like smart constructors (*http://www.haskell.org/haskellwiki/Smart_constructors*). For the purposes of this example, we've kept the code simple.

Defining a `PathMultiPiece` is just as simple. Let's say we want to have a wiki with at least two levels of hierarchy; we might define a data type such as:

```
data Page = Page Text Text [Text] -- 2 or more
instance PathMultiPiece Page where
    toPathMultiPiece (Page x y z) = x : y : z
    fromPathMultiPiece (x:y:z) = Just $ Page x y z
    fromPathMultiPiece _ = Nothing
```

Resource Name

Each resource pattern also has a name associated with it. That name will become the constructor for the *type safe URL* data type associated with your application. Therefore, it has to start with a capital letter. By convention, these resource names all end with a capital R. There is nothing forcing you to do this, it is just common practice.

The exact definition of our constructor depends upon the resource pattern it is attached to. Whatever data types are included in single and multi pieces of the pattern become arguments to the data type. This gives us a 1-to-1 correspondence between our type-safe URL values and valid URLs in our application.

> This doesn't necessarily mean that *every* value is a working page, just that it is a potentially valid URL. As an example, that value `PersonR "Michael"` may not resolve to a valid page if there is no Michael in the database.

Let's get some real examples going here. If you had the resource patterns `/person/#Text` named `PersonR`, `/year/#Int` named `YearR` and `/page/faq` named `FaqR`, you would end up with a route data type roughly looking like:

```
data MyRoute = PersonR Text
             | YearR Int
             | FaqR
```

If a user requests the relative URL of `/year/2009`, Yesod will convert it into the value `YearR 2009`. `/person/Michael` becomes `PersonR "Michael"` and `/page/faq` becomes `FaqR`. On the other hand, `/year/two-thousand-nine`, `/person/michael/snoyman` and `/page/FAQ` would all result in 404 errors without ever seeing your code.

Handler Specification

The last piece of the puzzle when declaring your resources is how they will be handled. There are three options in Yesod:

- A single handler function for all request methods on a given route.
- A separate handler function for each request method on a given route. Any other request method will generate a 405 Bad Method response.
- You want to pass off to a *subsite*.

The first two can be easily specified. A single handler function will be a line with just a resource pattern and the resource name, such as `/page/faq FaqR`. In this case, the handler function must be named `handleFaqR`.

A separate handler for each request method will be the same, plus a list of request methods. The request methods must be all capital letters. For example, `/person/#String PersonR GET POST DELETE`. In this case, you would need to define three handler functions: `getPersonR`, `postPersonR`, and `deletePersonR`.

Subsites are a very useful—but complicated—topic in Yesod. We will cover writing subsites later, but using them is not too difficult. The most commonly used subsite is the static subsite, which serves static files for your application. In order to serve static files from `/static`, you would need a resource line like:

```
/static StaticR Static getStatic
```

In this line, `/static` just says where in your URL structure to serve the static files from. There is nothing magical about the word static, you could easily replace it with `/my/non-dynamic/files`.

The next word, `StaticR`, gives the resource name. The next two words are what specify that we are using a subsite. `Static` is the name of the *subsite foundation data type*, and `getStatic` is a function that gets a `Static` value from a value of your master foundation data type.

Let's not get too caught up in the details of subsites now. We will look more closely at the static subsite in the scaffolded site chapter.

Dispatch

Once you have specified your routes, Yesod will take care of all the pesky details of URL dispatch for you. You just need to make sure to provide the appropriate *handler functions*. For subsite routes, you do not need to write any handler functions, but you do for the other two. We mentioned the naming rules above (`MyHandlerR GET` becomes `getMyHandlerR`, `MyOtherHandlerR` becomes `handleMyOtherHandlerR`). Now we need the type signature.

Return Type

Let's look at a simple handler function:

```
mkYesod "Simple" [parseRoutes|
/ HomeR GET
|]

getHomeR :: Handler RepHtml
getHomeR = defaultLayout [whamlet|<h1>This is simple
|]
```

Look at the type signature of `getHomeR`. The first component is `Handler`. `Handler` is a special monad that all handler functions live in. It provides access to request information, lets you send redirects, and lots of other stuff we'll get to soon.

Next we have `RepHtml`. When we discuss representations we will explore the *why* of things more; for now, we are just interested in the *how*.

As you might guess, `RepHtml` is a data type for HTML responses. And as you also may guess, websites need to return responses besides HTML. CSS, JavaScript, images, XML are all necessities of a website. Therefore, the return value of a handler function can be any instance of `HasReps`.

`HasReps` is a powerful concept that allows Yesod to automatically choose the correct representation of your data based on the client request. For now, we will focus just on simple instances such as `RepHtml`, which only provide one representation.

Arguments

Not every route is as simple as the `HomeR` we just defined. Take for instance our `PersonR` route from earlier. The name of the person needs to be passed to the handler function. This translation is very straightforward, and hopefully intuitive. For example:

```
mkYesod "Args" [parseRoutes|
/person/#Text PersonR GET
/year/#Integer/month/#Text/day/#Int DateR
/wiki/*Texts WikiR GET
|]

getPersonR :: Text -> Handler RepHtml
getPersonR name = defaultLayout [whamlet|<h1>Hello #{name}!|]

handleDateR :: Integer -> Text -> Int -> Handler RepPlain -- text/plain
handleDateR year month day =
    return $ RepPlain $ toContent $
        T.concat [month, " ", T.pack $ show day, ", ", T.pack $ show year]

getWikiR :: [Text] -> Handler RepPlain
getWikiR = return . RepPlain . toContent . T.unwords
```

The arguments have the types of the dynamic pieces for each route, in the order specified. Also, notice how we are able to use both `RepHtml` and `RepPlain`.

The Handler Monad

The vast majority of code you write in Yesod sits in the `Handler` monad. If you are approaching this from an MVC (Model-View-Controller) background, your `Handler` code is the Controller. Some important points to know about `Handler`:

- It is an instance of `MonadIO`, so you can run any IO action in your handlers with `liftIO`. By the way, `liftIO` is exported by the `Yesod` module for your convenience.
- Like `Widget`, `Handler` is a fake-monad-transformer. It wraps around a `ResourceT IO` monad. We discuss this type at length in the conduits appendix, but for now, we'll just say it let's you safely allocate resources.
- By "fake," I mean you can't use the standard `lift` function provided by the `transformers` package, you must use the Yesod-supplied one (just like with widgets).
- `Handler` is just a type synonym around `GHandler`. `GHandler` let's you specify exactly which subsite and master site you're using. The `Handler` synonym says that the sub and master sites are your application's type.
- `Handler` provides a lot of different functionality, such as:
    — Providing request information.
    — Keeping a list of the extra response headers you've added.
    — Allowing you to modify the user's session.

— Short-circuiting responses, for redirecting, sending static files, or reporting errors.

The remainder of this chapter will give a brief introduction to some of the most common functions living in the `Handler` monad. I am specifically *not* covering any of the session functions; that will be addressed in the sessions chapter.

Application Information

There are a number of functions that return information about your application as a whole, and give no information about individual requests. Some of these are:

getYesod
   Returns your application foundation value. If you store configuration values in your foundation, you will probably end up using this function a lot.

getYesodSub
   Get the subsite foundation value. Unless you are working in a subsite, this will return the same value as `getYesod`.

getUrlRender
   Returns the *URL rendering function*, which converts a type-safe URL into a `Text`. Most of the time—like with Hamlet—Yesod calls this function for you, but you may occasionally need to call it directly.

getUrlRenderParams
   A variant of `getUrlRender` that converts both a type-safe URL and a list of query-string parameters. This function handles all percent-encoding necessary.

Request Information

The most common information you will want to get about the current request is the requested path, the query string parameters and POSTed form data. The first of those is dealt with in the routing, as described above. The other two are best dealt with using the forms module.

That said, you will sometimes need to get the data in a more raw format. For this purpose, Yesod exposes the `Request` data type along with the `getRequest` function to retrieve it. This gives you access to the full list of GET parameters, cookies, and preferred languages. There are some convenient functions to make these lookups easier, such as `lookupGetParam`, `lookupCookie`, and `languages`. For raw access to the POST parameters, you should use `runRequest`.

If you need even more raw data, like request headers, you can use `waiRequest` to access the Web Application Interface (WAI) request value. See the WAI appendix for more details.

Short Circuiting

The following functions immediately end execution of a handler function and return a result to the user.

redirect
> Sends a redirect response to the user (a 303 response). If you want to use a different response code (e.g., a permanent 301 redirect), you can use `redirectWith`.

> Yesod uses a 303 response for HTTP/1.1 clients, and a 302 response for HTTP/1.0 clients. You can read up on this sordid saga in the HTTP spec.

notFound
> Return a 404 response. This can be useful if a user requests a database value that doesn't exist.

permissionDenied
> Return a 403 response with a specific error message.

invalidArgs
> A 400 response with a list of invalid arguments.

sendFile
> Sends a file from the filesystem with a specified content type. This is the preferred way to send static files, since the underlying WAI handler may be able to optimize this to a `sendfile` system call. Using `readFile` for sending static files should not be necessary.

sendResponse
> Send a normal `HasReps` response with a 200 status code. This is really just a convenience for when you need to break out of some deeply nested code with an immediate response.

sendWaiResponse
> When you need to get low-level and send out a raw WAI response. This can be especially useful for creating streaming responses or a technique like server-sent events.

Response Headers

setCookie
> Set a cookie on the client. Instead of taking an expiration date, this function takes a cookie duration in minutes. Remember, you won't see this cookie using `lookupCookie` until the *following* request.

deleteCookie
: Tells the client to remove a cookie. Once again, `lookupCookie` will not reflect this change until the next request.

setHeader
: Set an arbitrary response header.

setLanguage
: Set the preferred user language, which will show up in the result of the `languages` function.

cacheSeconds
: Set a Cache-Control header to indicate how many seconds this response can be cached. This can be particularly useful if you are using varnish on your server (*http://www.varnish-cache.org*).

neverExpires
: Set the Expires header to the year 2037. You can use this with content which should never expire, such as when the request path has a hash value associated with it.

alreadyExpired
: Sets the Expires header to the past.

expiresAt
: Sets the Expires header to the specified date/time.

Summary

Routing and dispatch is arguably the core of Yesod: it is from here that our type-safe URLs are defined, and the majority of our code is written within the `Handler` monad. This chapter covered some of the most important and central concepts of Yesod, so it is important that you properly digest it.

This chapter also hinted at a number of more complex Yesod topics that we will be covering later. But you should be able to write some very sophisticated web applications with just the knowledge you have learned up until here.

CHAPTER 8
Forms

I've mentioned the boundary issue already: whenever data enters or leaves an application, we need to validate it. Probably the most difficult place this occurs is forms. Coding forms is complex; in an ideal world, we'd like a solution that addresses the following problems:

- Ensure data is valid.
- Marshal string data in the form submission to Haskell data types.
- Generate HTML code for displaying the form.
- Generate JavaScript to do clientside validation and provide more user-friendly widgets, such as date pickers.
- Build up more complex forms by combining together simpler forms.
- Automatically assign names to our fields that are guaranteed to be unique.

The yesod-form package provides all these features in a simple, declarative API. It builds on top of Yesod's widgets to simplify styling of forms and applying JavaScript appropriately. And like the rest of Yesod, it uses Haskell's type system to make sure everything is working correctly.

Synopsis

```
{-# LANGUAGE QuasiQuotes, TemplateHaskell, MultiParamTypeClasses,
    OverloadedStrings, TypeFamilies #-}
import Yesod
import Yesod.Form.Jquery
import Data.Time (Day)
import Data.Text (Text)
import Control.Applicative ((<$>), (<*>))

data Synopsis = Synopsis

mkYesod "Synopsis" [parseRoutes|
/ RootR GET
/person PersonR POST
```

```haskell
    |]

instance Yesod Synopsis

-- Tells our application to use the standard English messages.
-- If you want i18n, then you can supply a translating function instead.
instance RenderMessage Synopsis FormMessage where
    renderMessage _ _ = defaultFormMessage

-- And tell us where to find the jQuery libraries. We'll just use the defaults,
-- which point to the Google CDN.
instance YesodJquery Synopsis

-- The data type we wish to receive from the form
data Person = Person
    { personName :: Text
    , personBirthday :: Day
    , personFavoriteColor :: Maybe Text
    , personEmail :: Text
    , personWebsite :: Maybe Text
    }
  deriving Show

-- Declare the form. The type signature is a bit intimidating, but here's the
-- overview:
--
-- * The Html parameter is used for encoding some extra information. See the
-- discussion regarding runFormGet and runFormPost below for further
-- explanation.
--
-- * We have the sub and master site types, as usual.
--
-- * FormResult can be in three states: FormMissing (no data available),
-- FormFailure (invalid data) and FormSuccess
--
-- * The Widget is the viewable form to place into the web page.
--
-- Note that the scaffolded site provides a convenient Form type synonym,
-- so that our signature could be written as:
--
-- > personForm :: Form Person
--
-- For our purposes, it's good to see the long version.
personForm :: Html -> MForm Synopsis Synopsis (FormResult Person, Widget)
personForm = renderDivs $ Person
    <$> areq textField "Name" Nothing
    <*> areq (jqueryDayField def
        { jdsChangeYear = True -- give a year dropdown
        , jdsYearRange = "1900:-5" -- 1900 till five years ago
        }) "Birthday" Nothing
    <*> aopt textField "Favorite color" Nothing
    <*> areq emailField "Email address" Nothing
    <*> aopt urlField "Website" Nothing

-- The GET handler displays the form
```

```
getRootR :: Handler RepHtml
getRootR = do
    -- Generate the form to be displayed
    ((_, widget), enctype) <- generateFormPost personForm
    defaultLayout [whamlet|
<p>The widget generated contains only the contents of the form, not the form tag itself. So...
<form method=post action=@{PersonR} enctype=#{enctype}>
    ^{widget}
    <p>It also doesn't include the submit button.
    <input type=submit>
|]

-- The POST handler processes the form. If it is successful, it displays the
-- parsed person. Otherwise, it displays the form again with error messages.
postPersonR :: Handler RepHtml
postPersonR = do
    ((result, widget), enctype) <- runFormPost personForm
    case result of
        FormSuccess person -> defaultLayout [whamlet|<p>#{show person}|]
        _ -> defaultLayout [whamlet|
<p>Invalid input, let's try again.
<form method=post action=@{PersonR} enctype=#{enctype}>
    ^{widget}
    <input type=submit>
|]

main :: IO ()
main = warpDebug 3000 Synopsis
```

Kinds of Forms

Before jumping into the types themselves, we should begin with an overview of the different kinds of forms. There are three categories:

Applicative
These are the most commonly used (it's what appeared in the synopsis). Applicative gives us some nice properties of letting error messages coalesce together and keep a very high-level, declarative approach. (For more information on applicative code, see the Haskell wiki (*http://www.haskell.org/haskellwiki/Applicative_func tor*).)

Monadic
A more powerful alternative to applicative. While this allows you more flexibility, it does so at the cost of being more verbose. Useful if you want to create forms that don't fit into the standard two-column look.

Input
Used only for receiving input. Does not generate any HTML for receiving the user input. Useful for interacting with existing forms.

In addition, there are a number of different variables that come into play for each form and field you will want to set up:

- Is the field required or optional?
- Should it be submitted with GET or POST?
- Does it have a default value, or not?

An overriding goal is to minimize the number of field definitions and let them work in as many contexts as possible. One result of this is that we end up with a few extra words for each field. In the synopsis, you may have noticed things like `areq` and that extra `Nothing` parameter. We'll cover why all of those exist in the course of this chapter, but for now realize that by making these parameters explicit, we are able to reuse the individual fields (like `intField`) in many different ways.

A quick note on naming conventions. Each form type has a one-letter prefix (A, M, and I) that is used in a few places, such as saying MForm. We also use req and opt to mean required and optional. Combining these, we create a required applicative field with `areq`, or an optional input field with `iopt`.

Types

The `Yesod.Form.Types` module declares a few types. Let's start off with some simple helpers:

Enctype
: The encoding type, either `UrlEncoded` or `Multipart`. This data type declares an instance of `ToHtml`, so you can use the enctype directly in Hamlet.

Env
: Maps a parameter name to a list of values.

FileEnv
: Maps a parameter name to the associated uploaded file.

Ints
: As mentioned in the introduction, `yesod-form` automatically assigns a unique name to each field. `Ints` is used to keep track of the next number to assign.

FormResult
: Has one of three possible states: `FormMissing` if no data was submitted, `FormFailure` if there was an error parsing the form (e.g., missing a required field, invalid content), or `FormSuccess` if everything went smoothly.

Next we have three data types used for defining individual fields.

> A field is a single piece of information, such as a number, a string, or an email address. Fields are combined together to build forms.

Field
: Defines two pieces of functionality: how to parse the text input from a user into a Haskell value, and how to create the widget to be displayed to the user. yesod-form defines a number of individual Fields in `Yesod.Form.Fields`.

FieldSettings
: Basic information on how a field should be displayed, such as the display name, an optional tooltip, and possibly hardcoded `id` and `name` attributes. (If none are provided, they are automatically generated.)

> `FieldSettings` provides an `IsString` instance, so when you need to provide a `FieldSettings` value, you can actually type in a literal string. That's how we interacted with it in the synopsis.

FieldView
: An intermediate format containing a bunch of view information on a field. This is hardly ever used directly by the user, we'll see more details later.

And finally, we get to the important stuff: the forms themselves. There are three types for this: `MForm` is for monadic forms, `AForm` for applicative, and `IForm` (declared in `IForm`) for input. `MForm` is actually a type synonym for a monad stack that provides the following features:

- A `Reader` monad giving us the parameters (`Env` and `FileEnv`), the master site argument and the list of languages the user supports. The last two are used for i18n (more on this later).
- A `Writer` monad keeping track of the `Enctype`. A form will always be `UrlEncoded`, unless there is a file input field, which will force us to use multipart instead.
- A `State` monad holding an `Ints` to keep track of the next unique name to produce.

An `AForm` is pretty similar. However, there are a few major differences:

- It produces a list of `FieldViews`. This allows us to keep an abstract idea of the form display, and then at the end of the day choose an appropriate function for laying it out on the page. In the synopsis, we used `renderDivs`, which creates a bunch of div tags. Another option would be `renderTable`.
- It does not provide a `Monad` instance. The goal of `Applicative` is to allow the entire form to run, grab as much information on each field as possible, and then create the final result. This cannot work in the context of `Monad`.

An `IForm` is even simpler: it returns either a list of error messages or a result.

Converting

"But wait a minute," you say. "You said the synopsis uses applicative forms, but I'm sure the type signature said `MForm`. Shouldn't it be Monadic?" That's true, the final form we produced was monadic. But what really happened is that we converted an applicative form to a monadic one.

Again, our goal is to reuse code as much as possible, and minimize the number of functions in the API. And Monadic forms are more powerful than Applicative, if more clumsy, so anything that can be expressed in an Applicative form could also be expressed in a Monadic form. There are two core functions that help out with this: `aformToForm` converts any applicative form to a monadic one, and `formToAForm` converts certain kinds of monadic forms to applicative forms.

"But wait **another** minute," you insist. "I didn't see any `aformToForm`!" Also true. The `renderDivs` function takes care of that for us.

Create AForms

Now that I've (hopefully) convinced you that in our synopsis we were really dealing with applicative forms, let's have a look and try to understand how these things get created. Let's take a simple example:

```
data Car = Car
    { carModel :: Text
    , carYear :: Int
    }
  deriving Show

carAForm :: AForm Synopsis Synopsis Car
carAForm = Car
    <$> areq textField "Model" Nothing
    <*> areq intField "Year" Nothing

carForm :: Html -> MForm Synopsis Synopsis (FormResult Car, Widget)
carForm = renderTable carAForm
```

Here, we've explicitly split up applicative and monadic forms. In `carAForm`, we use the `<$>` and `<*>` operators. This should not be surprising; these are almost always used in applicative-style code. And we have one line for each record in our `Car` data type. Perhaps unsurprisingly, we have a `textField` for the `Text` record, and an `intField` for the `Int` record.

Let's look a bit more closely at the `areq` function. Its (simplified) type signature is `Field a -> FieldSettings -> Maybe a -> AForm a`. So that first argument is going to determine the data type of this field, how to parse it, and how to render it. The next argument,

`FieldSettings`, tells us the label, tooltip, name, and ID of the field. In this case, we're using the previously mentioned `IsString` instance of `FieldSettings`.

And what's up with that `Maybe a`? It provides the optional default value. For example, if we want our form to fill in "2007" as the default car year, we would use `areq intField "Year" (Just 2007)`. We can even take this to the next level, and have a form that takes an optional parameter giving the default values.

Example 8-1. Form with default values

```
carAForm :: Maybe Car -> AForm Synopsis Synopsis Car
carAForm mcar = Car
    <$> areq textField "Model" (carModel <$> mcar)
    <*> areq intField "Year" (carYear <$> mcar)
```

Optional Fields

Suppose we wanted to have an optional field (like the car color). All we do instead is use the `aopt` function.

Example 8-2. Optional fields

```
data Car = Car
    { carModel :: Text
    , carYear :: Int
    , carColor :: Maybe Text
    }
    deriving Show

carAForm :: AForm Synopsis Synopsis Car
carAForm = Car
    <$> areq textField "Model" Nothing
    <*> areq intField "Year" Nothing
    <*> aopt textField "Color" Nothing
```

And like required fields, the last argument is the optional default value. However, this has two layers of Maybe wrapping. This may seem redundant (and it is), but it makes it much easier to write code that takes an optional default form parameter, such as in the next example.

Example 8-3. Default optional fields

```
data Car = Car
    { carModel :: Text
    , carYear :: Int
    , carColor :: Maybe Text
    }
    deriving Show

carAForm :: Maybe Car -> AForm Synopsis Synopsis Car
carAForm mcar = Car
    <$> areq textField "Model" (carModel <$> mcar)
    <*> areq intField  "Year"  (carYear  <$> mcar)
```

```
        <*> aopt textField "Color" (carColor <$> mcar)

carForm :: Html -> MForm Synopsis Synopsis (FormResult Car, Widget)
carForm = renderTable $ carAForm $ Just $ Car "Forte" 2010 $ Just "gray"
```

Validation

How would we make our form only accept cars created after 1990? If you remember, we said above that the `Field` itself contained the information on what is a valid entry. So all we need to do is write a new `Field`, right? Well, that would be a bit tedious. Instead, let's just modify an existing one:

```
carAForm :: Maybe Car -> AForm Synopsis Synopsis Car
carAForm mcar = Car
    <$> areq textField    "Model" (carModel <$> mcar)
    <*> areq carYearField "Year"  (carYear  <$> mcar)
    <*> aopt textField    "Color" (carColor <$> mcar)
  where
    errorMessage :: Text
    errorMessage = "Your car is too old, get a new one!"

    carYearField = check validateYear intField

    validateYear y
        | y < 1990 = Left errorMessage
        | otherwise = Right y
```

The trick here is the check function. It takes a function (`validateYear`) that returns either an error message or a modified field value. In this example, we haven't modified the value at all. That is usually going to be the case. This kind of checking is very common, so we have a shortcut:

```
    carYearField = checkBool (>= 1990) errorMessage intField
```

`checkBool` takes two parameters: a condition that must be fulfilled, and an error message to be displayed if it was not.

> You may have noticed the explicit `Text` type signature on `errorMessage`. In the presence of `OverloadedStrings`, this is necessary. In order to support i18n, messages can have many different data types, and GHC has no way of determining which instance of `IsString` you intended to use.

It's great to make sure the car isn't too old. But what if we want to make sure that the year specified is not from the future? In order to look up the current year, we'll need to run some IO. For such circumstances, we'll need checkM:

```
    carYearField = checkM inPast $ checkBool (>= 1990) errorMessage intField

    inPast y = do
```

```
        thisYear <- liftIO getCurrentYear
        return $ if y <= thisYear
            then Right y
            else Left ("You have a time machine!" :: Text)

getCurrentYear :: IO Int
getCurrentYear = do
    now <- getCurrentTime
    let today = utctDay now
    let (year, _, _) = toGregorian today
    return $ fromInteger year
```

inPast is a function that will return an Either result. However, it uses a Handler monad. We use liftIO getCurrentYear to get the current year and then compare it against the user-supplied year. Also, notice how we can chain together multiple validators.

> Since the checkM validator runs in the Handler monad, it has access to a lot of the stuff you can normally do in Yesod. This is especially useful for running database actions, which we'll cover in the Persistent chapter.

More Sophisticated Fields

Our color entry field is nice, but it's not exactly user-friendly. What we really want is a drop-down list.

Example 8-4. Drop-down lists

```
data Car = Car
    { carModel :: Text
    , carYear :: Int
    , carColor :: Maybe Color
    }
  deriving Show

data Color = Red | Blue | Gray | Black
    deriving (Show, Eq, Enum, Bounded)

carAForm :: Maybe Car -> AForm Synopsis Synopsis Car
carAForm mcar = Car
    <$> areq textField "Model" (carModel <$> mcar)
    <*> areq carYearField "Year" (carYear <$> mcar)
    <*> aopt (selectFieldList colors) "Color" (carColor <$> mcar)
  where
    colors :: [(Text, Color)]
    colors = [("Red", Red), ("Blue", Blue), ("Gray", Gray), ("Black", Black)]
```

selectFieldList takes a list of pairs. The first item in the pair is the text displayed to the user in the drop-down list, and the second item is the actual Haskell value. Of course, the code above looks really repetitive; we can get the same result using the Enum and Bounded instance GHC automatically derives for us.

Example 8-5. Uses Enum and Bounded

```
data Car = Car
    { carModel :: Text
    , carYear :: Int
    , carColor :: Maybe Color
    }
  deriving Show

data Color = Red | Blue | Gray | Black
    deriving (Show, Eq, Enum, Bounded)

carAForm :: Maybe Car -> AForm Synopsis Synopsis Car
carAForm mcar = Car
    <$> areq textField "Model" (carModel <$> mcar)
    <*> areq carYearField "Year" (carYear <$> mcar)
    <*> aopt (selectFieldList colors) "Color" (carColor <$> mcar)
  where
    colors = map (pack . show &&& id) $ [minBound..maxBound]
```

[minBound..maxBound] gives us a list of all the different Color values. We then apply a map and &&& (a.k.a., the fan-out operator) to turn that into a list of pairs.

Some people prefer radio buttons to drop-down lists. Fortunately, this is just a one-word change. For example, see Radio buttons:

Example 8-6. Radio buttons

```
data Car = Car
    { carModel :: Text
    , carYear :: Int
    , carColor :: Maybe Color
    }
  deriving Show

data Color = Red | Blue | Gray | Black
    deriving (Show, Eq, Enum, Bounded)

carAForm :: Maybe Car -> AForm Synopsis Synopsis Car
carAForm mcar = Car
    <$> areq textField "Model" (carModel <$> mcar)
    <*> areq carYearField "Year" (carYear <$> mcar)
    <*> aopt (radioFieldList colors) "Color" (carColor <$> mcar)
  where
    colors = map (pack . show &&& id) $ [minBound..maxBound]
```

Running Forms

At some point, we're going to need to take our beautiful forms and produce some results. There are a number of different functions available for this, each with its own purpose. I'll go through them, starting with the most common.

runFormPost
: This will run your form against any submitted `POST` parameters. If this is not a `POST` submission, it will return a `FormMissing`. This automatically inserts a security token as a hidden form field to avoid CSRF (*http://en.wikipedia.org/wiki/Cross-site_request_forgery*) attacks.

runFormGet
: Same as `runFormPost`, for GET parameters. In order to distinguish a normal GET page load from a `GET` submission, it includes an extra `_hasdata` hidden field in the form.

runFormPostNoNonce
: Same as `runFormPost`, but does not include (or require) the CSRF security token.

generateFormPost
: Instead of binding to existing `POST` parameters, acts as if there are none. This can be useful when you want to generate a new form after a previous form was submitted, such as in a wizard.

generateFormGet
: Same as `generateFormPost`, but for `GET`.

The return type from the first three is `((FormResult a, Widget), Enctype)`. The `Widget` will already have any validation errors and previously submitted values.

i18n

There have been a few references to i18n in this chapter. The topic will get more thorough coverage in its own chapter, but since it has such a profound effect on `yesod-form`, I wanted to give a brief overview. The idea behind i18n in Yesod is to have data types represent messages. Each site can have an instance of `RenderMessage` for a given data type which will translate that message based on a list of languages the user accepts. As a result of all this, there are a few things you should be aware of:

- There is an automatic instance of `RenderMessage` for `Text` in every site, so you can just use plain strings if you don't care about i18n support. However, you may need to use explicit type signatures occasionally.
- `yesod-form` expresses all of its messages in terms of the `FormMessage` data type. Therefore, to use `yesod-form`, you'll need to have an appropriate `RenderMessage` instance. A simple one that uses the default English translations would be:

```
instance RenderMessage MyApp FormMessage where
    renderMessage _ _ = defaultFormMessage
```

This is provided automatically by the scaffolded site.

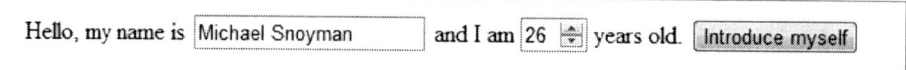

Figure 8-1. A non-standard form layout

Monadic Forms

Oftentimes, a simple form layout is adequate, and applicative forms excel at this approach. Sometimes, however, you'll want to have a more customized look to your form.

For these use cases, monadic forms fit the bill. They are a bit more verbose than their applicative cousins, but this verbosity allows you to have complete control over what the form will look like. In order to generate the form above, we could code something like this.

```
{-# LANGUAGE OverloadedStrings, TypeFamilies, QuasiQuotes,
            TemplateHaskell, MultiParamTypeClasses #-}
import Yesod
import Control.Applicative
import Data.Text (Text)

data MFormExample = MFormExample

mkYesod "MFormExample" [parseRoutes|
/ RootR GET
|]

instance Yesod MFormExample

instance RenderMessage MFormExample FormMessage where
    renderMessage _ _ = defaultFormMessage

data Person = Person { personName :: Text, personAge :: Int }
    deriving Show

personForm :: Html -> MForm MFormExample MFormExample (FormResult Person, Widget)
personForm extra = do
    (nameRes, nameView) <- mreq textField "this is not used" Nothing
    (ageRes, ageView) <- mreq intField "neither is this" Nothing
    let personRes = Person <$> nameRes <*> ageRes
    let widget = do
            toWidget [lucius|
##{fvId ageView} {
    width: 3em;
}
|]
            [whamlet|
#{extra}
<p>
    Hello, my name is #
    ^{fvInput nameView}
    \ and I am #
    ^{fvInput ageView}
```

80 | Chapter 8: Forms

```
        \ years old. #
    <input type=submit value="Introduce myself">
|]
    return (personRes, widget)

getRootR :: Handler RepHtml
getRootR = do
    ((res, widget), enctype) <- runFormGet personForm
    defaultLayout [whamlet|
<p>Result: #{show res}
<form enctype=#{enctype}>
    ^{widget}
|]

main :: IO ()
main = warpDebug 3000 MFormExample
```

Similar to the applicative `areq`, we use `mreq` for monadic forms. (And yes, there's also `mopt` for optional fields.) But there's a big difference: `mreq` gives us back a pair of values. Instead of hiding away the `FieldView` value and automatically inserting it into a widget, we get the control to insert it as we see fit.

`FieldView` has a number of pieces of information. The most important is `fvInput`, which is the actual form field. In this example, we also use `fvId`, which gives us back the HTML `id` attribute of the input tag. In our example, we use that to specify the width of the field.

You might be wondering what the story is with the "this is not used" and "neither is this" values. `mreq` takes a `FieldSettings` as its second argument. Since `FieldSettings` provides an `IsString` instance, the strings are essentially expanded by the compiler to:

```
fromString "this is not used" == FieldSettings
    { fsLabel = "this is not used"
    , fsTooltip = Nothing
    , fsId = Nothing
    , fsName = Nothing
    , fsClass = []
    }
```

In the case of applicative forms, the `fsLabel` and `fsTooltip` values are used when constructing your HTML. In the case of monadic forms, Yesod does not generate any of the "wrapper" HTML for you, and therefore these values are ignored. However, we still keep the `FieldSettings` parameter to allow you to override the `id` and `name` attributes of your fields if desired.

The other interesting bit is the `extra` value. GET forms include an extra field to indicate that they have been submitted, and POST forms include a security token to prevent CSRF attacks. If you don't include this extra hidden field in your form, Yesod will not accept it.

Other than that, things are pretty straightforward. We create our `personRes` value by combining together the `nameRes` and `ageRes` values, and then return a tuple of the person and the widget. And in the `getRootR` function, everything looks just like an applicative form. In fact, you could swap out our monadic form with an applicative one and the code would still work.

Input Forms

Applicative and monadic forms handle both the generation of your HTML code and the parsing of user input. Sometimes, you only want to do the latter, such as when there's an already-existing form in HTML somewhere, or if you want to generate a form dynamically using JavaScript. In such a case, you'll want input forms.

These work mostly the same as applicative and monadic forms, with some differences:

- You use `runInputPost` and `runInputGet`.
- You use `ireq` and `iopt`. These functions now only take two arguments: the field type and the name (i.e., HTML `name` attribute) of the field in question.
- After running a form, it returns the value. It doesn't return a widget or an encoding type.
- If there are any validation errors, the page returns an "invalid arguments" error page.

You can use input forms to recreate the previous example. Note, however, that the input version is less user friendly. If you make a mistake in an applicative or monadic form, you will be brought back to the same page, with your previously entered values in the form, and an error message explaining what you need to correct. With input forms, the user simply gets an error message.

```
{-# LANGUAGE OverloadedStrings, TypeFamilies, QuasiQuotes,
             TemplateHaskell, MultiParamTypeClasses #-}
import Yesod
import Control.Applicative
import Data.Text (Text)

data Input = Input

mkYesod "Input" [parseRoutes|
/ RootR GET
/input InputR GET
|]

instance Yesod Input

instance RenderMessage Input FormMessage where
    renderMessage _ _ = defaultFormMessage

data Person = Person { personName :: Text, personAge :: Int }
    deriving Show

getRootR :: Handler RepHtml
getRootR = defaultLayout [whamlet|
<form action=@{InputR}>
```

```
        <p>
            My name is #
            <input type=text name=name>
            \ and I am #
            <input type=text name=age>
            \ years old. #
            <input type=submit value="Introduce myself">
    |]

getInputR :: Handler RepHtml
getInputR = do
    person <- runInputGet $ Person
                <$> ireq textField "name"
                <*> ireq intField "age"
    defaultLayout [whamlet|<p>#{show person}|]

main :: IO ()
main = warpDebug 3000 Input
```

Custom Fields

The fields that come built-in with Yesod will likely cover the vast majority of your form needs. But occasionally, you'll need something more specialized. Fortunately, you can create new forms in Yesod yourself. The `Field` data type has two records: `fieldParse` takes a list of values submitted by the user and returns one of three results:

- An error message saying validation failed
- The parsed value
- Nothing, indicating that no data was supplied

That last case might sound surprising: shouldn't Yesod automatically know that no information is supplied when the input list is empty? Well, no, actually. Checkboxes, for instance, indicate an unchecked state by sending in an empty list.

Also, what's up with the list? Shouldn't it be a `Maybe`? Well, that's also not the case. With grouped checkboxes and multi-select lists, you'll have multiple widgets with the same name. We also use this trick in our example below.

The second record is `fieldView`, and it renders a widget to display to the user. This function has four arguments: the `id` attribute, the `name` attribute, the result, and a `Bool` indicating whether the field is required.

What did I mean by result? It's actually an `Either`, giving either the unparsed input (when parsing failed) or the successfully parsed value. `intField` is a great example of how this works. If you type in **42**, the value of result will be `Right 42`. But if you type in **turtle**, the result will be `Left "turtle"`. This lets you put in a value attribute on your input tag that will give the user a consistent experience.

As a small example, we'll create a new field type that is a password confirm field. This field has two text inputs—both with the same name attribute—and returns an error message if the values don't match. Note that, unlike most fields, it does *not* provide a value attribute on the input tags, as you don't want to send back a user-entered password in your HTML **ever**.

```
passwordConfirmField :: Field sub master Text
passwordConfirmField = Field
    { fieldParse = \rawVals ->
        case rawVals of
            [a, b]
                | a == b -> return $ Right $ Just a
                | otherwise -> return $ Left "Passwords don't match"
            [] -> return $ Right Nothing
            _ -> return $ Left "You must enter two values"
    , fieldView = \idAttr nameAttr _ eResult isReq -> [whamlet|
<input id=#{idAttr} name=#{nameAttr} type=password>
<div>Confirm:
<input id=#{idAttr}-confirm name=#{nameAttr} type=password>
|]
    }

getRootR :: Handler RepHtml
getRootR = do
    ((res, widget), enctype) <- runFormGet $ renderDivs
        $ areq passwordConfirmField "Password" Nothing
    defaultLayout [whamlet|
<p>Result: #{show res}
<form enctype=#{enctype}>
    ^{widget}
    <input type=submit value="Change password">
|]
```

Summary

Forms in Yesod are broken up into three groups. Applicative is the most common, as it provides a nice user interface with an easy-to-use API. Monadic forms give you more power, but are harder to use. Input forms are intended when you just want to read data from the user, not generate the input widgets.

There are a number of different `Fields` provided by Yesod out-of-the-box. In order to use these in your forms, you need to indicate the kind of form and whether the field is required or optional. The result is six helper functions: `areq`, `aopt`, `mreq`, `mopt`, `ireq`, and `iopt`.

Forms have significant power available. They can automatically insert JavaScript to help you leverage nicer UI controls, such as a jQuery UI date picker. Forms are also fully i18n-ready, so you can support a global community of users. And when you have more specific needs, you can slap on some validation functions to an existing field, or write a new one from scratch.

CHAPTER 9
Sessions

HTTP is a stateless protocol. While some view this as a disadvantage, advocates of RESTful web development laud this as a plus. When state is removed from the picture, it is easier to scale applications, caching can happen automatically, and many other nice side effects occur. You can draw many parallels with the non-mutable nature of Haskell in general.

As much as possible, RESTful applications should avoid storing state about an interaction with a client. However, it is sometimes unavoidable. Features like shopping carts are the classic example, but other more mundane interactions like proper login handling can be greatly enhanced by proper usage of sessions.

This chapter will describe how Yesod stores session data, how you can access this data, and some special functions to help you make the most of sessions.

Clientsession

One of the earliest packages spun off from Yesod was `clientsession`. This package uses encryption and signatures to store data in a client-side cookie. The encryption prevents the user from inspecting the data, and the signature ensures that the session can be neither hijacked nor tampered with.

It might sound like a bad idea from an efficiency standpoint to store data in a cookie: after all, this means that the data must be sent on every request. However, in practice, clientsession can be a great boon for performance.

- No server side database lookup is required to service a request.
- We can easily scale horizontally: each request contains all the information we need to send a response.
- To avoid undue bandwidth overhead, production sites can serve their static content from a separate domain name to avoid the overhead of transmitting the session cookie for each request.

Storing megabytes of information in the session will be a bad idea. But for that matter, most session implementations recommend against such practices. If you really need massive storage for a user, it is best to store a lookup key in the session, and put the actual data in a database.

All of the interaction with clientsession is handled by Yesod internally, but there are a few spots where you can tweak the behavior just a bit.

Controlling Sessions

There are three functions in the Yesod typeclass that control how sessions work. encryptKey returns the encryption key used. By default, it will take this from a local file, so that sessions can persist between database shutdowns. This file will be automatically created and filled with random data if it does not exist. And if you override this function to return Nothing, sessions will be disabled.

> Why disable sessions? They **do** introduce a performance overhead. Under normal circumstances, this overhead is minimal, especially compared to database access. However, when dealing with very basic tasks, the overhead can become noticeable. But be careful about disabling sessions: this will also disable such features as CSRF (Cross-Site Request Forgery) protection.

The next function is clientSessionDuration. This function gives the number of minutes that a session should be active. The default is 120 (2 hours).

This value ends up affecting the session cookie in two ways: first, it determines the expiration date for the cookie itself. More importantly, however, the session expiration timestamp is encoded inside the session signature. When Yesod decodes the signature, it checks whether the date is in the past; if so, it ignores the session values.

> Every time Yesod sends a response to the client, it sends an updated session cookie with a new expire date. This way, even if you do not change the session values themselves, a session will not time out if the user continues to browse your site.

And this leads very nicely to the last function: sessionIpAddress. By default, Yesod also encodes the client's IP address inside the cookie to prevent session hijacking. In general, this is a good thing. However, some ISPs are known for putting their users behind proxies that rewrite their IP addresses, sometimes changing the source IP in the middle of the session. If this happens, and you have sessionIpAddress enabled, the user's session will be reset. Turning this setting to False will allow a session to continue under such circumstances, at the cost of exposing a user to session hijacking.

Session Operations

Like most frameworks, a session in Yesod is a key-value store. The base session API boils down to four functions: `lookupSession` gets a value for a key (if available), `getSession` returns all of the key/value pairs, `setSession` sets a value for a key, and `deleteSession` clears a value for a key.

```
{-# LANGUAGE TypeFamilies, QuasiQuotes, TemplateHaskell, MultiParamTypeClasses,
OverloadedStrings #-}
import Yesod
import Control.Applicative ((<$>), (<*>))

data SessionExample = SessionExample

mkYesod "SessionExample" [parseRoutes|
/ Root GET POST
|]

getRoot :: Handler RepHtml
getRoot = do
    sess <- getSession
    hamletToRepHtml [hamlet|
<form method=post>
    <input type=text name=key>
    <input type=text name=val>
    <input type=submit>
<h1>#{show sess}
|]

postRoot :: Handler ()
postRoot = do
    (key, mval) <- runInputPost $ (,) <$> ireq textField "key" <*> iopt textField "val"
    case mval of
        Nothing -> deleteSession key
        Just val -> setSession key val
    liftIO $ print (key, mval)
    redirect Root

instance Yesod SessionExample where
    clientSessionDuration _ = 1

instance RenderMessage SessionExample FormMessage where
    renderMessage _ _ = defaultFormMessage

main :: IO ()
main = warpDebug 3000 SessionExample
```

Messages

One usage of sessions previously alluded to is messages. They come to solve a common problem in web development: the user performs a POST request, the web app makes a change, and then the web app wants to *simultaneously* redirect the user to a new page and send the user a success message. (This is known as Post/Redirect/Get.)

Yesod provides a pair of functions to make this very easy: setMessage stores a value in the session, and getMessage both reads the value most recently put into the session, and clears the old value so it does not accidently get displayed twice.

It is recommended to have a call to getMessage in defaultLayout so that any available message is shown to a user immediately, without having to remember to add getMessage calls to every handler.

```
{-# LANGUAGE OverloadedStrings, TypeFamilies, TemplateHaskell,
             QuasiQuotes, MultiParamTypeClasses #-}
import Yesod

data Messages = Messages

mkYesod "Messages" [parseRoutes|
/ RootR GET
/set-message SetMessageR POST
|]

instance Yesod Messages where
    defaultLayout widget = do
        pc <- widgetToPageContent widget
        mmsg <- getMessage
        hamletToRepHtml [hamlet|
$doctype 5
<html>
    <head>
        <title>#{pageTitle pc}
        ^{pageHead pc}
    <body>
        $maybe msg <- mmsg
            <p>Your message was: #{msg}
        ^{pageBody pc}
|]

instance RenderMessage Messages FormMessage where
    renderMessage _ _ = defaultFormMessage

getRootR :: Handler RepHtml
getRootR = defaultLayout [whamlet|
<form method=post action=@{SetMessageR}>
    My message is: #
    <input type=text name=message>
    <input type=submit>
|]

postSetMessageR :: Handler ()
postSetMessageR = do
    msg <- runInputPost $ ireq textField "message"
    setMessage $ toHtml msg
    redirect RootR
```

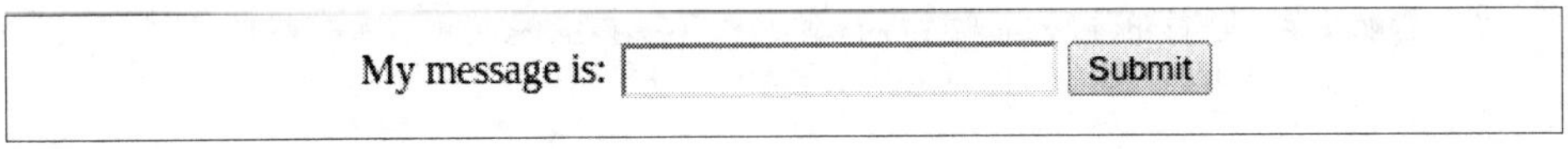

Figure 9-1. Initial page load, no message

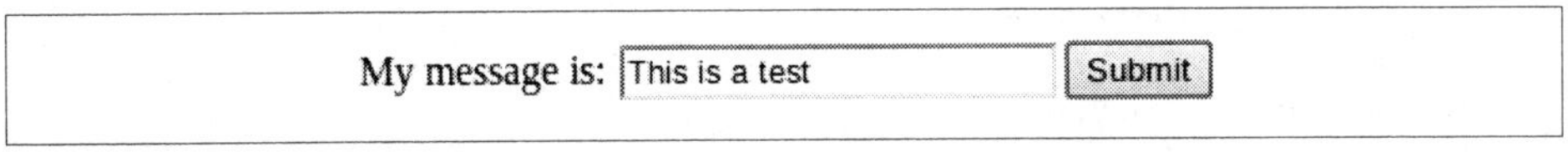

Figure 9-2. New message entered in text box

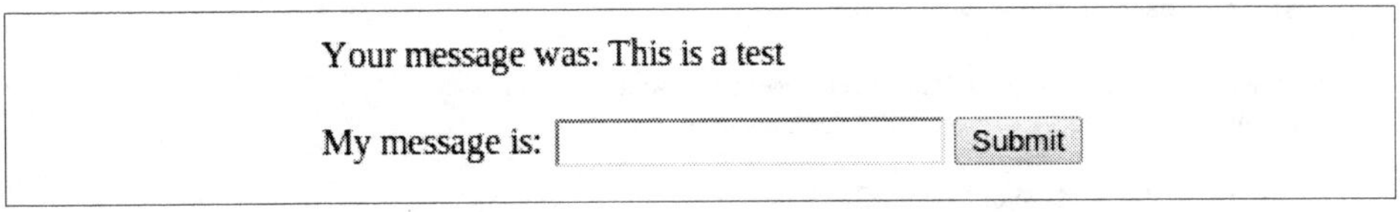

Figure 9-3. After form submit, message appears at top of page

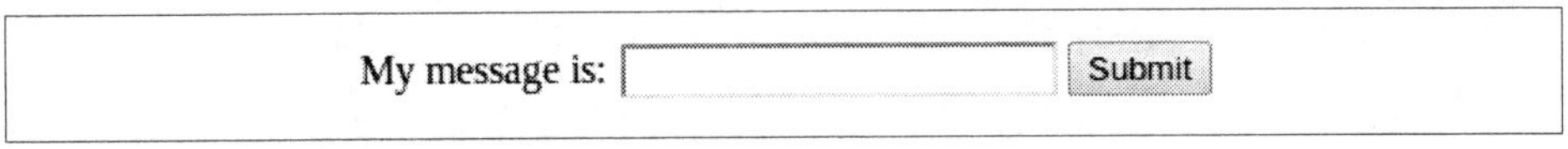

Figure 9-4. After refresh, the message is cleared

```
main :: IO ()
main = warpDebug 3000 Messages
```

Ultimate Destination

Not to be confused with a horror film, this concept is used internally in `yesod-auth`. Suppose a user requests a page that requires authentication. If the user is not yet logged in, you need to send him/her to the login page. A well-designed web app will then *send them back to the first page they requested*. That's what we call the ultimate destination.

`redirectUltDest` sends the user to the ultimate destination set in his/her session, clearing that value from the session. It takes a default destination as well, in case there is no destination set. For setting the session, there are three options:

- `setUltDest` sets the destination to the given URL.
- `setUltDestCurrent` sets the destination to the currently requested URL.
- `setUltDestReferer` sets the destination based on the `Referer` header (the page that led the user to the current page).

Let's look at a small sample app. It will allow the user to set his/her name in the session, and then tell the user his/her name from another route. If the name hasn't been set yet, the user will be redirected to the set name page, with an ultimate destination set to come back to the current page.

```haskell
{-# LANGUAGE OverloadedStrings, TypeFamilies, TemplateHaskell,
             QuasiQuotes, MultiParamTypeClasses #-}
import Yesod

data UltDest = UltDest

mkYesod "UltDest" [parseRoutes|
/ RootR GET
/setname SetNameR GET POST
/sayhello SayHelloR GET
|]

instance Yesod UltDest

instance RenderMessage UltDest FormMessage where
    renderMessage _ _ = defaultFormMessage

getRootR = defaultLayout [whamlet|
<p>
    <a href=@{SetNameR}>Set your name
<p>
    <a href=@{SayHelloR}>Say hello
|]

-- Display the set name form
getSetNameR = defaultLayout [whamlet|
<form method=post>
    My name is #
    <input type=text name=name>
    . #
    <input type=submit value="Set name">
|]

-- Retrieve the submitted name from the user
postSetNameR :: Handler ()
postSetNameR = do
    -- Get the submitted name and set it in the session
    name <- runInputPost $ ireq textField "name"
    setSession "name" name

    -- After we get a name, redirect to the ultimate destination.
    -- If no destination is set, default to the homepage
    redirectUltDest RootR

getSayHelloR = do
    -- Lookup the name value set in the session
    mname <- lookupSession "name"
    case mname of
        Nothing -> do
            -- No name in the session, set the current page as
            -- the ultimate destination and redirect to the
            -- SetName page
            setUltDestCurrent
            setMessage "Please tell me your name"
            redirect SetNameR
```

```
        Just name -> defaultLayout [whamlet|
<p>Welcome #{name}
|]

main :: IO ()
main = warpDebug 3000 UltDest
```

Summary

Sessions are the number one way we bypass the statelessness imposed by HTTP. We shouldn't consider this an escape hatch to perform whatever actions we want: statelessness in web applications is a virtue, and we should respect it whenever possible. However, there are specific cases where it is vital to retain some state.

The session API in Yesod is very simple. It provides a key-value store, and a few convenience functions built on top for common use cases. If used properly, with small payloads, sessions should be an unobtrusive part of your web development.

CHAPTER 10
Persistent

Forms deal with the boundary between the user and the application. Another boundary we need to deal with is between the application and the storage layer. Whether it be a SQL database, a YAML file, or a binary blob, odds are you have to work to get your storage layer to accept your application data types. Persistent is Yesod's answer to data storage—a type-safe, universal data store interface for Haskell.

Haskell has many different database bindings available. However, most of these have little knowledge of a schema and therefore do not provide useful static guarantees. They also force database-dependent APIs and data types on the programmer. Haskellers have attempted a more revolutionary route of creating Haskell-specific data stores to get around these flaws that allow one to easily store any Haskell type. These options are great for certain use cases, but they constrain one to the storage techniques provided by the library, do not interface well with other languages, and the flexibility can also mean one must write reams of code for querying data. In contrast, Persistent allows us to choose among existing databases that are highly tuned for different data storage use cases, interoperate with other programming languages, and to use a safe and productive query interface.

Persistent follows the guiding principles of type safety and concise, declarative syntax. Some other nice features are:

- Database-agnostic. There is first-class support for PostgreSQL, SQLite, and MongoDB, with experimental CouchDB and MySQL support in the works.
- By being non-relational in nature, we simultaneously are able to support a wider number of storage layers and are not constrained by some of the performance bottlenecks incurred through joins.
- A major source of frustration in dealing with SQL databases is changes to the schema. Persistent can automatically perform database migrations.

Synopsis

```haskell
{-# LANGUAGE QuasiQuotes, TemplateHaskell, TypeFamilies, OverloadedStrings #-}
{-# LANGUAGE GADTs, FlexibleContexts #-}
import Database.Persist
import Database.Persist.Sqlite
import Database.Persist.TH
import Control.Monad.IO.Class (liftIO)

share [mkPersist sqlSettings, mkMigrate "migrateAll"] [persist|
Person
    name String
    age Int Maybe
BlogPost
    title String
    authorId PersonId
|]

main :: IO ()
main = withSqliteConn ":memory:" $ runSqlConn $ do
    runMigration migrateAll

    johnId <- insert $ Person "John Doe" $ Just 35
    janeId <- insert $ Person "Jane Doe" Nothing

    insert $ BlogPost "My fr1st p0st" johnId
    insert $ BlogPost "One more for good measure" johnId

    oneJohnPost <- selectList [BlogPostAuthorId ==. johnId] [LimitTo 1]
    liftIO $ print (oneJohnPost :: [Entity BlogPost])

    john <- get johnId
    liftIO $ print (john :: Maybe Person)

    delete janeId
    deleteWhere [BlogPostAuthorId ==. johnId]
```

Solving the Boundary Issue

Suppose you are storing information on people in a SQL database. Your table might look something like:

```
CREATE TABLE Person(id SERIAL PRIMARY KEY, name VARCHAR NOT NULL, age INTEGER)
```

And if you are using a database like PostgreSQL, you can be guaranteed that the database will never store some arbitrary text in your age field. (The same cannot be said of SQLite, but let's forget about that for now.) To mirror this database table, you would likely create a Haskell data type that looks something like:

```haskell
data Person = Person
    { personName :: Text
    , personAge :: Int
    }
```

It looks like everything is type safe: the database schema matches our Haskell data types, the database ensures that invalid data can never make it into our data store, and everything is generally awesome. Well, until:

- You want to pull data from the database, and the database layer gives you the data in an untyped format.
- You want to find everyone older than 32, and you accidently write "thirtytwo" in your SQL statement. Guess what: that will compile just fine, and you won't find out you have a problem until runtime.
- You decide you want to find the first 10 people alphabetically. No problem...until you make a typo in your SQL. Once again, you don't find out until runtime.

In dynamic languages, the answers to these issues is unit testing. For everything that *can* go wrong, make sure you write a test case. But as I am sure you are aware by now, that doesn't jive well with the Yesod approach to things. We like to take advantage of Haskell's strong typing to save us wherever possible, and data storage is no exception.

So the question remains: how can we use Haskell's type system to save the day?

Types

Like routing, there is nothing intrinsically difficult about type-safe data access. It just requires a lot of monotonous, error prone, boiler plate code. As usual, this means we can use the type system to keep us honest. And to avoid some of the drudgery, we'll use a sprinkling of Template Haskell.

> Earlier versions of Persistent made much heavier usage of Template Haskell. Starting with 0.6, there is a new architecture inspired by the groundhog package. This approach uses phantom types to carry a lot of the burden.

`PersistValue` is the basic building block of Persistent. It is a sum type that can represent data that gets sent to and from a database. Its definition is:

```
data PersistValue = PersistText Text
                  | PersistByteString ByteString
                  | PersistInt64 Int64
                  | PersistDouble Double
                  | PersistBool Bool
                  | PersistDay Day
                  | PersistTimeOfDay TimeOfDay
                  | PersistUTCTime UTCTime
                  | PersistNull
                  | PersistList [PersistValue]
                  | PersistMap [(T.Text, PersistValue)]
                  | PersistForeignKey ByteString -- ^ intended especially for MongoDB
backend
```

Each Persistent backend needs to know how to translate the relevant values into something the database can understand. However, it would be awkward to have to express all of our data simply in terms of these basic types. The next layer is the `PersistField` typeclass, which defines how an arbitrary Haskell data type can be marshaled to and from a `PersistValue`. A `PersistField` correlates to a column in a SQL database. In our person example above, name and age would be our `PersistField`s.

To tie up the user side of the code, our last typeclass is `PersistEntity`. An instance of PersistEntity correlates with a table in a SQL database. This typeclass defines a number of functions and some associated types. To review, we have the following correspondence between Persistent and SQL:

SQL	Persistent
Data types (VARCHAR, INTEGER, etc)	PersistValue
Column	PersistField
Table	PersistEntity

Code Generation

In order to ensure that the PersistEntity instances match up properly with your Haskell data types, Persistent takes responsibility for both. This is also good from a DRY (don't repeat yourself) perspective: you only need to define your entities once. Let's see a quick example:

```
{-# LANGUAGE QuasiQuotes, TypeFamilies, GeneralizedNewtypeDeriving, TemplateHaskell,
    OverloadedStrings, GADTs #-}
import Database.Persist
import Database.Persist.TH
import Database.Persist.Sqlite
import Control.Monad.IO.Class (liftIO)

mkPersist sqlSettings [persist|
Person
    name String
    age Int
|]
```

We use a combination of Template Haskell and Quasi-Quotation (like when defining routes): `persist` is a quasi-quoter that converts a whitespace-sensitive syntax into a list of entity definitions. (You can also declare your entities in a separate file using `persistFile`.) `mkPersist` takes that list of entities and declares:

- One Haskell data type for each entity.
- A `PersistEntity` instance for each data type defined.

The example above generates code that looks like the following:

```
{-# LANGUAGE TypeFamilies, GeneralizedNewtypeDeriving, OverloadedStrings, GADTs #-}
import Database.Persist
```

```haskell
import Database.Persist.Store
import Database.Persist.Sqlite
import Database.Persist.EntityDef
import Control.Monad.IO.Class (liftIO)
import Control.Applicative

data Person = Person
    { personName :: String
    , personAge :: Int
    }
  deriving (Show, Read, Eq)

type PersonId = Key SqlPersist Person

instance PersistEntity Person where
    -- A Generalized Algebraic Data Type (GADT).
    -- This gives us a type-safe approach to matching fields with
    -- their data types.
    data EntityField Person typ where
        PersonId   :: EntityField Person PersonId
        PersonName :: EntityField Person String
        PersonAge  :: EntityField Person Int

    type PersistEntityBackend Person = SqlPersist

    toPersistFields (Person name age) =
        [ SomePersistField name
        , SomePersistField age
        ]

    fromPersistValues [nameValue, ageValue] = Person
        <$> fromPersistValue nameValue
        <*> fromPersistValue ageValue
    fromPersistValues _ = Left "Invalid fromPersistValues input"

    -- Information on each field, used internally to generate SQL statements
    persistFieldDef PersonId = FieldDef
        (HaskellName "Id")
        (DBName "id")
        (FTTypeCon Nothing "PersonId")
        []
    persistFieldDef PersonName = FieldDef
        (HaskellName "name")
        (DBName "name")
        (FTTypeCon Nothing "String")
        []
    persistFieldDef PersonAge = FieldDef
        (HaskellName "age")
        (DBName "age")
        (FTTypeCon Nothing "Int")
        []
```

As you might expect, our Person data type closely matches the definition we gave in the original Template Haskell version. We also have a Generalized Algebraic Data Type (GADT) that gives a separate constructor for each field. This GADT encodes both the type of the entity and the type of the field. We use its constructors throughout Persistent, such as to ensure that when we apply a filter, the types of the filtering value match the field.

We can use the generated `Person` type like any other Haskell type, and then pass it off to other Persistent functions.

```
main = withSqliteConn ":memory:" $ runSqlConn $ do
    michaelId <- insert $ Person "Michael" 26
    michael <- get michaelId
    liftIO $ print michael
```

We start off with some standard database connection code. In this case, we used the single-connection functions. Persistent also comes built in with connection pool functions, which we will generally want to use in production.

In this example, we have seen two functions: `insert` creates a new record in the database and returns its ID. Like everything else in Persistent, IDs are type safe. We'll get into more details of how these IDs work later. So when you call `insert $ Person "Michael" 25`, it gives you a value back of type `PersonId`.

The next function we see is `get`, which attempts to load a value from the database using an `Id`. In Persistent, you never need to worry that you are using the key from the wrong table: trying to load up a different entity (like `House`) using a `PersonId` will never compile.

PersistStore

One last detail is left unexplained from the previous example: what are those `withSqliteConn` and `runSqlConn` functions doing, and what is that monad that our database actions are running in?

All database actions need to occur within an instance of `PersistStore`. As its name implies, every data store (PostgreSQL, SQLite, MongoDB) has an instance of `PersistStore`. This is where all the translations from `PersistValue` to database-specific values occur, where SQL query generation happens, and so on.

> As you can imagine, even though `PersistStore` provides a safe, well-typed interface to the outside world, there are a lot of database interactions that could go wrong. However, by testing this code automatically and thoroughly in a single location, we can centralize our error-prone code and make sure it is as bug-free as possible.

`withSqliteConn` creates a single connection to a database using its supplied connection string. For our test cases, we will use `:memory:`, which uses an in-memory database. `runSqlConn` uses that connection to run the inner action. Both SQLite and PostgreSQL share the same instance of `PersistStore`: `SqlPersist`.

> There are actually a few other typeclasses: `PersistUpdate` and `PersistQuery`. Different typeclasses provide different functionality, which allows us to write backends that use simpler data stores (e.g., Redis) even though they can't provide us all the high-level functionality available in Persistent.

One important thing to note is that everything that occurs inside a single call to `runSqlConn` runs in a single transaction. This has two important implications:

- For many databases, committing a transaction can be a costly activity. By putting multiple steps into a single transaction, you can speed up code dramatically.
- If an exception is thrown anywhere inside a single call to `runSqlConn`, all actions will be rolled back (assuming your backend has rollback support).

Migrations

I'm sorry to tell you, but so far I have lied to you a bit: the example from the previous section does not actually work. If you try to run it, you will get an error message about a missing table.

For SQL databases, one of the major pains can be managing schema changes. Instead of leaving this to the user, Persistent steps in to help, but you have to *ask* it to help. Let's see what this looks like:

```
{-# LANGUAGE QuasiQuotes, TypeFamilies, GeneralizedNewtypeDeriving, TemplateHaskell,
             OverloadedStrings, GADTs, FlexibleContexts #-}
import Database.Persist
import Database.Persist.TH
import Database.Persist.Sqlite
import Control.Monad.IO.Class (liftIO)

share [mkPersist sqlSettings, mkSave "entityDefs"] [persist|
Person
    name String
    age Int
|]

main = withSqliteConn ":memory:" $ runSqlConn $ do
    runMigration $ migrate entityDefs (undefined :: Person) -- this line added: that's it!
    michaelId <- insert $ Person "Michael" 26
    michael <- get michaelId
    liftIO $ print michael
```

With this one little code change, Persistent will automatically create your `Person` table for you. This split between `runMigration` and `migrate` allows you to migrate multiple tables simultaneously.

This works when dealing with just a few entities, but can quickly get tiresome once we are dealing with a dozen entities. Instead of repeating yourself, Persistent provides a helper function, mkMigrate:

```
{-# LANGUAGE QuasiQuotes, TypeFamilies, GeneralizedNewtypeDeriving, TemplateHaskell,
             OverloadedStrings, GADTs, FlexibleContexts #-}
import Database.Persist
import Database.Persist.Sqlite
import Database.Persist.TH

share [mkPersist sqlSettings, mkMigrate "migrateAll"] [persist|
Person
    name String
    age Int
Car
    color String
    make String
    model String
|]

main = withSqliteConn ":memory:" $ runSqlConn $ do
    runMigration migrateAll
```

mkMigrate is a Template Haskell function that creates a new function that will automatically call migrate on all entities defined in the persist block. The share function is just a little helper that passes the information from the persist block to each Template Haskell function and concatenates the results.

Persistent has very conservative rules about what it will do during a migration. It starts by loading up table information from the database, complete with all defined SQL data types. It then compares that against the entity definition given in the code. For the following cases, it will automatically alter the schema:

- The data type of a field changed. However, the database may object to this modification if the data cannot be translated.
- A field was added. However, if the field is not null, no default value is supplied (we'll discuss defaults later) and there is already data in the database, the database will not allow this to happen.
- A field is converted from not null to null. In the opposite case, Persistent will attempt the conversion, contingent upon the database's approval.
- A brand new entity is added.

However, there are some cases that Persistent will not handle:

- Field or entity renames: Persistent has no way of knowing that "name" has now been renamed to "fullName": all it sees is an old field called name and a new field called fullName.

- Field removals: since this can result in data loss, Persistent by default will refuse to perform the action (you can force the issue by using `runMigrationUnsafe` instead of `runMigration`, though it is **not** recommended).

`runMigration` will print out the migrations it is running on `stderr` (you can bypass this by using `runMigrationSilent`). Whenever possible, it uses `ALTER TABLE` calls. However, in SQLite, `ALTER TABLE` has very limited abilities, and therefore Persistent must resort to copying the data from one table to another.

Finally, if instead of *performing* a migration, you want Persistent to give you hints about what migrations are necessary, use the `printMigration` function. This function will print out the migrations that `runMigration` would perform for you. This may be useful for performing migrations that Persistent is not capable of, for adding arbitrary SQL to a migration, or just to log what migrations occurred.

Uniqueness

In addition to declaring fields within an entity, you can also declare uniqueness constraints. A typical example would be requiring that a username be unique.

Example 10-1. Unique Username

```
User
    username Text
    UniqueUsername username
```

While each field name must begin with a lowercase letter, the uniqueness constraints must begin with an uppercase letter.

```
{-# LANGUAGE QuasiQuotes, TypeFamilies, GeneralizedNewtypeDeriving, TemplateHaskell,
             OverloadedStrings, GADTs, FlexibleContexts #-}
import Database.Persist
import Database.Persist.Sqlite
import Database.Persist.TH
import Data.Time
import Control.Monad.IO.Class (liftIO)

share [mkPersist sqlSettings, mkMigrate "migrateAll"] [persist|
Person
    firstName String
    lastName String
    age Int
    PersonName firstName lastName
|]

main = withSqliteConn ":memory:" $ runSqlConn $ do
    runMigration migrateAll
    insert $ Person "Michael" "Snoyman" 26
    michael <- getBy $ PersonName "Michael" "Snoyman"
    liftIO $ print michael
```

To declare a unique combination of fields, we add an extra line to our declaration. Persistent knows that it is defining a unique constructor, since the line begins with a capital letter. Each following word must be a field in this entity.

The main restriction on uniqueness is that it can only be applied non-null fields. The reason for this is that the SQL standard is ambiguous on how uniqueness should be applied to NULL (e.g., is NULL=NULL true or false?). Besides that ambiguity, most SQL engines in fact implement rules that would be *contrary* to what the Haskell data types anticipate (e.g., PostgreSQL says that NULL=NULL is false, whereas Haskell says Nothing == Nothing is True).

In addition to providing nice guarantees at the database level about consistency of your data, uniqueness constraints can also be used to perform some specific queries within your Haskell code, like the getBy demonstrated above. This happens via the Unique associated type. In the example above, we end up with a new constructor:

```
PersonName :: String -> String -> Unique Person
```

Queries

Depending on what your goal is, there are different approaches to querying the database. Some commands query based on a numeric ID, while others will filter. Queries also differ in the number of results they return: some lookups should return no more than one result (if the lookup key is unique) while others can return many results.

Persistent therefore provides a few different query functions. As usual, we try to encode as many invariants in the types as possible. For example, a query that can return only 0 or 1 results will use a Maybe wrapper, whereas a query returning many results will return a list.

Fetching by ID

The simplest query you can perform in Persistent is getting based on an ID. Since this value may or may not exist, its return type is wrapped in a Maybe.

Example 10-2. Using get

```
personId <- insert $ Person "Michael" "Snoyman" 26
maybePerson <- get personId
case maybePerson of
    Nothing -> liftIO $ putStrLn "Just kidding, not really there"
    Just person -> liftIO $ print person
```

This can be very useful for sites that provide URLs like */person/5*. However, in such a case, we don't usually care about the Maybe wrapper, and just want the value, returning a 404 message if it is not found. Fortunately, the get404 function helps us out here. We'll go into more details when we see integration with Yesod.

Fetching by Unique Constraint

`getBy` is almost identical to `get`, except it takes a uniqueness constraint instead of an ID it takes a Unique value.

Example 10-3. Using getBy

```
personId <- insert $ Person "Michael" "Snoyman" 26
maybePerson <- getBy $ UniqueName "Michael" "Snoyman"
case maybePerson of
    Nothing -> liftIO $ putStrLn "Just kidding, not really there"
    Just person -> liftIO $ print person
```

Like `get404`, there is also a `getBy404` function.

Select Functions

Most likely, you're going to want more powerful queries. You'll want to find everyone over a certain age; all cars available in blue; all users without a registered email address. For this, you need one of the select functions.

All the select functions use a similar interface, with slightly different outputs:

Function	Returns
selectSource	A Source containing all the IDs and values from the database. This allows you to write streaming code.
	We cover Sources in detail in the conduits appendix. Additionally, there's another function called selectSourceConn that allows you more control of connection allocation. We use this in the Sphinx case study.
selectList	A list containing all the IDs and values from the database. All records will be loaded into memory.
selectFirst	Takes just the first ID and value from the database, if available
selectKeys	Returns only the keys, without the values, as a Source.

`selectList` is the most commonly used, so we will cover it specifically. Understanding the others should be trivial after that.

`selectList` takes two arguments: a list of `Filters`, and a list of `SelectOpts`. The former is what limits your results based on characteristics; it allows for equals, less than, is member of, and such. `SelectOpts` provides for three different features: sorting, limiting output to a certain number of rows, and offsetting results by a certain number of rows.

> The combination of limits and offsets is very important; it allows for efficient pagination in your webapps.

Let's jump straight into an example of filtering, and then analyze it.

```
people <- selectList [PersonAge >. 25, PersonAge <=. 30] []
liftIO $ print people
```

As simple as that example is, we really need to cover three points:

1. PersonAge is a constructor for an associated phantom type. That might sound scary, but what's important is that it uniquely identifies the "age" column of the "person" table, and that it knows that the age field is an Int. (That's the phantom part.)
2. We have a bunch of Persistent filtering operators. They're all pretty straightforward: just tack a period to the end of what you'd expect. There are three gotchas here, I'll explain below.
3. The list of filters is ANDed together, so that our constraint means "age is greater than 25 AND age is less than or equal to 30". We'll describe ORing later.

The one operator that's surprisingly named is "not equals." We use !=., since /=. is used for updates (for "divide-and-set", described later). Don't worry: if you use the wrong one, the compiler will catch you. The other two surprising operators are the "is member" and "is not member". They are, respectively, <-. and /<-. (both end with a period).

And regarding ORs, we use the ||. operator. For example:

```
people <- selectList
    (    [PersonAge >. 25, PersonAge <=. 30]
     ||. [PersonFirstName /<-. ["Adam", "Bonny"]]
     ||. ([PersonAge ==. 50] ||. [PersonAge ==. 60])
    )
    []
liftIO $ print people
```

This (completely nonsensical) example means: find people who are 26-30, inclusive, OR whose names are neither Adam or Bonny, OR whose age is either 50 or 60.

SelectOpt

All of our selectList calls have included an empty list as the second parameter. That specifies no options, meaning: sort however the database wants, return all results, and don't skip any results. A SelectOpt has four constructors that can be used to change all that.

Asc
   Sort by the given column in ascending order. This uses the same phantom type as filtering, such as PersonAge.

Desc
   Same as Asc, in descending order.

LimitTo
   Takes an Int argument. Only return up to the specified number of results.

OffsetBy
   Takes an `Int` argument. Skip the specified number of results.

The following code defines a function that will break down results into pages. It returns all people aged 18 and over, and then sorts them by age (oldest person first). For people with the same age, they are sorted alphabetically by last name, then first name.

```
resultsForPage pageNumber = do
    let resultsPerPage = 10
    selectList
        [ PersonAge >=. 18
        ]
        [ Desc PersonAge
        , Asc PersonLastName
        , Asc PersonFirstName
        , LimitTo resultsPerPage
        , OffsetBy $ (pageNumber - 1) * resultsPerPage
        ]
```

Manipulation

Querying is only half the battle. We also need to be able to add data to and modify existing data in the database.

Insert

It's all well and good to be able to play with data in the database, but how does it get there in the first place? The answer is the `insert` function. You just give it a value, and it gives back an ID.

At this point, it makes sense to explain a bit of the philosophy behind Persistent. In many other ORM solutions, the data types used to hold data are opaque: you need to go through their defined interfaces to get at and modify the data. That's not the case with Persistent: we're using plain old Algebraic Data Types for the whole thing. This means you still get all the great benefits of pattern matching, currying, and everything else you're used to.

However, there are a few things we *can't* do. For one, there's no way to automatically update values in the database every time the record is updated in Haskell. Of course, with Haskell's normal stance of purity and immutability, this wouldn't make much sense anyway, so I don't shed any tears over it.

However, there is one issue that newcomers are often bothered by: why are IDs and values completely separate? It seems like it would be very logical to embed the ID inside the value. In other words, instead of having:

```
data Person = Person { name :: String }
```

have

```
data Person = Person { personId :: PersonId, name :: String }
```

Well, there's one problem with this right off the bat: how do we do an `insert`? If a Person needs to have an ID, and we get the ID by inserting, and an insert needs a Person, we have an impossible loop. We could solve this with `undefined`, but that's just asking for trouble.

OK, you say, let's try something a bit safer:

```
data Person = Person { personId :: Maybe PersonId, name :: String }
```

I definitely prefer `insert $ Person Nothing "Michael"` to `insert $ Person undefined "Michael"`. And now our types will be much simpler, right? For example, `selectList` could return a simple `[Person]` instead of that ugly `[Entity SqlPersist Person]`.

> Entity is a data type that ties together both the ID and value of an entity. Since IDs can be different based on backend, we also need to provide the Persistent backend we're using. The data type `Entity SqlPersist Person` can be read as "the ID and value of a person stored in a SQL database."

The problem is that the "ugliness" is incredibly useful. Having `Entity SqlPersist Person` makes it obvious, at the type level, that we're dealing with a value that exists in the database. Let's say we want to create a link to another page that requires the `PersonId` (not an uncommon occurrence as we'll discuss later). The `Entity SqlPersist Person` form gives us unambiguous access to that information; embedding `PersonId` within `Person` with a `Maybe` wrapper means an extra runtime check for `Just`, instead of a more error-proof compile time check.

Finally, there's a semantic mismatch with embedding the ID within the value. The `Person` is the value. Two people are identical (in the context of a database) if all their fields are the same. By embedding the ID in the value, we're no longer talking about a person, but about a row in the database. Equality is no longer really equality, it's identity: is this the *same person*, as opposed to an equivalent person.

In other words, there are some annoyances with having the ID separated out, but overall, it's the *right* approach, which in the grand scheme of things leads to better, less buggy code.

Update

Now, in the context of that discussion, let's think about updating. The simplest way to update is:

```
let michael = Person "Michael" 26
    michaelAfterBirthday = michael { personAge = 27 }
```

But that's not actually updating anything, it's just creating a new `Person` value based on the old one. When we say update, we're *not* talking about modifications to the values in Haskell. (We better not be of course, since Haskell data types are immutable.)

Instead, we're looking at ways of modifying rows in a table. And the simplest way to do that is with the `update` function.

```
personId <- insert $ Person "Michael" "Snoyman" 26
update personId [PersonAge =. 27]
```

`update` takes two arguments: an ID and a list of `Updates`. The simplest update is assignment, but it's not always the best. What if you want to increase someone's age by 1, but you don't have their current age? Persistent has you covered:

```
haveBirthday personId = update personId [PersonAge +=. 1]
```

And as you might expect, we have all the basic mathematical operators: +=., -=., *=., and /=. (full stop). These can be convenient for updating a single record, but they are also essential for proper ACID guarantees. Imagine the alternative: pull out a `Person`, increment the age, and update the new value. If you have two threads/processes working on this database at the same time, you're in for a world of hurt (hint: race conditions).

Sometimes you'll want to update many fields at once (give all your employees a 5% pay increase, for example). `updateWhere` takes two parameters: a list of filters and a list of updates to apply.

```
updateWhere [PersonFirstName ==. "Michael"] [PersonAge *=. 2] -- it's been a long day
```

Occassionally, you'll just want to completely replace the value in a database with a different value. For that, you use (surprise) the `replace` function.

```
personId <- insert $ Person "Michael" "Snoyman" 26
replace personId $ Person "John" "Doe" 20
```

Delete

As much as it pains us, sometimes we must part with our data. To do so, we have three functions:

delete
    Delete based on an ID

deleteBy
    Delete based on a unique constraint

deleteWhere
    Delete based on a set of filters

```
personId <- insert $ Person "Michael" "Snoyman" 26
delete personId
```

```
deleteBy $ UniqueName "Michael" "Snoyman"
deleteWhere [PersonFirstName ==. "Michael"]
```

We can even use deleteWhere to wipe out all the records in a table, we just need to give some hints to GHC as to what table we're interested in:

```
deleteWhere ([] :: [Filter Person])
```

Attributes

So far, we have seen a basic syntax for our persist blocks: a line for the name of our entities, and then an indented line for each field with two words: the name of the field and the data type of the field. Persistent handles more than this: you can assign an arbitrary list of attributes after the first two words on a line.

Suppose we want to have a Person entity with an (optional) age and the timestamp of when he/she was added to the system. For entities already in the database, we want to just use the current date-time for that timestamp.

```
{-# LANGUAGE QuasiQuotes, TypeFamilies, GeneralizedNewtypeDeriving, TemplateHaskell,
            OverloadedStrings, GADTs, FlexibleContexts #-}
import Database.Persist
import Database.Persist.Sqlite
import Database.Persist.TH
import Data.Time
import Control.Monad.IO.Class

share [mkPersist sqlSettings, mkMigrate "migrateAll"] [persist|
Person
    name String
    age Int Maybe
    created UTCTime default=now()
|]

main = withSqliteConn ":memory:" $ runSqlConn $ do
    time <- liftIO getCurrentTime
    runMigration migrateAll
    insert $ Person "Michael" (Just 26) time
    insert $ Person "Greg" Nothing time
```

Maybe is a built-in, single-word attribute. It makes the field optional. In Haskell, this means it is wrapped in a Maybe. In SQL, it makes the column nullable.

The default attribute is backend specific, and uses whatever syntax is understood by the database. In this case, it uses the database's built-in now() function. Suppose that we now want to add a field for a person's favorite programming language:

```
{-# LANGUAGE QuasiQuotes, TypeFamilies, GeneralizedNewtypeDeriving, TemplateHaskell,
            OverloadedStrings, GADTs, FlexibleContexts #-}
import Database.Persist
import Database.Persist.Sqlite
import Database.Persist.TH
import Data.Time
```

```
share [mkPersist sqlSettings, mkMigrate "migrateAll"] [persist|
Person
    name String
    age Int Maybe
    created UTCTime default=now()
    language String default='Haskell'
|]

main = withSqliteConn ":memory:" $ runSqlConn $ do
    runMigration migrateAll
```

> The `default` attribute has absolutely no impact on the Haskell code itself; you still need to fill in all values. This will only affect the database schema and automatic migrations.

We need to surround the string with single quotes so that the database can properly interpret it. Finally, Persistent can use double quotes for containing white space, so if we want to set someone's default home country to be El Salvador:

```
{-# LANGUAGE QuasiQuotes, TypeFamilies, GeneralizedNewtypeDeriving, TemplateHaskell,
            OverloadedStrings, GADTs, FlexibleContexts #-}
import Database.Persist
import Database.Persist.Sqlite
import Database.Persist.TH
import Data.Time

share [mkPersist sqlSettings, mkMigrate "migrateAll"] [persist|
Person
    name String
    age Int Maybe
    created UTCTime default=now()
    language String default='Haskell'
    country String "default='El Salvador'"
|]

main = withSqliteConn ":memory:" $ runSqlConn $ do
    runMigration migrateAll
```

One last trick you can do with attributes is to specify the names to be used for the SQL tables and columns. This can be convenient when interacting with existing databases.

```
share [mkPersist sqlSettings, mkMigrate "migrateAll"] [persist|
Person sql=the-person-table
    firstName String sql=first_name
    lastName String sql=fldLastName
    age Int Gt Desc "sql=The Age of the Person"
    UniqueName firstName lastName
|]
```

Relations

Persistent allows references between your data types in a manner that is consistent with supporting non-SQL databases. We do this by embedding an ID in the related entity. So if a person has many cars:

```
{-# LANGUAGE QuasiQuotes, TypeFamilies, GeneralizedNewtypeDeriving, TemplateHaskell,
            OverloadedStrings, GADTs, FlexibleContexts #-}
import Database.Persist
import Database.Persist.Sqlite
import Database.Persist.TH
import Control.Monad.IO.Class (liftIO)
import Data.Time

share [mkPersist sqlSettings, mkMigrate "migrateAll"] [persist|
Person
    name String
Car
    ownerId PersonId Eq
    name String
|]

main = withSqliteConn ":memory:" $ runSqlConn $ do
    runMigration migrateAll
    bruce <- insert $ Person "Bruce Wayne"
    insert $ Car bruce "Bat Mobile"
    insert $ Car bruce "Porsche"
    -- this could go on a while
    cars <- selectList [CarOwnerId ==. bruce] []
    liftIO $ print cars
```

Using this technique, you can define one-to-many relationships. To define many-to-many relationships, we need a join entity, which has a one-to-many relationship with each of the original tables. It is also a good idea to use uniqueness constraints on these. For example, to model a situation where we want to track which people have shopped in which stores:

```
{-# LANGUAGE QuasiQuotes, TypeFamilies, GeneralizedNewtypeDeriving, TemplateHaskell,
            OverloadedStrings, GADTs, FlexibleContexts #-}
import Database.Persist
import Database.Persist.Sqlite
import Database.Persist.TH
import Data.Time

share [mkPersist sqlSettings, mkMigrate "migrateAll"] [persist|
Person
    name String
Store
    name String
PersonStore
    personId PersonId
    storeId StoreId
    UniquePersonStore personId storeId
|]
```

```
main = withSqliteConn ":memory:" $ runSqlConn $ do
    runMigration migrateAll

    bruce <- insert $ Person "Bruce Wayne"
    michael <- insert $ Person "Michael"

    target <- insert $ Store "Target"
    gucci <- insert $ Store "Gucci"
    sevenEleven <- insert $ Store "7-11"

    insert $ PersonStore bruce gucci
    insert $ PersonStore bruce sevenEleven

    insert $ PersonStore michael target
    insert $ PersonStore michael sevenEleven
```

Closer Look at Types

So far, we've spoken about `Person` and `PersonId` without really explaining what they are. In the simplest sense, for a SQL-only system, the `PersonId` could just be `type PersonId = Int64`. However, that means there is nothing binding a `PersonId` at the type level to the `Person` entity. As a result, you could accidentally use a `PersonId` and get a `Car`. In order to model this relationship, we use phantom types. So, our next naive step would be:

```
newtype Key entity = Key Int64
type PersonId = Key Person
```

> Prior to Persistent 0.6, we used associated types instead of phantom types. You could solve the problem in that direction as well, but phantoms worked out better.

And that works out really well, until you get to a backend that doesn't use Int64 for its IDs. And that's not just a theoretical question; MongoDB uses `ByteStrings` instead. So what we need is a key value that can contain an `Int` and a `ByteString`. Seems like a great time for a sum type:

```
data Key entity = KeyInt Int64 | KeyByteString ByteString
```

But that's just asking for trouble. Next we'll have a backend that uses timestamps, so we'll need to add another constructor to `Key`. This could go on for a while. Fortunately, we already have a sum type intended for representing arbitrary data: `PersistValue`:

```
newtype Key entity = Key PersistValue
```

But this has another problem. Let's say we have a web application that takes an ID as a parameter from the user. It will need to receive that parameter as `Text` and then try to convert it to a Key. Well, that's simple: write a function to convert a Text to a PersistValue, and then wrap the result in the Key constructor, right?

Wrong. We tried this, and there's a big problem. We end up getting Keys that could never be. For example, if we're dealing with SQL, a key must be an integer. But the approach described above would allow arbitrary textual data in. The result was a bunch of 500 server errors as the database choked on comparing an integer column to text.

So what we need is a way to convert text to a Key, but have it dependent on the rules of the backend in question. And once phrased that way, the answer is simple: just add another phantom. The real, actual definition of Key in Persistent is:

```
newtype Key backend entity = Key { unKey :: PersistValue }
```

This works great: we can have a Text -> Key MongoDB entity function and a Text -> Key SqlPersist entity function, and everything runs smoothly. But now we have a new problem: relations. Let's say we want to represent blogs and blog posts. We would use the entity definition:

```
Blog
    title Text
Post
    title Text
    blogId BlogId
```

But what would that look like in terms of our Key data type?

```
data Blog = Blog { blogTitle :: Text }
data Post = Post { postTitle :: Text, postBlogId :: Key <what goes here?> Blog }
```

We need something to fill in as the backend. In theory, we could hardcode this to SqlPersist, or Mongo, but then our data types will only work for a single backend. For an individual application, that might be acceptable, but what about libraries defining data types to be used by multiple applications, using multiple backends?

So things got a little more complicated. Our types are actually:

```
data BlogGeneric backend = Blog { blogTitle :: Text }
data PostGeneric backend = Post { postTitle :: Text, postBlogId :: Key backend
    (BlogGeneric backend) }
```

Notice that we still keep the short names for the constructors and the records. Finally, to give a simple interface for normal code, we define some type synonyms:

```
type Blog = BlogGeneric SqlPersist
type BlogId = Key SqlPersist Blog
type Post = PostGeneric SqlPersist
type PostId = Key SqlPersist Post
```

And no, SqlPersist isn't hard-coded into Persistent anywhere. That sqlSettings parameter you've been passing to mkPersist is what tells us to use SqlPersist. Mongo code will use mongoSettings instead.

This might be quite complicated under the surface, but user code hardly ever touches this. Look back through this whole chapter: not once did we need to deal with the Key or Generic stuff directly. The most common place for it to pop up is in compiler error messages. So it's important to be aware that this exists, but it shouldn't affect you on a day-to-day basis.

Custom Fields

Occassionally, you will want to define a custom field to be used in your datastore. The most common case is an enumeration, such as employment status. For this, Persistent provides a helper Template Haskell function:

```
{-# LANGUAGE QuasiQuotes, TypeFamilies, GeneralizedNewtypeDeriving, TemplateHaskell,
            OverloadedStrings, GADTs, FlexibleContexts #-}
import Database.Persist
import Database.Persist.Sqlite
import Database.Persist.TH

data Employment = Employed | Unemployed | Retired
    deriving (Show, Read, Eq)
derivePersistField "Employment"

share [mkPersist sqlSettings, mkMigrate "migrateAll"] [persist|
Person
    name String
    employment Employment
|]

main = withSqliteConn ":memory:" $ runSqlConn $ do
    runMigration migrateAll

    insert $ Person "Bruce Wayne" Retired
    insert $ Person "Peter Parker" Unemployed
    insert $ Person "Michael" Employed
```

derivePersistField stores the data in the database using a string field, and performs marshaling using the Show and Read instances of the data type. This may not be as efficient as storing via an integer, but it is much more future proof: even if you add extra constructors in the future, your data will still be valid.

Persistent: Raw SQL

The Persistent package provides a type-safe interface to data stores. It tries to be back-end-agnostic, such as not relying on relational features of SQL. My experience has been that you can easily perform 95% of what you need to do with the high-level interface. (In fact, most of my web apps use the high-level interface exclusively.)

But occassionally you'll want to use a feature that's specific to a backend. One feature I've used in the past is full text search. In this case, we'll use the SQL "LIKE" operator, which is not modeled in Persistent. We'll get all people with the last name "Snoyman" and print the records out.

> Actually, you *can* express a LIKE operator directly in the normal syntax due to a feature added in Persistent 0.6, which allows backend-specific operators. But this is still a good example, so let's roll with it.

```
{-# LANGUAGE OverloadedStrings, TemplateHaskell, QuasiQuotes, TypeFamilies #-}
{-# LANGUAGE GeneralizedNewtypeDeriving, GADTs, FlexibleContexts #-}
import Database.Persist.Sqlite (withSqliteConn)
import Database.Persist.TH (mkPersist, persist, share, mkMigrate, sqlSettings)
import Database.Persist.GenericSql (runSqlConn, runMigration, SqlPersist)
import Database.Persist.GenericSql.Raw (withStmt)
import Data.Text (Text)
import Database.Persist
import Database.Persist.Store (PersistValue)
import Control.Monad.IO.Class (liftIO)
import qualified Data.Conduit as C
import qualified Data.Conduit.List as CL

share [mkPersist sqlSettings, mkMigrate "migrateAll"] [persist|
Person
    name Text
|]

main :: IO ()
main = withSqliteConn ":memory:" $ runSqlConn $ do
    runMigration migrateAll
    insert $ Person "Michael Snoyman"
    insert $ Person "Miriam Snoyman"
    insert $ Person "Eliezer Snoyman"
    insert $ Person "Gavriella Snoyman"
    insert $ Person "Greg Weber"
    insert $ Person "Rick Richardson"

    -- Persistent does not provide the LIKE keyword, but we'd like to get the
    -- whole Snoyman family...
    let sql = "SELECT name FROM Person WHERE name LIKE '%Snoyman'"
    C.runResourceT $ withStmt sql []
              C.$$ CL.mapM_ $ liftIO . print
```

There is also higher-level support that allows for automated data marshaling. Please see the Haddock API docs for more details.

Integration with Yesod

So you've been convinced of the power of Persistent. How do you integrate it with your Yesod application? If you use the scaffolding, most of the work is done for you already. But as we normally do, we'll build up everything manually here to point out how it works under the surface.

The `yesod-persistent` package provides the meeting point between Persistent and
Yesod. It provides the `YesodPersist` typeclass, which standardizes access to the database via the `runDB` method. Let's see this in action.

```haskell
{-# LANGUAGE QuasiQuotes, TypeFamilies, GeneralizedNewtypeDeriving, FlexibleContexts #-}
{-# LANGUAGE TemplateHaskell, OverloadedStrings, GADTs, MultiParamTypeClasses #-}
import Yesod
import Database.Persist.Sqlite

-- Define our entities as usual
share [mkPersist sqlSettings, mkMigrate "migrateAll"] [persist|
Person
    firstName String
    lastName String
    age Int Gt Desc
|]

-- We keep our connection pool in the foundation. At program initialization, we
-- create our initial pool, and each time we need to perform an action we check
-- out a single connection from the pool.
data PersistTest = PersistTest ConnectionPool

-- We'll create a single route, to access a person. It's a very common
-- occurrence to use an Id type in routes.
mkYesod "PersistTest" [parseRoutes|
/person/#PersonId PersonR GET
|]

-- Nothing special here
instance Yesod PersistTest

-- Now we need to define a YesodPersist instance, which will keep track of
-- which backend we're using and how to run an action.
instance YesodPersist PersistTest where
    type YesodPersistBackend PersistTest = SqlPersist

    runDB action = do
        PersistTest pool <- getYesod
        runSqlPool action pool

-- We'll just return the show value of a person, or a 404 if the Person doesn't
-- exist.
getPersonR :: PersonId -> Handler RepPlain
getPersonR personId = do
    person <- runDB $ get404 personId
    return $ RepPlain $ toContent $ show person

openConnectionCount :: Int
openConnectionCount = 10

main :: IO ()
main = withSqlitePool "test.db3" openConnectionCount $ \pool -> do
    runSqlPool (runMigration migrateAll) pool
```

```
runSqlPool (insert $ Person "Michael" "Snoyman" 26) pool
warpDebug 3000 $ PersistTest pool
```

There are two important pieces here for general use. `runDB` is used to run a DB action from within a `Handler`. Within the `runDB`, you can use any of the functions we've spoken about so far, such as `insert` and `selectList`.

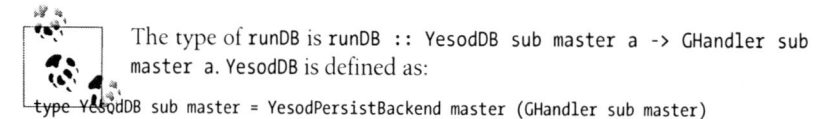

> The type of `runDB` is `runDB :: YesodDB sub master a -> GHandler sub master a`. `YesodDB` is defined as:
>
> `type YesodDB sub master = YesodPersistBackend master (GHandler sub master)`
>
> Since it is built on top of the `YesodPersistBackend` associated type, it uses the appropriate database backend based on the current site.

The other new feature is `get404`. It works just like `get`, but instead of returning a `Nothing` when a result can't be found, it returns a 404 message page. The `getPersonR` function is a very common approach used in real-world Yesod applications: `get404` a value and then return a response based on it.

Summary

Persistent brings the type safety of Haskell to your data access layer. Instead of writing error-prone, untyped data access, or manually writing boilerplate marshal code, you can rely on Persistent to automate the process for you.

The goal is to provide everything you need, *most* of the time. For the times when you need something a bit more powerful, Persistent gives you direct access to the underlying data store, so you can write whatever five-way joins you want.

Persistent integrates directly into the general Yesod workflow. Not only do helper packages like `yesod-persistent` provide a nice layer, but packages like `yesod-form` and `yesod-auth` also leverage Persistent's features as well.

CHAPTER 11
Deploying Your Webapp

I can't speak for others, but I personally prefer programming to system administration. But the fact is that, eventually, you need to serve your app somehow, and odds are that you'll need to be the one to set it up.

There are some promising initiatives in the Haskell web community towards making deployment easier. In the future, we may even have a service that allows you to deploy your app with a single command.

But we're not there yet. And even if we were, such a solution will never work for everyone. This chapter covers the different options you have for deployment, and gives some general recommendations on what you should choose in different situations.

Compiling

First things first: how do you build your production application? If you're using the scaffolded site, it's as simple as `cabal build`. I also recommend cleaning beforehand to make sure there is no cached information, so a simple combination to build your executable is:

```
cabal clean && cabal configure && cabal build
```

Warp

As we have mentioned before, Yesod is built on the Web Application Interface (WAI), allowing it to run on any WAI backend. At the time of writing, the following backends are available:

- Warp
- FastCGI
- SCGI
- CGI

- Webkit
- Development server

The last two are not intended for production deployments. Of the remaining four, all can be used for production deployment in theory. In practice, a CGI backend will likely be horribly inefficient, since a new process must be spawned for each connection. And SCGI is not nearly as well supported by frontend web servers as Warp (via reverse proxying) or FastCGI.

So between the two remaining choices, Warp gets a very strong recommendation because:

- It is significantly faster.
- Like FastCGI, it can run behind a frontend server like Nginx, using reverse HTTP proxy.
- In addition, it is a fully capable server of its own accord, and can therefore be used without any frontend server.

So that leaves one last question: should Warp run on its own, or via reverse proxy behind a frontend server? For most use cases, I recommend the latter, because:

- As fast as Warp is, it is still optimized as an application server, not a static file server.
- Using Nginx, you can set up virtual hosting to serve your static contents from a separate domain. (It's possible to do this with Warp, but a bit more involved).
- You can use Nginx as either a load balancer or a SSL proxy. (Though with `warp-tls` it's entirely possible to run an https site on Warp alone.)

So my final recommendation is: set up Nginx to reverse proxy to Warp.

> A number of people in the Yesod community disagree with me here, and believe that the increased performance and decreased complexity of skipping the Nginx step make standalone Warp a better choice. Feel free to follow either approach; they are both perfectly valid.

Configuration

In general, Nginx will listen on port 80 and your Yesod/Warp app will listen on some unprivileged port (lets say 4321). You will then need to provide a *nginx.conf* file, such as:

```
daemon off; # Don't run nginx in the background, good for monitoring apps
events {
    worker_connections 4096;
}

http {
    server {
```

```
        listen 80; # Incoming port for Nginx
        server_name www.myserver.com;
        location / {
            proxy_pass http://127.0.0.1:4321; # Reverse proxy to your Yesod app
        }
    }
}
```

You can add as many server blocks as you like. A common addition is to ensure that users always access your pages with the www prefix on the domain name, ensuring the RESTful principle of canonical URLs. (You could just as easily do the opposite and always strip the www, just make sure that your choice is reflected in both the nginx config and the approot of your site.) In this case, we would add the block:

```
server {
    listen 80;
    server_name myserver.com;
    rewrite ^/(.*) http://www.myserver.com/$1 permanent;
}
```

A highly recommended optimization is to serve static files from a separate domain name, therefore bypassing the cookie transfer overhead. Assuming that our static files are stored in the static folder within our site folder, and the site folder is located at /home/michael/sites/mysite, this would look like:

```
server {
    listen 80;
    server_name static.myserver.com;
    root /home/michael/sites/mysite/static;
    # Since yesod-static appends a content hash in the query string,
    # we are free to set expiration dates far in the future without
    # concerns of stale content.
    expires max;
}
```

In order for this to work, your site must properly rewrite static URLs to this alternate domain name. The scaffolded site is set up to make this fairly simple via the Settings.staticRoot function and the definition of urlRenderOverride. However, if you just want to get the benefit of nginx's faster static file serving without dealing with separate domain names, you can instead modify your original server block like so:

```
server {
    listen 80; # Incoming port for Nginx
    server_name www.myserver.com;
    location / {
        proxy_pass http://127.0.0.1:4321; # Reverse proxy to your Yesod app
    }
    location /static {
        root /home/michael/sites/mysite; # Notice that we do *not* include /static
        expires max;
    }
}
```

Server Process

Many people are familiar with an Apache/mod_php or Lighttpd/FastCGI kind of setup, where the web server automatically spawns the web application. With nginx, either for reverse proxying or FastCGI, this is not the case: you are responsible for running your own process. I strongly recommend a monitoring utility that will automatically restart your application in case it crashes. There are many great options out there, such as **angel** or daemontools.

To give a concrete example, here is an Upstart config file. The file must be placed in /etc/init/mysite.conf:

```
description "My awesome Yesod application"
start on runlevel [2345];
stop on runlevel [!2345];
respawn
chdir /home/michael/sites/mysite
exec /home/michael/sites/mysite/dist/build/mysite/mysite
```

Once this is in place, bringing up your application is as simple as `sudo start mysite`.

FastCGI

Some people may prefer using FastCGI for deployment. In this case, you'll need to add an extra tool to the mix. FastCGI works by receiving new connections from a file descriptor. The C library assumes that this file descriptor will be 0 (standard input), so you need to use the spawn-fcgi program to bind your application's standard input to the correct socket.

It can be very convenient to use Unix named sockets for this instead of binding to a port, especially when hosting multiple applications on a single host. A possible script to load up your app could be:

```
spawn-fcgi \
    -d /home/michael/sites/mysite \
    -s /tmp/mysite.socket \
    -n \
    -M 511 \
    -u michael \
    -- /home/michael/sites/mysite/dist/build/mysite-fastcgi/mysite-fastcgi
```

You will also need to configure your frontend server to speak to your app over FastCGI. This is relatively painless in Nginx:

```
server {
    listen 80;
    server_name www.myserver.com;
    location / {
        fastcgi_pass unix:/tmp/mysite.socket;
    }
}
```

That should look pretty familiar from above. The only last trick is that, with Nginx, you need to manually specify all of the FastCGI variables. It is recommended to store these in a separate file (say, fastcgi.conf) and then add `include fastcgi.conf;` to the end of your http block. The contents of the file, to work with WAI, should be:

```
fastcgi_param  QUERY_STRING       $query_string;
fastcgi_param  REQUEST_METHOD     $request_method;
fastcgi_param  CONTENT_TYPE       $content_type;
fastcgi_param  CONTENT_LENGTH     $content_length;
fastcgi_param  PATH_INFO          $fastcgi_script_name;
fastcgi_param  SERVER_PROTOCOL    $server_protocol;
fastcgi_param  GATEWAY_INTERFACE  CGI/1.1;
fastcgi_param  SERVER_SOFTWARE    nginx/$nginx_version;
fastcgi_param  REMOTE_ADDR        $remote_addr;
fastcgi_param  SERVER_ADDR        $server_addr;
fastcgi_param  SERVER_PORT        $server_port;
fastcgi_param  SERVER_NAME        $server_name;
```

Desktop

Another nifty backend is `wai-handler-webkit`. This backend combines Warp and QtWebkit to create an executable that a user simply double-clicks. This can be a convenient way to provide an offline version of your application.

One of the very nice conveniences of Yesod for this is that your templates are all compiled into the executable, and thus do not need to be distributed with your application. Static files do, however.

> There's actually support for embedding your static files directly in the executable as well; see the `yesod-static` docs for more details.

A similar approach, without requiring the QtWebkit library, is `wai-handler-launch`, which launches a Warp server and then opens up the user's default web browser. There's a little trickery involved here: in order to know that the user is still using the site, `wai-handler-launch` inserts a "ping" JavaScript snippet to every HTML page it serves. If `wai-handler-launch` doesn't receive a ping for two minutes, it shuts down.

CGI on Apache

CGI and FastCGI work almost identically on Apache, so it should be fairly straightforward to port this configuration. You essentially need to accomplish two goals:

1. Get the server to serve your file as (Fast)CGI.
2. Rewrite all requests to your site to go through the (Fast)CGI executable.

Here is a configuration file for serving a blog application, with an executable named
"bloggy.cgi," living in a subfolder named "blog" of the document root. This example
was taken from an application living in the path /f5/snoyman/public/blog.

```
Options +ExecCGI
AddHandler cgi-script .cgi
Options +FollowSymlinks

RewriteEngine On
RewriteRule ^/f5/snoyman/public/blog$ /blog/ [R=301,S=1]
RewriteCond $1 !^bloggy.cgi
RewriteCond $1 !^static/
RewriteRule ^(.*) bloggy.cgi/$1 [L]
```

The first RewriteRule is to deal with subfolders. In particular, it redirects a request
for /blog to /blog/. The first RewriteCond prevents directly requesting the executable,
the second allows Apache to serve the static files, and the last line does the actual
rewriting.

FastCGI on lighttpd

For this example, I've left off some of the basic FastCGI settings like mime-types. I also
have a more complex file in production that prepends "www." when absent and serves
static files from a separate domain. However, this should serve to show the basics.

Here, "/home/michael/fastcgi" is the fastcgi application. The idea is to rewrite all requests to start with "/app," and then serve everything beginning with "/app" via the
FastCGI executable.

```
server.port = 3000
server.document-root = "/home/michael"
server.modules = ("mod_fastcgi", "mod_rewrite")

url.rewrite-once = (
  "(.*)" => "/app/$1"
)

fastcgi.server = (
    "/app" => ((
        "socket" => "/tmp/test.fastcgi.socket",
        "check-local" => "disable",
        "bin-path" => "/home/michael/fastcgi", # full path to executable
        "min-procs" => 1,
        "max-procs" => 30,
        "idle-timeout" => 30
    ))
)
```

CGI on lighttpd

This is basically the same as the FastCGI version, but tells lighttpd to run a file ending in ".cgi" as a CGI executable. In this case, the file lives at "/home/michael/myapp.cgi".

```
server.port = 3000
server.document-root = "/home/michael"
server.modules = ("mod_cgi", "mod_rewrite")

url.rewrite-once = (
    "(.*)" => "/myapp.cgi/$1"
)

cgi.assign = (".cgi" => "")
```

PART II
Advanced

CHAPTER 12
RESTful Content

One of the stories from the early days of the Web is how search engines wiped out entire websites. When dynamic web sites were still a new concept, developers didn't appreciate the difference between a GET and POST request. As a result, they created pages —accessed with the GET method—that would delete pages. When search engines started crawling these sites, they could wipe out all the content.

If these web developers had followed the HTTP spec properly, this would not have happened. A GET request is supposed to cause no side effects (you know, like wiping out a site). Recently, there has been a move in web development to properly embrace Representational State Transfer, also known as REST. This chapter describes the RESTful features in Yesod and how you can use them to create more robust web applications.

Request Methods

In many web frameworks, you write one handler function per resource. In Yesod, the default is to have a separate handler function for each *request method*. The two most common request methods you will deal with in creating websites are GET and POST. These are the most well-supported methods in HTML, since they are the only ones supported by web forms. However, when creating RESTful APIs, the other methods are very useful.

Technically speaking, you can create whichever request methods you like, but it is strongly recommended to stick to the ones spelled out in the HTTP spec. The most common of these are:

GET
: Read-only requests. Assuming no other changes occur on the server, calling a GET request multiple times should result in the same response, barring such things as "current time" or randomly assigned results.

POST
: A general mutating request. A POST request should never be submitted twice by the user. A common example of this would be to transfer funds from one bank account to another.

PUT
: Create a new resource on the server, or replace an existing one. This method *is* safe to be called multiple times.

DELETE
: Just like it sounds: wipe out a resource on the server. Calling multiple times should be OK.

To a certain extent, this fits in very well with Haskell philosophy: a GET request is similar to a pure function, which cannot have side effects. In practice, your GET functions will probably perform IO, such as reading information from a database, logging user actions, and so on.

See the routing and handlers chapter for more information on the syntax of defining handler functions for each request method.

Representations

Suppose we have a Haskell data type and value:

```
data Person = Person { name :: String, age :: Int }
michael = Person "Michael" 25
```

We could represent that data as HTML:

```
<table>
    <tr>
        <th>Name</th>
        <td>Michael</td>
    </tr>
    <tr>
        <th>Age</th>
        <td>25</td>
    </tr>
</table>
```

or we could represent it as JSON:

```
{"name":"Michael","age":25}
```

or as XML:

```
<person>
    <name>Michael</name>
    <age>25</age>
</person>
```

Oftentimes, web applications will use a different URL to get each of these representations; perhaps /person/michael.html, /person/michael.json, etc. Yesod follows the RESTful principle of a single URL for each *resource*. So in Yesod, all of these would be accessed from /person/michael.

Then the question becomes how do we determine *which* representation to serve. The answer is the HTTP Accept header: it gives a prioritized list of content types the client is expecting. Yesod will automatically determine which representation to serve based upon this header.

Let's make that last sentence a bit more concrete with some code:

```
type ChooseRep = [ContentType] -> IO (ContentType, Content)
class HasReps a where
    chooseRep :: a -> ChooseRep
```

The chooseRep function takes two arguments: the value we are getting representations for and a list of content types that the client will accept. We determine this by reading the Accept request header. chooseRep returns a tuple containing the content type of our response and the actual content.

This typeclass is the core of Yesod's RESTful approach to representations. Every handler function must return an instance of HasReps. When Yesod generates the dispatch function, it automatically applies chooseRep to each handler, essentially giving all functions the type Handler ChooseRep. After running the Handler and obtaining the ChooseRep result, it is applied to the list of content types parsed from the Accept header.

Yesod provides a number of instances of HasReps out of the box. When we use default Layout, for example, the return type is RepHtml, which looks like:

```
newtype RepHtml = RepHtml Content
instance HasReps RepHtml where
    chooseRep (RepHtml content) _ = return ("text/html", content)
```

Notice that we ignore entirely the list of expected content types. A number of the built-in representations (RepHtml, RepPlain, RepJson, RepXml) in fact only support a single representation, and therefore what the client requests in the Accept header is irrelevant.

RepHtmlJson

An example to the contrary is RepHtmlJson, which provides either an HTML or JSON representation. This instance helps greatly in programming AJAX applications that degrade nicely. Here is an example that returns either HTML or JSON data, depending on what the client wants.

```
{-# LANGUAGE QuasiQuotes, TypeFamilies, OverloadedStrings #-}
{-# LANGUAGE MultiParamTypeClasses, TemplateHaskell #-}
import Yesod
data R = R
mkYesod "R" [parseRoutes|
/ RootR GET
/#String NameR GET
|]
instance Yesod R
```

```
getRootR = defaultLayout $ do
    setTitle "Homepage"
    addScriptRemote "http://ajax.googleapis.com/ajax/libs/jquery/1.4/jquery.min.js"
    addJulius [julius|
$(function(){
    $("#ajax a").click(function(){
        jQuery.getJSON($(this).attr("href"), function(o){
            $("div").text(o.name);
        });
        return false;
    });
});
|]
    let names = words "Larry Moe Curly"
    addHamlet [hamlet|
<h2>AJAX Version
<div #results>
    AJAX results will be placed here when you click #
    the names below.
<ul #ajax>
    $forall name <- names
        <li>
            <a href=@{NameR name}>#{name}

<h2>HTML Version
<p>
    Clicking the names below will redirect the page #
    to an HTML version.
<ul #html>
    $forall name <- names
        <li>
            <a href=@{NameR name}>#{name}

|]

getNameR name = do
    let widget = do
            setTitle $ toHtml name
            addHamlet [hamlet|Looks like you have Javascript off. Name: #{name}|]
    let json = object ["name" .= name]
    defaultLayoutJson widget json

main = warpDebug 4000 R
```

Our getRootR handler creates a page with three links and some JavaScript that intercept clicks on the links and performs asynchronous requests. If the user has JavaScript enabled, clicking on the link will cause a request to be sent with an Accept header of application/json. In that case, getNameR will return the JSON representation instead.

If the user disables JavaScript, clicking on the link will send the user to the appropriate URL. A web browser places priority on an HTML representation of the data, and therefore the page defined by the widget will be returned.

We can of course extend this to work with XML, Atom feeds, or even binary representations of the data. A fun exercise could be writing a web application that serves data simply using the default Show instances of data types, and then writing a web client that parses the results using the default Read instances.

> You might be concerned about efficiency here. Doesn't this approach mean we have to generate both an HTML and JSON response for each request? Thanks to laziness, that's not the case. In getNameR, neither widget nor json will be evaluated until the appropriate response type has been selected, and therefore only one of them will ever be run.

News Feeds

A great, practical example of multiple representations is the yesod-newsfeed package. There are two major formats for news feeds on the Web: RSS and Atom. They contain almost exactly the same information, but are just packaged differently.

The yesod-newsfeed package defines a Feed data type that contains information like title, description, and last updated time. It then provides two separate sets of functions for displaying this data: one for RSS, one for Atom. They each define their own representation data types:

```
newtype RepAtom = RepAtom Content
instance HasReps RepAtom where
    chooseRep (RepAtom c) _ = return (typeAtom, c)
newtype RepRss = RepRss Content
instance HasReps RepRss where
    chooseRep (RepRss c) _ = return (typeRss, c)
```

But there's a third module that defines another data type:

```
data RepAtomRss = RepAtomRss RepAtom RepRss
instance HasReps RepAtomRss where
    chooseRep (RepAtomRss (RepAtom a) (RepRss r)) = chooseRep
        [ (typeAtom, a)
        , (typeRss, r)
        ]
```

This data type will automatically serve whichever representation the client prefers, defaulting to Atom. If a client connects that only understands RSS, assuming it provides the correct HTTP headers, Yesod will provide RSS output.

Other Request Headers

There are a great deal of other request headers available. Some of them only affect the transfer of data between the server and client, and should not affect the application at all. For example, Accept-Encoding informs the server which compression schemes the client understands, and Host informs the server which virtual host to serve up.

Other headers *do* affect the application, but are automatically read by Yesod. For example, the `Accept-Language` header specifies which human language (English, Spanish, German, Swiss-German) the client prefers. See the i18n chapter for details on how this header is used.

Stateless

I've saved this section for the last, not because it is less important, but rather because there are no specific features in Yesod to enforce this.

HTTP is a stateless protocol: each request is to be seen as the beginning of a conversation. This means, for instance, it doesn't matter to the server if you requested five pages previously, it will treat your sixth request as if it's your first one.

On the other hand, some features on websites won't work without some kind of state. For example, how can you implement a shopping cart without saving information about items in between requests?

The solution to this is cookies, and built on top of this, sessions. We have a whole section addressing the sessions features in Yesod. However, I cannot stress enough that this should be used sparingly.

Let me give you an example. There's a popular bug-tracking system that I deal with on a daily basis that horribly abuses sessions. There's a little drop-down on every page to select the current project. Seems harmless, right? What that dropdown does is set the current project in your session.

The result of all this is that clicking on the "view issues" link is entirely dependent on the last project you selected. There's no way to create a bookmark to your "Yesod" issues and a separate link for your "Hamlet" issues.

The proper RESTful approach to this is to have one resource for all of the Yesod issues and a separate one for all the Hamlet issues. In Yesod, this is easily done with a route definition like:

```
/ ProjectsR GET
/projects/#ProjectID ProjectIssuesR GET
/issues/#IssueID IssueR GET
```

Be nice to your users: proper stateless architecture means that basic features like bookmarks, permalinks, and the back/forward button will always work.

Summary

Yesod adheres to the following tenets of REST:

- Use the correct request method.
- Each resource should have precisely one URL.

- Allow multiple representations of data on the same URL.
- Inspect request headers to determine extra information about what the client wants.

This makes it easy to use Yesod not just for building websites, but for building APIs. In fact, using techniques such as RepHtmlJson, you can serve both a user-friendly HTML page and a machine-friendly JSON page from the same URL.

CHAPTER 13
Yesod's Monads

As you've read through this book, there have been a number of monads that have appeared: `Handler`, `Widget`, and `YesodDB` (for Persistent). As with most monads, each one provides some specific functionality: `Handler` gives access to the request and allows you to send responses, a `Widget` contains HTML, CSS, and JavaScript, and `YesodDB` let's you make database queries. In Model-View-Controller (MVC) terms, we could consider `YesodDB` to be the model, `Widget` to be the view, and `Handler` to be the controller.

So far, we've presented some very straightforward ways to use these monads: your main handler will run in `Handler`, using `runDB` to execute a `YesodDB` query, and `defaultLayout` to return a `Widget`, which in turn was created by calls to `toWidget`.

However, if we have a deeper understanding of these types, we can achieve some fancier results.

Monad Transformers

> Monads are like onions. Monads are *not* like cakes. [Shrek, more or less]

Before we get into the heart of Yesod's monads, we need to understand a bit about monad transformers. (If you already know all about monad transformers, you can likely skip this section.) Different monads provide different functionality: `Reader` allows read-only access to some piece of data throughout a computation, `Error` allows you to short-circuit computations, and so on.

Oftentimes, however, you would like to be able to combine a few of these features together. After all, why not have a computation with read-only access to some settings variable, which could error out at any time? One approach to this would be to write a new monad like `ReaderError`, but this has the obvious downside of exponential complexity: you'll need to write a new monad for every single possible combination.

Instead, we have monad transformers. In addition to `Reader`, we have `ReaderT`, which adds reader functionality to any other monad. So we could represent our `ReaderError` as (conceptually):

```
type ReaderError = ReaderT Error
```

In order to access our settings variable, we can use the `ask` function. But what about short-circuiting a computation? We'd like to use `throwError`, but that won't exactly work. Instead, we need to `lift` our call into the next monad up. In other words:

```
throwError :: errValue -> Error
lift . throwError :: errValue -> ReaderT Error
```

There are a few things you should pick up here:

- A transformer can be used to add functionality to an existing monad.
- A transformer must always wrap around an existing monad.
- The functionality available in a wrapped monad will be dependent not only on the monad transformer, but also on the inner monad that is being wrapped.

A great example of that last point is the `IO` monad. No matter how many layers of transformers you have around an `IO`, there's still an `IO` at the core, meaning you can perform I/O in any of these *monad transformer stacks*. You'll often see code that looks like `liftIO $ putStrLn "Hello There!"`.

The Three Transformers

We've already discussed two of our transformers previously: `Handler` and `Widget`. Just to recap, there are two special things about these transformers:

1. In order to simplify error messages, they are not actual transformers. Instead, they are newtypes that hard-code their inner monads.

   > Remember, this is why Yesod provides a specialized `lift` function, which works for `Handler` and `Widget`.

2. In reality they have extra type parameters for the sub and master site. As a result, the Yesod libraries provide `GHandler sub master a` and `GWidget sub master a`, and each site gets a pair of type synonyms `type Handler = GHandler MyApp MyApp` and `type Widget = GWidget MyApp My App ()`.

In `persistent`, we have a typeclass called `PersistStore`. This typeclass defines all of the primitive operations you can perform on a database, like `get`. This typeclass essentially looks like `class (Monad (b m)) => PersistStore b m`. `b` is the backend itself, and is in fact a monad transformer, while `m` is the inner monad that `b` wraps around. Both SQL and MongoDB have their own instances; in the case of SQL, it looks like:

```
instance MonadBaseControl IO m => PersistBackend SqlPersist m
```

This means that you can run a SQL database with any underlying monad, so long as that underlying monad supports `MonadBaseControl IO`, which allows you to properly deal with exceptions in a monad stack. That basically means any transformer stack built around `IO` (besides exceptional cases like `ContT`). Fortunately for us, that includes both `Handler` and `Widget`. The takeaway here is that we can layer our Persistent transformer on top of `Handler` or `Widget`.

> This wasn't always the case. Before Yesod 0.10, Yesod was built on top of enumerators, which do not support `MonadBaseControl`. In Yesod 0.10, we moved over to `conduit`, which greatly simplified everything we're discussing here.

In order to make it simpler to refer to the relevant Persistent transformer, the `yesod-persistent` package defines the `YesodPersistBackend` associated type. For example, if I have a site called `MyApp` and it uses SQL, I would define something like `type instance YesodPersistBackend MyApp = SqlPersist`.

When we want to run our database actions, we'll have a `SqlPersist` wrapped around a `Handler` or `Widget`. We can then use the standard Persistent unwrap functions (like `runSqlPool`) to run the action and get back a normal `Handler`/`Widget`. To automate this, we provide the `runDB` function. Putting it all together, we can now run database actions inside our handlers and widgets.

Most of the time in Yesod code, and especially thus far in this book, widgets have been treated as actionless containers that simply combine together HTML, CSS, and JavaScript. But if you look at that last paragraph again, you'll realize that's not the way things have to be. Since a widget is a transformer on top of a handler, anything you do in a handler can be done in a widget, including database actions. All you have to do is `lift`.

Example: Database-Driven Navbar

Let's put some of this new knowledge into action. We want to create a `Widget` that generates its output based on the contents of the database. Previously, our approach would have been to load up the data in a `Handler`, and then pass that data into a `Widget`. Now, we'll do the loading of data in the `Widget` itself. This is a boon for modularity, as this `Widget` can be used in any `Handler` we want, without any need to pass in the database contents.

```
{-# LANGUAGE OverloadedStrings, TypeFamilies, TemplateHaskell, FlexibleContexts,
             QuasiQuotes, TypeFamilies, MultiParamTypeClasses, GADTs #-}
import Yesod
import Database.Persist.Sqlite
import Data.Text (Text)
import Data.Time

share [mkPersist sqlSettings, mkMigrate "migrateAll"] [persist|
Link
```

```
        title Text
        url Text
        added UTCTime
|]

data LinksExample = LinksExample ConnectionPool

mkYesod "LinksExample" [parseRoutes|
/ RootR GET
/add-link AddLinkR POST
|]

instance Yesod LinksExample

instance RenderMessage LinksExample FormMessage where
    renderMessage _ _ = defaultFormMessage

instance YesodPersist LinksExample where
    type YesodPersistBackend LinksExample = SqlPersist
    runDB db = do
        LinksExample pool <- getYesod
        runSqlPool db pool

getRootR :: Handler RepHtml
getRootR = defaultLayout [whamlet|
<form method=post action=@{AddLinkR}>
    <p>
        Add a new link to #
        <input type=url name=url value=http://>
        \ titled #
        <input type=text name=title>
        \ #
        <input type=submit value="Add link">
<h2>Existing links
^{existingLinks}
|]

existingLinks :: Widget
existingLinks = do
    links <- lift $ runDB $ selectList [] [LimitTo 5, Desc LinkAdded]
    [whamlet|
<ul>
    $forall Entity _ link <- links
        <li>
            <a href=#{linkUrl link}>#{linkTitle link}
|]

postAddLinkR :: Handler ()
postAddLinkR = do
    url <- runInputPost $ ireq urlField "url"
    title <- runInputPost $ ireq textField "title"
    now <- liftIO getCurrentTime
    runDB $ insert $ Link title url now
    setMessage "Link added"
    redirect RootR
```

```
main :: IO ()
main = withSqlitePool "links.db3" 10 $ \pool -> do
    runSqlPool (runMigration migrateAll) pool
    warpDebug 3000 $ LinksExample pool
```

Pay attention in particular to the `existingLinks` function. Notice how all we needed to do was apply `lift` to a normal database action. And from within `getRootR`, we treated `existingLinks` like any ordinary `Widget`, no special parameters at all. See the figure for the output of this app.

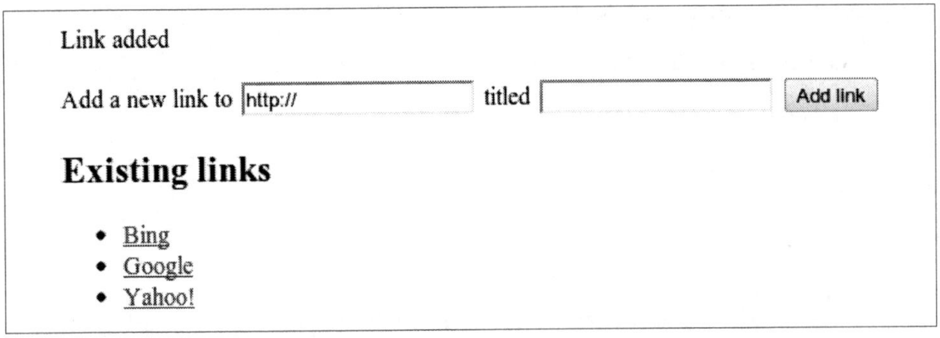

Figure 13-1. Screenshot of the navbar

Example: Request Information

Likewise, you can get request information inside a `Widget`. Here we can determine the sort order of a list based on a GET parameter.

```
{-# LANGUAGE OverloadedStrings, TypeFamilies, TemplateHaskell,
             QuasiQuotes, TypeFamilies, MultiParamTypeClasses, GADTs #-}
import Yesod
import Data.Text (Text)
import Data.List (sortBy)
import Data.Ord (comparing)

data Person = Person
    { personName :: Text
    , personAge :: Int
    }

people :: [Person]
people =
    [ Person "Miriam" 25
    , Person "Eliezer" 3
    , Person "Michael" 26
    , Person "Gavriella" 1
    ]

data People = People
```

```
mkYesod "People" [parseRoutes|
/ RootR GET
|]

instance Yesod People

instance RenderMessage People FormMessage where
    renderMessage _ _ = defaultFormMessage

getRootR :: Handler RepHtml
getRootR = defaultLayout [whamlet|
<p>
    <a href="?sort=name">Sort by name
    \ | #
    <a href="?sort=age">Sort by age
    \ | #
    <a href="?">No sort
^{showPeople}
|]

showPeople :: Widget
showPeople = do
    msort <- lift $ runInputGet $ iopt textField "sort"
    let people' =
            case msort of
                Just "name" -> sortBy (comparing personName) people
                Just "age"  -> sortBy (comparing personAge)  people
                _           -> people
    [whamlet|
<dl>
    $forall person <- people'
        <dt>#{personName person}
        <dd>#{show $ personAge person}
|]

main :: IO ()
main = warpDebug 3000 People
```

Once again, all we need to do is `lift` our normal `Handler` code (in this case, `runInput Get`) to have it run in our `Widget`.

Summary

If you completely ignore this chapter, you'll still be able to use Yesod to great benefit. The advantage of understanding how Yesod's monads interact is to be able to produce cleaner, more modular code. Being able to perform arbitrary actions in a `Widget` can be a powerful tool, and understanding how Persistent and your `Handler` code interact can help you make more informed design decisions in your app.

CHAPTER 14
Authentication and Authorization

Authentication and authorization are two very related, and yet separate, concepts. While the former deals with identifying a user, the latter determines what a user is allowed to do. Unfortunately, since both terms are often abbreviated as "auth," the concepts are often conflated.

Yesod provides built-in support for a number of third-party authentication systems, such as OpenID, BrowserID, and OAuth. These are systems where your application trusts some external system for validating a user's credentials. Additionally, there is support for more commonly used username/password and email/password systems. The former route ensures simplicity for users (no new passwords to remember) and implementors (no need to deal with an entire security architecture), while the latter gives the developer more control.

On the authorization side, we are able to take advantage of REST and type-safe URLs to create simple, declarative systems. Additionally, since all authorization code is written in Haskell, you have the full flexibility of the language at your disposal.

This chapter will cover how to set up an "auth" solution in Yesod and discuss some trade-offs in the different authentication options.

Overview

The `yesod-auth` package provides a unified interface for a number of different authentication plug-ins. The only real requirement for these backends is that they identify a user based on some unique string. In OpenID, for instance, this would be the actual OpenID value. In BrowserID, it's the email address. For HashD, which uses a database of hashed passwords, it's the username.

Each authentication plug-in provides its own system for logging in, whether it be via passing tokens with an external site or a email/password form. After a successful login, the plug-in sets a value in the user's session to indicate his/her `AuthId`. This `AuthId` is usually a Persistent ID from a table used for keeping track of users.

There are a few functions available for querying a user's `AuthId`, most commonly `maybeAuthId`, `requireAuthId`, `maybeAuth`, and `requireAuth`. The required versions will redirect to a login page if the user is not logged in, while the second set of functions (the ones **not** ending in `Id`) give both the table ID *and* entity value.

Since all of the storage of `AuthId` is built on top of sessions, all of the rules from there apply. In particular, the data is stored in an encrypted HMACed client cookie, which automatically times out after a certain configurable period of inactivity. Additionally, since there is no server-side component to sessions, logging out simply deletes the data from the session cookie; if a user reuses an older cookie value, the session will still be valid.

> There are plans to add in a server-side component to sessions, which would allow forced logout. This will almost certainly be implemented before a 1.0 release of Yesod.

On the flip side, authorization is handled by a few methods inside the `Yesod` typeclass. For every request, these methods are run to determine if access should be allowed or denied, or if the user needs to be authenticated. By default, these methods allow access for every request. Alternatively, you can implement authorization in a more ad hoc way by adding calls to `requireAuth` and the like within individual handler functions, though this undermines many of the benefits of a declarative authorization system.

Authenticate Me

Let's jump right in with an example of authentication.

```
{-# LANGUAGE OverloadedStrings, TemplateHaskell, TypeFamilies,
             MultiParamTypeClasses, QuasiQuotes #-}
import Yesod
import Yesod.Auth
import Yesod.Auth.BrowserId
import Yesod.Auth.GoogleEmail
import Data.Text (Text)
import Network.HTTP.Conduit (Manager, newManager, def)

data MyAuthSite = MyAuthSite
    { httpManager :: Manager
    }

mkYesod "MyAuthSite" [parseRoutes|
/ RootR GET
/auth AuthR Auth getAuth
|]

instance Yesod MyAuthSite where
    -- Note: In order to log in with BrowserID, you must correctly
```

```
    -- set your hostname here.
    approot = ApprootStatic "http://localhost:3000"

instance YesodAuth MyAuthSite where
    type AuthId MyAuthSite = Text
    getAuthId = return . Just . credsIdent

    loginDest _  = RootR
    logoutDest _ = RootR

    authPlugins _ =
        [ authBrowserId
        , authGoogleEmail
        ]

    authHttpManager = httpManager

instance RenderMessage MyAuthSite FormMessage where
    renderMessage _ _ = defaultFormMessage

getRootR :: Handler RepHtml
getRootR = do
    maid <- maybeAuthId
    defaultLayout [whamlet|
<p>Your current auth ID: #{show maid}
$maybe _ <- maid
    <p>
        <a href=@{AuthR LogoutR}>Logout
$nothing
    <p>
        <a href=@{AuthR LoginR}>Go to the login page
|]

main :: IO ()
main = do
    man <- newManager def
    warpDebug 3000 $ MyAuthSite man
```

We'll start with the route declarations. First we declare our standard RootR route, and then we set up the authentication subsite. Remember that a subsite needs four parameters: the path to the subsite, the route name, the subsite name, and a function to get the subsite value. In other words, based on the line:

```
/auth AuthR Auth getAuth
```

We need to have getAuth :: MyAuthSite -> Auth. While we haven't written that function ourselves, yesod-auth provides it automatically. With other subsites (like static files), we provide configuration settings in the subsite value, and therefore need to specify the get function. In the auth subsite, we specify these settings in a separate typeclass, YesodAuth.

> Why not use the subsite value? There are a number of settings we would like to give for an auth subsite, and doing so from a record type would be inconvenient. Also, since we want to have an `AuthId` associated type, a typeclass is more natural. On the flip side, why not use a typeclass for all subsites? It comes with a downside: you can then only have a single instance per site, disallowing serving different sets of static files from different routes. Also, the subsite value works better when we want to load data at app initialization.

So what exactly goes in this YesodAuth instance? There are six required declarations:

- `AuthId` is an associated type. This is the value `yesod-auth` will give you when you ask if a user is logged in (via `maybeAuthId` or `requireAuthId`). In our case, we're simply using `Text`, to store the raw identifier—an email address, as we'll soon see.
- `getAuthId` gets the actual `AuthId` from the `Creds` (credentials) data type. This type has three pieces of information: the authentication backend used (browserid or googleemail in our case), the actual identifier, and an associated list of arbitrary extra information. Each backend provides different extra information; see their docs for more information.
- `loginDest` gives the route to redirect to after a successful login.
- Likewise, `logoutDest` gives the route to redirect to after a logout.
- `authPlugins` is a list of individual authentication backends to use. In our example, we're using BrowserID, which logs in via Mozilla's BrowserID system, and Google Email, which authenticates a user's email address using their Google account. The nice thing about these two backends is:
    - They require no setup, as opposed to Facebook or OAuth, which require users to establish credentials.
    - They use email addresses as identifiers, which people are comfortable with, as opposed to OpenID, which uses a URL.
- `authHttpManager` gets an HTTP connection manager from the foundation type. This allow authentication backends which use HTTP connections (i.e., almost all third-party login systems) to share connections, avoiding the cost of restarting a TCP connection for each request.

In our `RootR` handler, we have some simple links to the login and logout pages, depending on whether or not the user is logged in. Notice how we construct these subsite links: first we give the subsite route name (`AuthR`), followed by the route within the subsite (`LoginR` and `LogoutR`).

The figures below show what the login process looks like from a user perspective.

Your current auth ID: Nothing

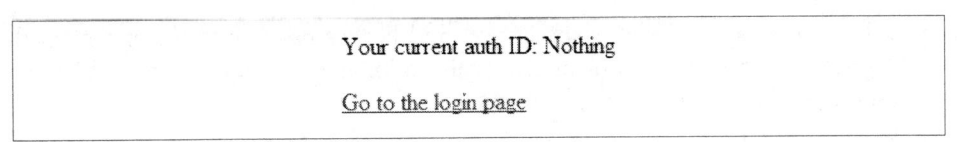

Go to the login page

Figure 14-1. Initial page load

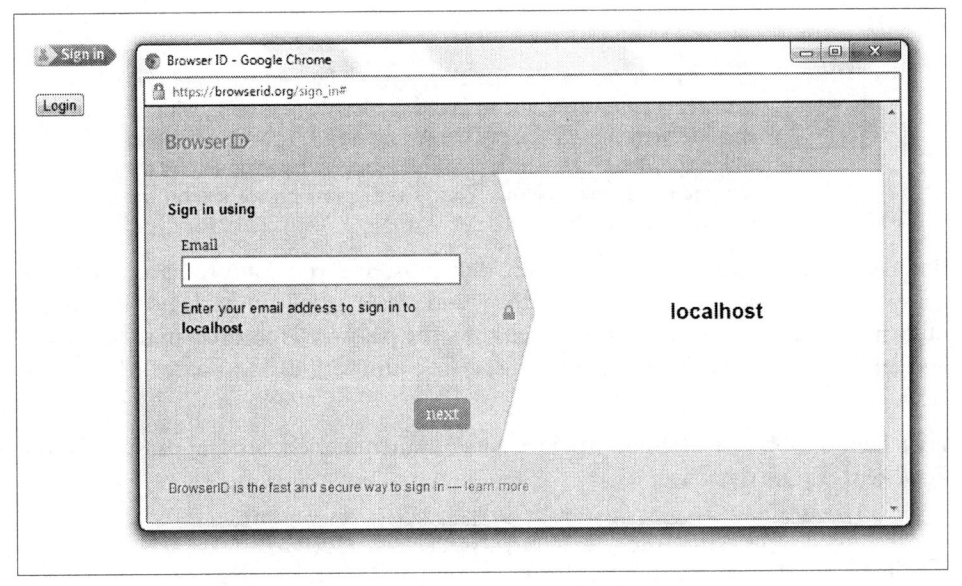

Figure 14-2. BrowserID login screen

You are now logged in

Your current auth ID: Just "michael@snoyman.com"

Logout

Figure 14-3. Homepage after logging in

Email

For many use cases, third-party authentication of email will be sufficient. Occasionally, you'll want users to actually create passwords on your site. The scaffolded site does not include this setup, because:

- In order to securely accept passwords, you need to be running over SSL. Many users are not serving their sites over SSL.

- While the email backend properly salts and hashes passwords, a compromised database could still be problematic. Again, we make no assumptions that Yesod users are following secure deployment practices.
- You need to have a working system for sending email. Many web servers these days are not equipped to deal with all of the spam protection measures used by mail servers.

> The example below will use the system's built-in *sendmail* executable. If you would like to avoid the hassle of dealing with an email server yourself, you can use Amazon SES. There is a package called `mime-mail-ses`, which provides a drop-in replacement for the sendmail code used below. This is the approach we use on the Haskellers.com site.

But assuming you are able to meet these demands, and you want to have a separate password login specifically for your site, Yesod offers a built-in backend. It requires quite a bit of code to set up, since it needs to store passwords securely in the database and send a number of different emails to users (account verification, password retrieval, etc.).

Let's have a look at a site that provides email authentication, storing passwords in a Persistent SQLite database.

```
{-# LANGUAGE OverloadedStrings, TypeFamilies, QuasiQuotes, GADTs,
             TemplateHaskell, MultiParamTypeClasses, FlexibleContexts #-}
import Yesod
import Yesod.Auth
import Yesod.Auth.Email
import Database.Persist.Sqlite
import Database.Persist.TH
import Data.Text (Text)
import Network.Mail.Mime
import qualified Data.Text.Lazy.Encoding
import Text.Shakespeare.Text (stext)
import Text.Blaze.Renderer.Utf8 (renderHtml)
import Text.Hamlet (shamlet)
import Data.Maybe (isJust)
import Control.Monad (join)

share [mkPersist sqlSettings, mkMigrate "migrateAll"] [persist|
User
    email Text
    password Text Maybe -- Password may not be set yet
    verkey Text Maybe -- Used for resetting passwords
    verified Bool
    UniqueUser email
|]

data MyEmailApp = MyEmailApp Connection

mkYesod "MyEmailApp" [parseRoutes|
```

```
/ RootR GET
/auth AuthR Auth getAuth
|]

instance Yesod MyEmailApp where
    -- Emails will include links, so be sure to include an approot so that
    -- the links are valid!
    approot = ApprootStatic "http://localhost:3000"

instance RenderMessage MyEmailApp FormMessage where
    renderMessage _ _ = defaultFormMessage

-- Set up Persistent
instance YesodPersist MyEmailApp where
    type YesodPersistBackend MyEmailApp = SqlPersist
    runDB f = do
        MyEmailApp conn <- getYesod
        runSqlConn f conn

instance YesodAuth MyEmailApp where
    type AuthId MyEmailApp = UserId

    loginDest _ = RootR
    logoutDest _ = RootR
    authPlugins _ = [authEmail]

    -- Need to find the UserId for the given email address.
    getAuthId creds = runDB $ do
        x <- insertBy $ User (credsIdent creds) Nothing Nothing False
        return $ Just $
            case x of
                Left (Entity userid _) -> userid -- newly added user
                Right userid -> userid -- existing user

    authHttpManager = error "Email doesn't need an HTTP manager"

-- Here's all of the email-specific code
instance YesodAuthEmail MyEmailApp where
    type AuthEmailId MyEmailApp = UserId

    addUnverified email verkey =
        runDB $ insert $ User email Nothing (Just verkey) False

    sendVerifyEmail email _ verurl =
        liftIO $ renderSendMail (emptyMail $ Address Nothing "noreply")
            { mailTo = [Address Nothing email]
            , mailHeaders =
                [ ("Subject", "Verify your email address")
                ]
            , mailParts = [[textPart, htmlPart]]
            }
      where
        textPart = Part
            { partType = "text/plain; charset=utf-8"
            , partEncoding = None
```

```
                    , partFilename = Nothing
                    , partContent = Data.Text.Lazy.Encoding.encodeUtf8 [stext|
Please confirm your email address by clicking on the link below.

\#{verurl}

Thank you
|]
                    , partHeaders = []
                    }
            htmlPart = Part
                { partType = "text/html; charset=utf-8"
                , partEncoding = None
                , partFilename = Nothing
                , partContent = renderHtml [shamlet|
<p>Please confirm your email address by clicking on the link below.
<p>
    <a href=#{verurl}>#{verurl}
<p>Thank you
|]
                    , partHeaders = []
                    }
    getVerifyKey = runDB . fmap (join . fmap userVerkey) . get
    setVerifyKey uid key = runDB $ update uid [UserVerkey =. Just key]
    verifyAccount uid = runDB $ do
        mu <- get uid
        case mu of
            Nothing -> return Nothing
            Just u -> do
                update uid [UserVerified =. True]
                return $ Just uid
    getPassword = runDB . fmap (join . fmap userPassword) . get
    setPassword uid pass = runDB $ update uid [UserPassword =. Just pass]
    getEmailCreds email = runDB $ do
        mu <- getBy $ UniqueUser email
        case mu of
            Nothing -> return Nothing
            Just (Entity uid u) -> return $ Just EmailCreds
                { emailCredsId = uid
                , emailCredsAuthId = Just uid
                , emailCredsStatus = isJust $ userPassword u
                , emailCredsVerkey = userVerkey u
                }
    getEmail = runDB . fmap (fmap userEmail) . get

getRootR :: Handler RepHtml
getRootR = do
    maid <- maybeAuthId
    defaultLayout [whamlet|
<p>Your current auth ID: #{show maid}
$maybe _ <- maid
    <p>
        <a href=@{AuthR LogoutR}>Logout
$nothing
    <p>
```

```
            <a href=@{AuthR LoginR}>Go to the login page
|]

main :: IO ()
main = withSqliteConn "email.db3" $ \conn -> do
    runSqlConn (runMigration migrateAll) conn
    warpDebug 3000 $ MyEmailApp conn
```

Authorization

Once you can authenticate your users, you can use their credentials to *authorize* requests. Authorization in Yesod is simple and declarative: most of the time, you just need to add the authRoute and isAuthorized methods to your Yesod typeclass instance. Let's see an example.

```
{-# LANGUAGE OverloadedStrings, TemplateHaskell, TypeFamilies,
             MultiParamTypeClasses, QuasiQuotes #-}
import Yesod
import Yesod.Auth
import Yesod.Auth.Dummy -- just for testing, don't use in real life!!!
import Data.Text (Text)
import Network.HTTP.Conduit (Manager, newManager, def)

data MyAuthSite = MyAuthSite
    { httpManager :: Manager
    }

mkYesod "MyAuthSite" [parseRoutes|
/ RootR GET POST
/admin AdminR GET
/auth AuthR Auth getAuth
|]

instance Yesod MyAuthSite where
    authRoute _ = Just $ AuthR LoginR

    -- route name, then a boolean indicating if it's a write request
    isAuthorized RootR True = isAdmin
    isAuthorized AdminR _ = isAdmin

    -- anyone can access other pages
    isAuthorized _ _ = return Authorized

isAdmin = do
    mu <- maybeAuthId
    return $ case mu of
        Nothing -> AuthenticationRequired
        Just "admin" -> Authorized
        Just _ -> Unauthorized "You must be an admin"

instance YesodAuth MyAuthSite where
    type AuthId MyAuthSite = Text
    getAuthId = return . Just . credsIdent
```

```
    loginDest  _ = RootR
    logoutDest _ = RootR

    authPlugins _ = [authDummy]

    authHttpManager = httpManager

instance RenderMessage MyAuthSite FormMessage where
    renderMessage _ _ = defaultFormMessage

getRootR :: Handler RepHtml
getRootR = do
    maid <- maybeAuthId
    defaultLayout [whamlet|
<p>Note: Log in as "admin" to be an administrator.
<p>Your current auth ID: #{show maid}
$maybe _ <- maid
    <p>
        <a href=@{AuthR LogoutR}>Logout
<p>
    <a href=@{AdminR}>Go to admin page
<form method=post>
    Make a change (admins only)
    \ #
    <input type=submit>
|]

postRootR :: Handler ()
postRootR = do
    setMessage "You made some change to the page"
    redirect RootR

getAdminR :: Handler RepHtml
getAdminR = defaultLayout [whamlet|
<p>I guess you're an admin!
<p>
    <a href=@{RootR}>Return to homepage
|]

main :: IO ()
main = do
    manager <- newManager def
    warpDebug 3000 $ MyAuthSite manager
```

authRoute should be your login page, almost always AuthR LoginR. isAuthorized is a function that takes two parameters: the requested route, and whether or not the request was a "write" request. You can actually change the meaning of what a write request is using the isWriteRequest method, but the out-of-the-box version follows RESTful principles: anything but a GET, HEAD, OPTIONS, or TRACE request is a write request.

What's convenient about the body of isAuthorized is that you can run any Handler code you want. This means you can:

- Access the filesystem (normal IO)
- Lookup values in the database
- Pull any session or request values you want

Using these techniques, you can develop as sophisticated an authorization system as you like, or even tie into existing systems used by your organization.

Conclusion

This chapter covered the basics of setting up user authentication, as well as how the built-in authorization functions provide a simple, declarative approach for users. While these are complicated concepts with many approaches, Yesod should provide you with the building blocks you need to create your own customized auth solution.

CHAPTER 15
Scaffolding and the Site Template

So you're tired of running small examples, and ready to write a real site? Then you're at the right chapter. Even with the entire Yesod library at your fingertips, there are still a lot of steps you need to go through to get a production-quality site setup:

- Config file parsing
- Signal handling (*nix)
- More efficient static file serving
- A good file layout

The scaffolded site is a combination of many Yesoders' best practices brought together into a ready-to-use skeleton for your sites. It is highly recommended for all sites. This chapter will explain the overall structure of the scaffolding, how to use it, and some of its less-than-obvious features.

For the most part, this chapter will not contain code samples. It is recommended that you follow along with an actual scaffolded site.

> Due to the nature of the scaffolded site, it is the most fluid component of Yesod, and can change from version to version. It is possible that the information in this chapter is slightly outdated.

How to Scaffold

The `yesod` package installs both a library and an executable (conveniently named *yesod* as well). This executable provides a few commands (run *yesod* by itself to get a list). In order to generate a scaffolding, the command is *yesod init*. This will start a question-and-answer process where you get to provide basic details (your name, the project name, etc). After answering the questions, you will have a site template in a subfolder with the name of your project.

The most important of these questions is the database backend. You get four choices here: SQLite, PostgreSQL, MongoDB, and tiny. tiny is not a database backend; instead, it is specifying that you do not want to use any database. This option also turns off a few extra dependencies, giving you a leaner site overall. The remainder of this chapter will focus on the scaffoldings for one of the database backends. There will be minor differences for the tiny backend.

After creating your files, the scaffolder will print a message about getting started. It gives two sets of options for commands: one using *cabal*, and the other using *cabal-dev*. *cabal-dev* is basically a wrapper around cabal that causes all dependencies to be built in a sandbox. Using it is a good way to ensure that installing other packages will not break your site setup. It is strongly recommended. If you don't have *cabal-dev*, you can install it by running *cabal install cabal-dev*.

Note that you really do need to use the *cabal install --only-dependencies* (or *cabal-dev install --only-dependencies*) command. Most likely, you do not yet have all the dependencies your site needs in place. For example, neither the database backends nor the Javascript minifier (`hjsmin`) are included when installing the `yesod` package.

Finally, to launch your development site, you would use *yesod devel* (or *yesod --dev devel*). This site will automatically rebuild and reload whenever you change your code.

File Structure

The scaffolded site is built as a fully cabalized Haskell package. In addition to source files, config files, templates, and static files are produced as well.

Cabal File

Whether directly using *cabal*, or indirectly using *yesod devel*, building your code will always go through the cabal file. If you open the file, you'll see there are both library and executable blocks. Only one of these is built at a time, depending on the value of the `library-only` flag. If `library-only` is turned on, then the library is built, which is how *yesod devel* calls your app. Otherwise, the executable is built.

The `library-only` flag should only be used by *yesod devel*; you should never be explicitly passing it into *cabal*. There is an additional flag, `dev`, that allows cabal to build an executable, but turns on some of the same features as the library-only flag, i.e., no optimizations and reload versions of the Shakespearean template functions.

In general, you will build as follows:

- When developing, use *yesod devel* exclusively.
- When building a production build, perform *cabal clean && cabal configure && cabal build*. This will produce an optimized executable in your *dist* folder.

> In the past we had a `-fproduction` flag. If you produced a scaffolded site in the past, you may have to use this flag to get a production build.

You'll also notice that we specify all language extensions in the cabal file. The extensions are specified *twice*: once for the executable, and once for the library. If you add any extensions to the list, add it to both places.

You might be surprised to see the `NoImplicitPrelude` extension. We turn this on since the site includes its own module, `Import`, with a few changes to the Prelude that make working with Yesod a little more convenient.

The last thing to note is the exported-modules list. If you add any modules to your application, you **must** update this list to get yesod devel to work correctly. Unfortunately, neither Cabal nor GHC will give you a warning if you forgot to make this update, and instead you'll get a very scary-looking error message from yesod devel.

> One of our planned improvements to *yesod devel* is to check if there are any missing modules.

Routes and Entities

Multiple times in this book, you've seen a comment like "We're declaring our routes/entities with quasiquotes for convenience. In a production site, you should use an external file." The scaffolding uses such an external file.

Routes are defined in *config/routes*, and entities in *config/models*. They have the exact same syntax as the quasiquoting you've seen throughout the book, and *yesod devel* knows to automatically recompile the appropriate modules when these files change.

The *models* files is referenced by `Model.hs`. You are free to declare whatever you like in this file, but here are some guidelines:

- Any data types used in *entities* **must** be imported/declared in *Model.hs*, above the `persistFile` call.
- Helper utilities should either be declared in `Import.hs` or, if very model-centric, in a file within the `Model` folder and imported into *Import.hs*.

Foundation and Application Modules

The `mkYesod` function, which we have used throughout the book, declares a few things:

- Route type
- Route render function

- Dispatch function

The dispatch function refers to all of the handler functions. Therefore, all of those must either be defined in the same file as the dispatch function, or be imported by the dispatch function.

Meanwhile, the handler functions will almost certainly refer to the route type. Therefore, *they* must be either in the same file where the route type is defined, or must import that file. If you follow the logic here, your entire application must essentially live in a single file!

Clearly, this isn't what we want. So instead of using `mkYesod`, the scaffolding site uses a decomposed version of the function. Foundation calls `mkYesodData`, which declares the route type and render function. Since it does not declare the dispatch function, the handler functions need not be in scope. `Import.hs` imports `Foundation.hs`, and all the handler modules import `Import.hs`.

In `Application.hs`, we call `mkYesodDispatch`, which creates our dispatch function. For this to work, all handler functions must be in scope, so be sure to add an import statement for any new handler modules you create.

Other than that, *Application.hs* is pretty simple. It provides two functions: `withDevelAppPort` is used by *yesod devel* to launch your app, and `getApplication` is used by the executable to launch.

Foundation.hs is much more exciting. It:

- Declares your foundation data type
- Declares a number of instances, such as `Yesod`, `YesodAuth`, and `YesodPersist`
- Imports the messages files. If you look for the line starting with `mkMessage`, you will see that it specifies the folder containing the messages (*messages*) and the default language (en, for English)

This is the right file for adding extra instances for your foundation, such as `YesodAuthEmail` or `YesodBreadcrumbs`.

We'll be referring back to this file later, as we discussed some of the special implementations of `Yesod` typeclass methods.

Import

The `Import` module was born out of a few commonly recurring patterns.

- I want to define some helper functions (maybe the `<> = mappend` operator) to be used by all handlers.
- I'm always adding the same five import statements (`Data.Text`, `Control.Applicative`, etc) to every handler module.
- I want to make sure I never use some evil function (`head`, `readFile`, ...) from `Prelude`.

> Yes, evil is hyperbole. If you're wondering why I listed those functions as bad: `head` is partial, and throws exceptions on an empty list, and `readFile` uses lazy I/O, which doesn't close file handles quickly enough. Also, `readFile` uses `String` instead of `Text`.

The solution is to turn on the `NoImplicitPrelude` language extension, re-export the parts of `Prelude` we want, add in all the other stuff we want, define our own functions as well, and then import this file in all handlers.

Handler Modules

Handler modules should go inside the *Handler* folder. The site template includes one module: *Handler/Root.hs*. How you split up your handler functions into individual modules is your decision, but a good rule of thumb is:

- Different methods for the same route should go in the same file, e.g., `getBlogR` and `postBlogR`.
- Related routes can also usually go in the same file, e.g., `getPeopleR` and `getPersonR`.

Of course, it's entirely up to you. When you add a new handler file, make sure you do the following:

- Add it to version control (you *are* using version control, right?).
- Add it to the cabal file.
- Add it to the *Application.hs* file.
- Put a module statement at the top, and an `import Import` line below it.

> One of the planned improvements to the *yesod* executable is to automate these four steps.

widgetFile

It's very common to want to include CSS and JavaScript specific to a page. You don't want to have to remember to include those Lucius and Julius files manually every time you refer to a Hamlet file. For this, the site template provides the `widgetFile` function.

If you have a handler function:

    getRootR = defaultLayout $(widgetFile "homepage")

, Yesod will look for the following files:

- *templates/homepage.hamlet*
- *templates/homepage.lucius*

- *templates/homepage.cassius*
- *templates/homepage.julius*

If any of those files are present, they will be automatically included in the output.

> Due to the nature of how this works, if you launch your app with *yesod devel*, and then create a new file (e.g., *templates/homepage.julius*), the contents will *not* be included until the file calling `widgetFile` is recompiled. In such a case, you may need to force a save of that file to get *yesod devel* to recompile.

defaultLayout

One of the first things you're going to want to customize is the look of your site. The layout is actually broken up into two files:

- *templates/default-layout-wrapper.hamlet* contains just the basic shell of a page. This file is interpreted as plain Hamlet, not as a Widget, and therefore cannot refer to other widgets, embed i18n strings, or add extra CSS/JS.
- *templates/default-layout.hamlet* is where you would put the bulk of your page. You **must** remember to include the `widget` value in the page, as that contains the per-page contents. This file is interpreted as a Widget.

Also, since default-layout is included via the `widgetFile` function, any Lucius, Cassius, or Julius files named *default-layout.** will automatically be included as well.

Static Files

The scaffolded site automatically includes the static file subsite, optimized for serving files that will not change over the lifetime of the current build. What this means is that:

- When your static file identifiers are generated (e.g., *static/mylogo.png* becomes `mylogo_png`), a query-string parameter is added to it with a hash of the contents of the file. All of this happens at compile time.
- When `yesod-static` serves your static files, it sets expiration headers far in the future, and includes an etag based on a hash of your content.
- Whenever you embed a link to `mylogo_png`, the rendering includes the query-string parameter. If you change the logo, recompile, and launch your new app, the query string will have changed, causing users to ignore the cached copy and download a new version.

Additionally, you can set a specific static root in your *Settings.hs* file to serve from a different domain name. This has the advantage of not requiring transmission of cookies for static file requests, and also lets you offload static file hosting to a CDN or a service like Amazon S3. See the comments in the file for more details.

Another optimization is that CSS and JavaScript included in your widgets will not be included inside your HTML. Instead, their contents will be written to an external file, and a link given. This file will be named based on a hash of the contents as well, meaning:

1. Caching works properly.
2. Yesod can avoid an expensive disk write of the CSS/JavaScript file contents if a file with the same hash already exists.

Finally, all of your JavaScript is automatically minified via `hjsmin`.

Conclusion

The purpose of this chapter was not to explain every line that exists in the scaffolded site, but instead to give a general overview of how it works. The best way to become more familiar with it is to jump right in and start writing a Yesod site with it.

CHAPTER 16
Internationalization

Users expect our software to speak their language. Unfortunately for us, there will likely be more than one language involved. While doing simple string replacement isn't too involved, correctly dealing with all the grammar issues can be tricky. After all, who wants to see "List 1 file(s)" from a program output?

But a real i18n solution needs to do more than just provide a means of achieving the correct output. It needs to make this process easy for both the programmer and the translator, and be relatively error-proof. Yesod's answer to the problem gives you:

- Intelligent guessing of the user's desired language based on request headers, with the ability to override.
- A simple syntax for giving translations, which requires no Haskell knowledge. (After all, most translators aren't programmers.)
- The ability to bring in the full power of Haskell for tricky grammar issues as necessary, along with a default selection of helper functions to cover most needs.
- Absolutely no issues at all with word order.

Synopsis

```
-- @messages/en.msg
Hello: Hello
EnterItemCount: I would like to buy:
Purchase: Purchase
ItemCount count@Int: You have purchased #{showInt count} #{plural count "item" "items"}.
SwitchLanguage: Switch language to:
Switch: Switch

-- @messages/he.msg
Hello: שלום
EnterItemCount: אני רוצה לקנות:
Purchase: קנה
ItemCount count: קנית #{showInt count} #{plural count "דברים" "דבר"}.
```

```
SwitchLanguage: ‏החלף שפה ל‎:
Switch: ‏החלף‎

-- @i18n-synopsis.hs
{-# LANGUAGE OverloadedStrings, QuasiQuotes, TemplateHaskell, TypeFamilies,
    MultiParamTypeClasses #-}
import Yesod

data I18N = I18N

mkMessage "I18N" "messages" "en"

plural :: Int -> String -> String -> String
plural 1 x _ = x
plural _ _ y = y

showInt :: Int -> String
showInt = show

instance Yesod I18N

instance RenderMessage I18N FormMessage where
    renderMessage _ _ = defaultFormMessage

mkYesod "I18N" [parseRoutes|
/ RootR GET
/buy BuyR GET
/lang LangR POST
|]

getRootR :: Handler RepHtml
getRootR = defaultLayout [whamlet|
<h1>_{MsgHello}
<form action=@{BuyR}>
    _{MsgEnterItemCount}
    <input type=text name=count>
    <input type=submit value=_{MsgPurchase}>
<form action=@{LangR} method=post>
    _{MsgSwitchLanguage}
    <select name=lang>
        <option value=en>English
        <option value=he>Hebrew
    <input type=submit value=_{MsgSwitch}>
|]

getBuyR :: Handler RepHtml
getBuyR = do
    count <- runInputGet $ ireq intField "count"
    defaultLayout [whamlet|
<p>_{MsgItemCount count}
|]

postLangR :: Handler ()
postLangR = do
    lang <- runInputPost $ ireq textField "lang"
    setLanguage lang
```

```
    redirect RootR

main :: IO ()
main = warpDebug 3000 I18N
```

Overview

Most existing i18n solutions out there, like gettext or Java message bundles, work on the principle of string lookups. Usually some form of printf-interpolation is used to interpolate variables into the strings. In Yesod, as you might guess, we instead rely on types. This gives us all of our normal advantages, such as the compiler automatically catching mistakes.

Let's take a concrete example. Suppose our application has two things it wants to say to a user: say hello, and state how many users are logged into the system. This can be modeled with a sum type:

```
data MyMessage = MsgHello | MsgUsersLoggedIn Int
```

I can also write a function to turn this data type into an English representation:

```
toEnglish :: MyMessage -> String
toEnglish MsgHello = "Hello there!"
toEnglish (MsgUsersLoggedIn 1) = "There is 1 user logged in."
toEnglish (MsgUsersLoggedIn i) = "There are " ++ show i ++ " users logged in."
```

We can also write similar functions for other languages. The advantage to this inside-Haskell approach is that we have the full power of Haskell for addressing tricky grammar issues, especially pluralization.

> You may think pluralization isn't so complicated: you have one version for 1 item, and another for any other count. That might be true in English, but it's not true for every language. Russian, for example, has six different forms, and you need to use some modulus logic to determine which one to use.

The downside, however, is that you have to write all of this inside of Haskell, which won't be very translator-friendly. To solve this, Yesod introduces the concept of message files. We'll cover that in a little bit.

Assuming we have this full set of translation functions, how do we go about using them? What we need is a new function to wrap them all up together, and then choose the appropriate translation function based on the user's selected language. Once we have that, Yesod can automatically choose the most relevant render function and call it on the values you provide.

In order to simplify things a bit, Hamlet has a special interpolation syntax, _{...}, which handles all the calls to the render functions. And in order to associate a render function with your application, you use the `YesodMessage` typeclass.

Message Files

The simplest approach to creating translations is via *message files*. The setup is simple: there is a single folder containing all of your translation files, with a single file for each language. Each file is named based on its language code, e.g., *en.msg*. And each line in a file handles one phrase, which correlates to a single constructor in your message data type.

> The scaffolded site already includes a fully configured message folder.

So firstly, a word about language codes. There are really two choices available: using a two-letter language code, or a language-LOCALE code. For example, when I load up a page in my web browser, it sends two language codes: en-US and en. What my browser is saying is "if you have American English, I like that the most. If you have English, I'll take that instead."

So which format should you use in your application? Most likely two-letter codes, unless you are actually creating separate translations by locale. This ensures that someone asking for Canadian English will still see your English. Behind the scenes, Yesod will add the two-letter codes where relevant. For example, suppose a user has the following language list:

    pt-BR, es, he

What this means is "I like Brazilian Portuguese, then Spanish, and then Hebrew." Suppose your application provides the languages pt (general Portuguese) and English, with English as the default. Strictly following the user's language list would result in the user being served English. Instead, Yesod translates that list into:

    pt-BR, es, he, pt

In other words: unless you're giving different translations based on locale, just stick to the two-letter language codes.

Now what about these message files? The syntax should be very familiar after your work with Hamlet and Persistent. The line starts off with the name of the message. Since this is a data constructor, it must start with a capital letter. Next, you can have individual parameters, which must be given in lowercase. These will be arguments to the data constructor.

The argument list is terminated by a colon, and then followed by the translated string, which allows usage of our typical variable interpolation syntax #{myVar}. By referring to the parameters defined before the colon, and using translation helper functions to deal with issues like pluralization, you can create all the translated messages you need.

Specifying Types

Since we will be creating a data type out of our message specifications, each parameter to a data constructor must be given a data type. We use a @-syntax for this. For example, to create the data type data MyMessage = MsgHello | MsgSayAge Int, we would write:

```
Hello: Hi there!
SayAge age@Int: Your age is: #{show age}
```

But there are two problems with this:

1. It's not very DRY (don't repeat yourself) to have to specify this data type in every file.
2. Translators will be confused having to specify these data types.

So instead, the type specification is only required in the main language file. This is specified as the third argument in the mkMessage function. This also specifies what the backup language will be, to be used when none of the languages provided by your application match the user's language list.

RenderMessage Typeclass

Your call to mkMessage creates an instance of the RenderMessage typeclass, which is the core of Yesod's i18n. It is defined as:

```
class RenderMessage master message where
    renderMessage :: master
                  -> [Text] -- ^ languages
                  -> message
                  -> Text
```

Notice that there are two parameters to the RenderMessage class: the master site and the message type. In theory, we could skip the master type here, but that would mean that every site would need to have the same set of translations for each message type. When it comes to shared libraries like forms, that would not be a workable solution.

The renderMessage function takes a parameter for each of the class's type parameters: master and message. The extra parameter is a list of languages the user will accept, in descending order of priority. The method then returns a user-ready Text that can be displayed.

A simple instance of `RenderMessage` may involve no actual translation of strings; instead, it will just display the same value for every language. For example:

```
data MyMessage = Hello | Greet Text
instance RenderMessage MyApp MyMessage where
    renderMessage _ _ Hello = "Hello"
    renderMessage _ _ (Greet name) = "Welcome, " <> name <> "!"
```

Notice how we ignore the first two parameters to `renderMessage`. We can now extend this to support multiple languages:

```
renderEn Hello = "Hello"
renderEn (Greet name) = "Welcome, " <> name <> "!"
renderHe Hello = "שלום"
renderHe (Greet name) = "ברוכים הבאים, " <> name <> "!"
instance RenderMessage MyApp MyMessage where
    renderMessage _ ("en":_) = renderEn
    renderMessage _ ("he":_) = renderHe
    renderMessage master (_:langs) = renderMessage master langs
    renderMessage _ [] = renderEn
```

The idea here is fairly straightforward: we define helper functions to support each language. We then add a clause to catch each of those languages in the renderMessage definition. We then have two final cases: if no languages matched, continue checking with the next language in the user's priority list. If we've exhausted all languages the user specified, then use the default language (in our case, English).

But odds are that you will never need to worry about writing this stuff manually, as the message file interface does all this for you. But it's always a good idea to have an understanding of what's going on under the surface.

Interpolation

One way to use your new `RenderMessage` instance would be to directly call the `renderMessage` function. This would work, but it's a bit tedious: you need to pass in the foundation value and the language list manually. Instead, Hamlet provides a specialized i18n interpolation, which looks like _{...}.

> Why the underscore? Underscore is already a well-established character for i18n, as it is used in the gettext library.

Hamlet will then automatically translate that to a call to `renderMessage`. Once Hamlet gets the output `Text` value, it uses the `toHtml` function to produce an `Html` value, meaning that any special characters (<, &, >) will be automatically escaped.

Phrases, Not Words

As a final note, I'd just like to give some general i18n advice. Let's say you have an application for selling turtles. You're going to use the word "turtle" in multiple places, like "You have added 4 turtles to your cart." and "You have purchased 4 turtles, congratulations!" As a programmer, you'll immediately notice the code reuse potential: we have the phrase "4 turtles" twice. So you might structure your message file as:

```
AddStart: You have added
AddEnd: to your cart.
PurchaseStart: You have purchased
PurchaseEnd: , congratulations!
Turtles count@Int: #{show count} #{plural "turtle" "turtles"}
```

STOP RIGHT THERE! This is all well and good from a programming perspective, but translations are *not* programming. There are a many things that could go wrong with this, such as:

- Some languages might put "to your cart" before "You have added."
- Maybe "added" will be constructed differently depending whether you added 1 or more turtles.
- There are a bunch of whitespace issues as well.

So the general rule is: translate entire phrases, not just words.

CHAPTER 17
Creating a Subsite

How many sites provide authentication systems? Or need to provide Create, Read, Update, Delete (CRUD) management of some objects? Or a blog? Or a wiki?

The theme here is that many websites include common components that can be reused throughout multiple sites. However, it is often quite difficult to get code to be modular enough to be truly plug-and-play: a component will require hooks into the routing system, usually for multiple routes, and will need some way of sharing styling information with the master site.

In Yesod, the solution is subsites. A subsite is a collection of routes and their handlers that can be easily inserted into a master site. By using type classes, it is easy to ensure that the master site provides certain capabilities, and to access the default site layout. And with type-safe URLs, it's easy to link from the master site to subsites.

Hello World

Writing subsites is a little bit tricky, involving a number of different types. Let's start off with a simple Hello World subsite:

```
{-# LANGUAGE QuasiQuotes, TypeFamilies, MultiParamTypeClasses #-}
{-# LANGUAGE TemplateHaskell, FlexibleInstances, OverloadedStrings #-}
import Yesod

-- Subsites have foundations just like master sites.
data HelloSub = HelloSub

-- We have a familiar analogue from mkYesod, with just one extra parameter.
-- We'll discuss that later.
mkYesodSub "HelloSub" [] [parseRoutes|
/ SubRootR GET
|]

-- And we'll spell out the handler type signature.
getSubRootR :: Yesod master => GHandler HelloSub master RepHtml
getSubRootR = defaultLayout [whamlet|Welcome to the subsite!|]
```

```
-- And let's create a master site that calls it.
data Master = Master
    { getHelloSub :: HelloSub
    }

mkYesod "Master" [parseRoutes|
/ RootR GET
/subsite SubsiteR HelloSub getHelloSub
|]

instance Yesod Master

-- Spelling out type signature again.
getRootR :: GHandler sub Master RepHtml -- could also replace sub with Master
getRootR = defaultLayout [whamlet|
<h1>Welcome to the homepage
<p>
    Feel free to visit the #
    <a href=@{SubsiteR SubRootR}>subsite
    \ as well.
|]

main = warpDebug 3000 $ Master HelloSub
```

This very simple example actually shows most of the complications involved in creating a subsite. Like a normal Yesod application, everything in a subsite is centered around a foundation data type, HelloSub in our case. We then use mkYesodSub, in much the same way that we use mkYesod, to create the route data type and the dispatch/render functions. (We'll come back to that extra parameter in a second.)

What's interesting is the type signature of getSubRootR. Up until now, we have tried to ignore the GHandler data type, or *if* we need to acknowledge its existence, pretend the first two type arguments are always the same. Now we get to finally acknowledge the truth about this funny data type.

A handler function always has two foundation types associated with it: the subsite and the master site. When you write a normal application, **those two data types are the same**. However, when you are working in a subsite, they will necessarily be different. So the type signature for getSubRootR uses HelloSub for the first argument and master for the second.

The defaultLayout function is part of the Yesod typeclass. Therefore, in order to call it, the master type argument must be an instance of Yesod. The advantage of this approach is that any modifications to the master site's defaultLayout method will automatically be reflected in subsites.

When we embed a subsite in our master site route definition, we need to specify four pieces of information: the route to use as the base of the subsite (in this case, /sub site), the constructor for the subsite routes (SubsiteR), the subsite foundation data type (`HelloSub`), and a function that takes a master foundation value and returns a subsite foundation value (`getHelloSub`).

In the definition of getRootR, we can see how the route constructor gets used. In a sense, `SubsiteR` promotes any subsite route to a master site route, making it possible to safely link to it from any master site template.

PART III
Examples

CHAPTER 18
Blog: i18n, Authentication, Authorization, and Database

This is a simple blog app. It allows an admin to add blog posts via a rich-text editor (nicedit), allows logged-in users to comment, and has full i18n support. It is also a good example of using a Persistent database, leveraging Yesod's authorization system, and templates.

While in general we recommend placing templates, Persistent entity definitions, and routing in separate files, we'll keep it all in one file here for convenience. The one exception you'll see below will be i18n messages.

We'll start off with our language extensions. In scaffolded code, the language extensions are specified in the cabal file, so you won't need to put this in your individual Haskell files.

```
> {-# LANGUAGE OverloadedStrings, TypeFamilies, QuasiQuotes,
>              TemplateHaskell, GADTs, FlexibleContexts,
>              MultiParamTypeClasses #-}
```

Now our imports.

```
> import Yesod
> import Yesod.Auth
> import Yesod.Form.Nic (YesodNic, nicHtmlField)
> import Yesod.Auth.BrowserId (authBrowserId)
> import Data.Text (Text)
> import Network.HTTP.Conduit (Manager, newManager, def)
> import Database.Persist.Sqlite
>     ( ConnectionPool, SqlPersist, runSqlPool, runMigration
>     , createSqlitePool
>     )
> import Data.Time (UTCTime, getCurrentTime)
> import Control.Applicative ((<$>), (<*>), pure)
```

First we'll set up our Persistent entities. We're going to create both our data types (via mkPersist) and a migration function, which will automatically create and update our SQL schema. If you were using the MongoDB backend, migration would not be needed.

```
> share [mkPersist sqlSettings, mkMigrate "migrateAll"] [persistLowerCase|
```

Keeps track of users. In a more robust application, we would also keep account creation date, display name, etc.

```
> User
>     email Text
>     UniqueUser email
```

An individual blog entry (I've avoided using the word "post" due to the confusion with the request method POST).

```
> Entry
>     title Text
>     posted UTCTime
>     content Html
```

We need to tack on this "deriving" line since Html doesn't specify instances for Read, Show, or Eq. If you get an error message about "cannot derive" in your own code, try adding the deriving statement.

```
>     deriving
```

And a comment on the blog post.

```
> Comment
>     entry EntryId
>     posted UTCTime
>     user UserId
>     name Text
>     text Textarea
> |]
```

Every site has a foundation data type. This value is initialized before launching your application, and is available throughout. We'll store a database connection pool and HTTP connection manager in ours. See the very end of this file for how those are initialized.

```
> data Blog = Blog
>     { connPool :: ConnectionPool
>     , httpManager :: Manager
>     }
```

To make i18n easy and translator friendly, we have a special file format for translated messages. There is a single file for each language, and each file is named based on the language code (e.g., en, es, de-DE) and placed in that folder. We also specify the main language file (here, "en") as a default language.

```
> mkMessage "Blog" "../messages-blog" "en"
```

Our en message file contains the following content:

    NotAnAdmin: You must be an administrator to access this page.

    WelcomeHomepage: Welcome to the homepage
    SeeArchive: See the archive

    NoEntries: There are no entries in the blog
    LoginToPost: Admins can login to post
    NewEntry: Post to blog
    NewEntryTitle: Title
    NewEntryContent: Content

    PleaseCorrectEntry: Your submitted entry had some errors, please correct and try again.
    EntryCreated title@Text: Your new blog post, #{title}, has been created

    EntryTitle title@Text: Blog post: #{title}
    CommentsHeading: Comments
    NoComments: There are no comments
    AddCommentHeading: Add a Comment
    LoginToComment: You must be logged in to comment
    AddCommentButton: Add comment

    CommentName: Your display name
    CommentText: Comment
    CommentAdded: Your comment has been added
    PleaseCorrectComment: Your submitted comment had some errors, please correct and try again.

    HomepageTitle: Yesod Blog Demo
    BlogArchiveTitle: Blog Archive

Now we're going to set up our routing table. We have four entries: a homepage, an entry list page (BlogR), an individual entry page (EntryR) and our authentication subsite. Note that BlogR and EntryR both accept GET and POST methods. The POST methods are for adding a new blog post and adding a new comment, respectively.

> mkYesod "Blog" [parseRoutes|
> / RootR GET
> /blog BlogR GET POST
> /blog/#EntryId EntryR GET POST
> /auth AuthR Auth getAuth
> |]

Every foundation needs to be an instance of the Yesod typeclass. This is where we configure various settings.

> instance Yesod Blog where

The base of our application. Note that in order to make BrowserID work properly, this must be a valid URL.

>   approot = ApprootStatic "http://localhost:3000"

Our authorization scheme. We want to have the following rules:

* Only admins can add a new entry.
* Only logged in users can add a new comment.
* All other pages can be accessed by anyone.

We set up our routes in a RESTful way, where the actions that could make changes are always using a POST method. As a result, we can simply check for whether or not a request is a write request, given by the True in the second field.

First, we'll authorize requests to add a new entry.

> isAuthorized BlogR True = do
>   mauth <- maybeAuth
>   case mauth of
>   Nothing -> return AuthenticationRequired
>   Just (Entity _ user)
> | isAdmin user -> return Authorized
> | otherwise   -> unauthorizedI MsgNotAnAdmin

Now we'll authorize requests to add a new comment.

> isAuthorized (EntryR _) True = do
>   mauth <- maybeAuth
>   case mauth of
>   Nothing -> return AuthenticationRequired
>   Just _ -> return Authorized

And for all other requests, the result is always authorized.

> isAuthorized _ _ = return Authorized

Where a user should be redirected to if they get an AuthenticationRequired.

> authRoute _ = Just (AuthR LoginR)

This is where we define our site look-and-feel. The function is given the content for the individual page, and wraps it up with a standard template.

> defaultLayout inside = do

Yesod encourages the get-following-post pattern, where after a POST, the user is redirected to another page. In order to allow the POST page to give the user some kind of feedback, we have the getMessage and setMessage functions. It's a good idea to always check for pending messages in your defaultLayout function.

>   mmsg <- getMessage

We use widgets to compose together HTML, CSS, and JavaScript. At the end of the day, we need to unwrap all of that into simple HTML. That's what the widgetToPageContent function is for. We're going to give it a widget consisting of the content we received from the individual page (inside), plus a standard CSS for all pages. We'll use the Lucius template language to create the latter.

>   pc <- widgetToPageContent $ do
>   toWidget [lucius|

```
> body {
>     width: 760px;
>     margin: 1em auto;
>     font-family: sans-serif;
> }
> textarea {
>     width: 400px;
>     height: 200px;
> }
> #message {
>   color: #900;
> }
> |]
>           inside
```

And finally we'll use a new Hamlet template to wrap up the individual components (title, head data and body data) into the final output.

```
>           hamletToRepHtml [hamlet|
> $doctype 5
> <html>
>     <head>
>         <title>#{pageTitle pc}
>         ^{pageHead pc}
>     <body>
>         $maybe msg <- mmsg
>             <div #message>#{msg}
>         ^{pageBody pc}
> |]
```

This is a simple function to check if a user is the admin. In a real application, we would likely store the admin bit in the database itself, or check with some external system. For now, I've just hardcoded my own email address.

```
> isAdmin :: User -> Bool
> isAdmin user = userEmail user == "michael@snoyman.com"
```

In order to access the database, we need to create a YesodPersist instance, which says which backend we're using and how to run an action.

```
> instance YesodPersist Blog where
>     type YesodPersistBackend Blog = SqlPersist
>     runDB f = do
>         master <- getYesod
>         let pool = connPool master
>         runSqlPool f pool
```

This is a convenience synonym. It is defined automatically for you in the scaffolding.

```
> type Form x = Html -> MForm Blog Blog (FormResult x, Widget)
```

In order to use yesod-form and yesod-auth, we need an instance of RenderMessage for FormMessage. This allows us to control the i18n of individual form messages.

```
> instance RenderMessage Blog FormMessage where
>     renderMessage _ _ = defaultFormMessage
```

In order to use the built-in Nic HTML editor, we need this instance. We just take the default values, which use a CDN-hosted version of Nic.

```
> instance YesodNic Blog
```

In order to use yesod-auth, we need a YesodAuth instance.

```
> instance YesodAuth Blog where
>     type AuthId Blog = UserId
>     loginDest _ = RootR
>     logoutDest _ = RootR
>     authHttpManager = httpManager
```

We'll use [BrowserID](https://browserid.org/), which is a third-party system using email addresses as your identifier. This makes it easy to switch to other systems in the future, such as locally authenticated email addresses (also included with yesod-auth).

```
>     authPlugins _ = [authBrowserId]
```

This function takes someone's login credentials (i.e., his/her email address) and gives back a user ID.

```
>     getAuthId creds = do
>         let email = credsIdent creds
>             user = User email
>         res <- runDB $ insertBy user
>         return $ Just $ either entityKey id res
```

Homepage handler. The one important detail here is our usage of `setTitleI`, which allows us to use i18n messages for the title. We also use this message with a `_{Msg...}` interpolation in Hamlet.

```
> getRootR :: Handler RepHtml
> getRootR = defaultLayout $ do
>     setTitleI MsgHomepageTitle
>     [whamlet|
> <p>_{MsgWelcomeHomepage}
> <p>
>     <a href=@{BlogR}>_{MsgSeeArchive}
> |]
```

Define a form for adding new entries. We want the user to provide the title and content, and then fill in the post date automatically via `getCurrentTime`.

```
> entryForm :: Form Entry
> entryForm = renderDivs $ Entry
>     <$> areq textField (fieldSettingsLabel MsgNewEntryTitle) Nothing
>     <*> aformM (liftIO getCurrentTime)
>     <*> areq nicHtmlField (fieldSettingsLabel MsgNewEntryContent) Nothing
```

Get the list of all blog entries, and present an admin with a form to create a new entry.

```
> getBlogR :: Handler RepHtml
> getBlogR = do
>     muser <- maybeAuth
>     entries <- runDB $ selectList [] [Desc EntryPosted]
>     ((_, entryWidget), enctype) <- generateFormPost entryForm
>     defaultLayout $ do
>         setTitleI MsgBlogArchiveTitle
>         [whamlet|
> $if null entries
>     <p>_{MsgNoEntries}
> $else
>     <ul>
>         $forall Entity entryId entry <- entries
>             <li>
>                 <a href=@{EntryR entryId}>#{entryTitle entry}
```

We have three possibilities: the user is logged in as an admin, the user is logged in and is not an admin, and the user is not logged in. In the first case, we should display the entry form. In the second, we'll do nothing. In the third, we'll provide a login link.

```
> $maybe Entity _ user <- muser
>     $if isAdmin user
>         <form method=post enctype=#{enctype}>
>             ^{entryWidget}
>             <div>
>                 <input type=submit value=_{MsgNewEntry}>
> $nothing
>     <p>
>         <a href=@{AuthR LoginR}>_{MsgLoginToPost}
> |]
```

Process an incoming entry addition. We don't do any permissions checking, since isAuthorized handles it for us. If the form submission was valid, we add the entry to the database and redirect to the new entry. Otherwise, we ask the user to try again.

```
> postBlogR :: Handler RepHtml
> postBlogR = do
>     ((res, entryWidget), enctype) <- runFormPost entryForm
>     case res of
>         FormSuccess entry -> do
>             entryId <- runDB $ insert entry
>             setMessageI $ MsgEntryCreated $ entryTitle entry
>             redirect $ EntryR entryId
>         _ -> defaultLayout $ do
>             setTitleI MsgPleaseCorrectEntry
>             [whamlet|
> <form method=post enctype=#{enctype}>
>     ^{entryWidget}
>     <div>
```

```
>             <input type=submit value=_{MsgNewEntry}>
> |]
```

A form for comments, very similar to our entryForm above. It takes the
EntryId of the entry the comment is attached to. By using pure, we embed
this value in the resulting Comment output, without having it appear in the
generated HTML.

```
> commentForm :: EntryId -> Form Comment
> commentForm entryId = renderDivs $ Comment
>     <$> pure entryId
>     <*> aformM (liftIO getCurrentTime)
>     <*> aformM requireAuthId
>     <*> areq textField (fieldSettingsLabel MsgCommentName) Nothing
>     <*> areq textareaField (fieldSettingsLabel MsgCommentText) Nothing
```

Show an individual entry, comments, and an add comment form if the user is
logged in.

```
> getEntryR :: EntryId -> Handler RepHtml
> getEntryR entryId = do
>     (entry, comments) <- runDB $ do
>         entry <- get404 entryId
>         comments <- selectList [] [Asc CommentPosted]
>         return (entry, map entityVal comments)
>     muser <- maybeAuth
>     ((_, commentWidget), enctype) <-
>         generateFormPost (commentForm entryId)
>     defaultLayout $ do
>         setTitleI $ MsgEntryTitle $ entryTitle entry
>         [whamlet|
> <h1>#{entryTitle entry}
> <article>#{entryContent entry}
>     <section .comments>
>         <h1>_{MsgCommentsHeading}
>         $if null comments
>             <p>_{MsgNoComments}
>         $else
>             $forall Comment _entry posted _user name text <- comments
>                 <div .comment>
>                     <span .by>#{name}
>                     <span .at>#{show posted}
>                     <div .content>#{text}
>     <section>
>         <h1>_{MsgAddCommentHeading}
>         $maybe _ <- muser
>             <form method=post enctype=#{enctype}>
>                 ^{commentWidget}
>                 <div>
>                     <input type=submit value=_{MsgAddCommentButton}>
>         $nothing
>             <p>
>                 <a href=@{AuthR LoginR}>_{MsgLoginToComment}
> |]
```

Receive an incoming comment submission.

```
> postEntryR :: EntryId -> Handler RepHtml
> postEntryR entryId = do
>     ((res, commentWidget), enctype) <-
>         runFormPost (commentForm entryId)
>     case res of
>         FormSuccess comment -> do
>             _ <- runDB $ insert comment
>             setMessageI MsgCommentAdded
>             redirect $ EntryR entryId
>         _ -> defaultLayout $ do
>             setTitleI MsgPleaseCorrectComment
>             [whamlet|
> <form method=post enctype=#{enctype}>
>     ^{commentWidget}
>     <div>
>         <input type=submit value=_{MsgAddCommentButton}>
> |]
```

Finally, our main function.

```
> main :: IO ()
> main = do
>     pool <- createSqlitePool "blog.db3" 10 -- create a new pool
>     -- perform any necessary migration
>     runSqlPool (runMigration migrateAll) pool
>     manager <- newManager def -- create a new HTTP manager
>     warpDebug 3000 $ Blog pool manager -- start our server
```

CHAPTER 19
Wiki: Markdown, Chat Subsite, Event Source

This example will tie together a few different ideas. We'll start with a chat subsite, which allows us to embed a chat widget on any page. We'll use the HTML5 event source API to handle sending events from the server to the client.

```haskell
-- @Chat.hs
{-# LANGUAGE OverloadedStrings, TypeFamilies, QuasiQuotes,
             TemplateHaskell, FlexibleInstances, MultiParamTypeClasses,
             FlexibleContexts
  #-}
-- | This module defines a subsite that allows you to insert a chat box on
-- any page of your site. It uses eventsource for sending the messages from
-- the server to the browser.
module Chat where

import Yesod
import Control.Concurrent.Chan (Chan, dupChan, writeChan)
import Data.Text (Text)
import Network.Wai.EventSource (ServerEvent (..), eventSourceAppChan)
import Language.Haskell.TH.Syntax (Type (VarT), Pred (ClassP), mkName)
import Blaze.ByteString.Builder.Char.Utf8 (fromText)
import Data.Monoid (mappend)

-- | Our subsite foundation. We keep a channel of events that all connections
-- will share.
data Chat = Chat (Chan ServerEvent)

-- | We need to know how to check if a user is logged in and how to get
-- his/her username (for printing messages).
class (Yesod master, RenderMessage master FormMessage)
        => YesodChat master where
    getUserName :: GHandler sub master Text
    isLoggedIn :: GHandler sub master Bool

-- Now we set up our subsite. The first argument is the subsite, very similar
-- to how we've used mkYesod in the past. The second argument is specific to
-- subsites. What it means here is "the master site must be an instance of
```

```haskell
-- YesodChat".
--
-- We define two routes: a route for sending messages from the client to the
-- server, and one for opening up the event stream to receive messages from
-- the server.
mkYesodSub "Chat"
    [ ClassP ''YesodChat [VarT $ mkName "master"]
    ] [parseRoutes|
/send SendR POST
/recv ReceiveR GET
|]

-- | Get a message from the user and send it to all listeners.
postSendR :: YesodChat master => GHandler Chat master ()
postSendR = do
    from <- getUserName

    -- Note that we're using GET parameters for simplicity of the Ajax code.
    -- This could easily be switched to POST. Nonetheless, our overall
    -- approach is still RESTful since this route can only be accessed via a
    -- POST request.
    body <- runInputGet $ ireq textField "message"

    -- Get the channel
    Chat chan <- getYesodSub

    -- Send an event to all listeners with the user's name and message.
    liftIO $ writeChan chan $ ServerEvent Nothing Nothing $ return $
        fromText from `mappend` fromText ": " `mappend` fromText body

-- | Send an eventstream response with all messages streamed in.
getReceiveR :: GHandler Chat master ()
getReceiveR = do
    -- First we get the main channel
    Chat chan0 <- getYesodSub

    -- We duplicated the channel, which allows us to create broadcast
    -- channels.
    chan <- liftIO $ dupChan chan0

    -- Now we use the event source API. eventSourceAppChan takes two parameters:
    -- the channel of events to read from, and the WAI request. It returns a
    -- WAI response, which we can return with sendWaiResponse.
    req <- waiRequest
    res <- lift $ eventSourceAppChan chan req
    sendWaiResponse res

-- | Provide a widget that the master site can embed on any page.
chatWidget :: YesodChat master
           => (Route Chat -> Route master)
           -> GWidget sub master ()
-- This toMaster argument tells us how to convert a Route Chat into a master
-- route. You might think this is redundant information, but taking this
-- approach means we can have multiple chat subsites in a single site.
chatWidget toMaster = do
```

```
    -- Get some unique identifiers to help in creating our HTML/CSS. Remember,
    -- we have no idea what the master site's HTML will look like, so we
    -- should not assume we can make up identifiers that won't be reused.
    -- Also, it's possible that multiple chatWidgets could be embedded in the
    -- same page.
    chat <- lift newIdent   -- the containing div
    output <- lift newIdent -- the box containing the messages
    input <- lift newIdent  -- input field from the user

    ili <- lift isLoggedIn  -- check if we're already logged in
    if ili
        then do
            -- Logged in: show the widget
            [whamlet|
<div ##{chat}>
    <h2>Chat
    <div ##{output}>
    <input ##{input} type=text placeholder="Enter Message">
|]
            -- Just some CSS
            toWidget [lucius|
##{chat} {
    position: absolute;
    top: 2em;
    right: 2em;
}
##{output} {
    width: 200px;
    height: 300px;
    border: 1px solid #999;
    overflow: auto;
}
|]
            -- And now that JavaScript
            toWidgetBody [julius|
// Set up the receiving end
var output = document.getElementById("#{output}");
var src = new EventSource("@{toMaster ReceiveR}");
src.onmessage = function(msg) {
    // This function will be called for each new message.
    var p = document.createElement("p");
    p.appendChild(document.createTextNode(msg.data));
    output.appendChild(p);

    // And now scroll down within the output div so the most recent message
    // is displayed.
    output.scrollTop = output.scrollHeight;
};

// Set up the sending end: send a message via Ajax whenever the user hits
// enter.
var input = document.getElementById("#{input}");
input.onkeyup = function(event) {
    var keycode = (event.keyCode ? event.keyCode : event.which);
    if (keycode == '13') {
```

```
                var xhr = new XMLHttpRequest();
                var val = input.value;
                input.value = "";
                var params = "?message=" + encodeURI(val);
                xhr.open("POST", "@{toMaster SendR}" + params);
                xhr.send(null);
            }
        }
|]
                else do
                    -- User isn't logged in, give a not-logged-in message.
                    master <- lift getYesod
                    [whamlet|
<p>
    You must be #
    $maybe ar <- authRoute master
        <a href=@{ar}>logged in
    $nothing
        logged in
    \ to chat.
|]
```

This module stands on its own, and can be used in any application. Next we'll provide such a driver application: a wiki. Our wiki will have a hardcoded homepage, and then a wiki section of the site. We'll be using *multiple dynamic pieces* to allow an arbitrary hierarchy of pages within the wiki.

For storage, we'll just use a mutable reference to a `Map`. For a production application, this should be replaced with a proper database. The content will be stored and served as Markdown. yesod-auth's dummy plugin will provide us with (fake) authentication.

```
{-# LANGUAGE OverloadedStrings, TypeFamilies, QuasiQuotes,
             TemplateHaskell, FlexibleInstances, MultiParamTypeClasses,
             FlexibleContexts
  #-}
import Yesod
import Yesod.Auth
import Yesod.Auth.Dummy (authDummy)
import Chat
import Control.Concurrent.Chan (Chan, newChan)
import Network.Wai.Handler.Warp (run)
import Data.Text (Text)
import qualified Data.Text.Lazy as TL
import qualified Data.IORef as I
import qualified Data.Map as Map
import Text.Markdown (markdown, def)

-- | Our foundation type has both the chat subsite and a mutable reference to
-- a map of all our wiki contents. Note that the key is a list of Texts, since
-- a wiki can have an arbitrary hierarchy.
--
-- In a real application, we would want to store this information in a
-- database of some sort.
data Wiki = Wiki
    { getChat :: Chat
```

```haskell
    , wikiContent :: I.IORef (Map.Map [Text] Text)
    }

-- Set up our routes as usual.
mkYesod "Wiki" [parseRoutes|
/ RootR GET                     -- the homepage
/wiki/*Texts WikiR GET POST     -- note the multipiece for the wiki hierarchy
/chat ChatR Chat getChat        -- the chat subsite
/auth AuthR Auth getAuth        -- the auth subsite
|]

instance Yesod Wiki where
    authRoute _ = Just $ AuthR LoginR -- get a working login link

    -- Our custom defaultLayout will add the chat widget to every page.
    -- We'll also add login and logout links to the top.
    defaultLayout widget = do
        pc <- widgetToPageContent $ widget >> chatWidget ChatR
        mmsg <- getMessage
        hamletToRepHtml [hamlet|
$doctype 5
<html>
    <head>
        <title>#{pageTitle pc}
        ^{pageHead pc}
    <body>
        $maybe msg <- mmsg
            <div .message>#{msg}
        <nav>
            <a href=@{AuthR LoginR}>Login
            \ | #
            <a href=@{AuthR LogoutR}>Logout
        ^{pageBody pc}
|]

-- Fairly standard YesodAuth instance. We'll use the dummy plugin so that you
-- can create any name you want, and store the login name as the AuthId.
instance YesodAuth Wiki where
    type AuthId Wiki = Text
    authPlugins _ = [authDummy]
    loginDest _ = RootR
    logoutDest _ = RootR
    getAuthId = return . Just . credsIdent
    authHttpManager = error "authHttpManager" -- not used by authDummy

-- Just implement authentication based on our yesod-auth usage.
instance YesodChat Wiki where
    getUserName = requireAuthId
    isLoggedIn = do
        ma <- maybeAuthId
        return $ maybe False (const True) ma

instance RenderMessage Wiki FormMessage where
    renderMessage _ _ = defaultFormMessage
```

```haskell
-- Nothing special here, just giving a link to the root of the wiki.
getRootR :: Handler RepHtml
getRootR = defaultLayout [whamlet|
<p>Welcome to the Wiki!
<p>
    <a href=@{wikiRoot}>Wiki root
|]
  where
    wikiRoot = WikiR []

-- A form for getting wiki content
wikiForm mtext = renderDivs $ areq textareaField "Page body" mtext

-- Show a wiki page and an edit form
getWikiR :: [Text] -> Handler RepHtml
getWikiR page = do
    -- Get the reference to the contents map
    icontent <- fmap wikiContent getYesod

    -- And read the map from inside the reference
    content <- liftIO $ I.readIORef icontent

    -- Lookup the contents of the current page, if available
    let mtext = Map.lookup page content

    -- Generate a form with the current contents as the default value.
    -- Note that we use the Textarea wrapper to get a <textarea>.
    ((_, form), _) <- generateFormPost $ wikiForm $ fmap Textarea mtext
    defaultLayout $ do
        case mtext of
            -- We're treating the input as markdown. The markdown package
            -- automatically handles XSS protection for us.
            Just text -> toWidget $ markdown def $ TL.fromStrict text
            Nothing -> [whamlet|<p>Page does not yet exist|]
        [whamlet|
<h2>Edit page
<form method=post>
    ^{form}
    <div>
        <input type=submit>
|]

-- Get a submitted wiki page and updated the contents.
postWikiR :: [Text] -> Handler RepHtml
postWikiR page = do
    icontent <- fmap wikiContent getYesod
    content <- liftIO $ I.readIORef icontent
    let mtext = Map.lookup page content
    ((res, form), _) <- runFormPost $ wikiForm $ fmap Textarea mtext
    case res of
        FormSuccess (Textarea t) -> do
            liftIO $ I.atomicModifyIORef icontent $
                \m -> (Map.insert page t m, ())
            setMessage "Page updated"
            redirect $ WikiR page
```

```
                _ -> defaultLayout [whamlet|
<form method=post>
    ^{form}
    <div>
        <input type=submit>
|]

main :: IO ()
main = do
    -- Create our server event channel
    chan <- newChan

    -- Initially have a blank database of wiki pages
    icontent <- I.newIORef Map.empty

    -- Run our app
    warpDebug 3000 $ Wiki (Chat chan) icontent
```

CHAPTER 20
JSON Web Service

Let's create a very simple web service: it takes a JSON request and returns a JSON response. We're going to write the server in WAI/Warp, and the client in `http-conduit`. We'll be using `aeson` for JSON parsing and rendering. We could also write the server in Yesod itself, but for such a simple example, the extra features of Yesod don't add much.

Server

WAI uses the `conduit` package to handle streaming request bodies, and efficiently generates responses using `blaze-builder`. `aeson` uses `attoparsec` for parsing; by using `attoparsec-conduit` we get easy interoperability with WAI. This plays out as:

```
{-# LANGUAGE OverloadedStrings #-}
import Network.Wai (Response, responseLBS, Application, requestBody)
import Network.HTTP.Types (status200, status400)
import Network.Wai.Handler.Warp (run)
import Data.Aeson.Parser (json)
import Data.Conduit.Attoparsec (sinkParser)
import Control.Monad.IO.Class (liftIO)
import Data.Aeson (Value, encode, object, (.=))
import Control.Exception (SomeException)
import Data.ByteString (ByteString)
import Data.Conduit (ResourceT, ($$))
import Control.Exception.Lifted (handle)

main :: IO ()
main = run 3000 app

app :: Application
app req = handle invalidJson $ do
    value <- requestBody req $$ sinkParser json
    newValue <- liftIO $ modValue value
    return $ responseLBS
        status200
        [("Content-Type", "application/json")]
```

193

```
            $ encode newValue

    invalidJson :: SomeException -> ResourceT IO Response
    invalidJson ex = return $ responseLBS
        status400
        [("Content-Type", "application/json")]
        $ encode $ object
            [ ("message" .= show ex)
            ]

    -- Application-specific logic would go here.
    modValue :: Value -> IO Value
    modValue = return
```

Client

`http-conduit` was written as a companion to WAI. It too uses `conduit` and `blaze-builder` pervasively, meaning we once again get easy interop with `aeson`. A few extra comments for those not familiar with `http-conduit`:

- A `Manager` is present to keep track of open connections, so that multiple requests to the same server use the same connection. You usually want to use the `withManager` function to create and clean up this `Manager`, since it is exception safe.
- We need to know the size of our request body, which can't be determined directly from a `Builder`. Instead, we convert the `Builder` into a lazy `ByteString` and take the size from there.
- There are a number of different functions for initiating a request. We use `http`, which allows us to directly access the data stream. There are other higher level functions (such as `httpLbs`) that let you ignore the issues of sources and get the entire body directly.

```
{-# LANGUAGE OverloadedStrings #-}
import Network.HTTP.Conduit
    ( http, parseUrl, withManager, RequestBody (RequestBodyLBS)
    , requestBody, method, Response (..)
    )
import Data.Aeson (Value (Object, String))
import Data.Aeson.Parser (json)
import Data.Conduit (($$))
import Data.Conduit.Attoparsec (sinkParser)
import Control.Monad.IO.Class (liftIO)
import Data.Aeson (encode, (.=), object)

main :: IO ()
main = withManager $ \manager -> do
    value <- liftIO makeValue
    -- We need to know the size of the request body, so we convert to a
    -- ByteString
    let valueBS = encode value
    req' <- liftIO $ parseUrl "http://localhost:3000/"
```

```
    let req = req' { method = "POST", requestBody = RequestBodyLBS valueBS }
    Response status headers body <- http req manager
    resValue <- body $$ sinkParser json
    liftIO $ handleResponse resValue

-- Application-specific function to make the request value
makeValue :: IO Value
makeValue = return $ object
    [ ("foo" .= ("bar" :: String))
    ]

-- Application-specific function to handle the response from the server
handleResponse :: Value -> IO ()
handleResponse = print
```

CHAPTER 21
Case Study: Sphinx-Based Search

Sphinx (*http://sphinxsearch.com/*) is a search server, and powers the search feature on many sites, including Yesod's own site. While the actual code necessary to integrate Yesod with Sphinx is relatively short, it touches on a number of complicated topics, and is therefore a great case study in how to play with some of the under-the-surface details of Yesod.

There are essentially three different pieces at play here:

- Storing the content we wish to search. This is fairly straightforward Persistent code, and we won't dwell on it much in this chapter.
- Accessing Sphinx search results from inside Yesod. Thanks to the `sphinx` package, this is actually very easy.
- Providing the document content to Sphinx. This is where the interesting stuff happens, and will show how to deal with streaming content from a database directly to XML, which gets sent directly over the wire to the client.

Sphinx Setup

Unlike many of our other examples, to start with here we'll need to actually configure and run our external Sphinx server. I'm not going to go into all the details of Sphinx, partly because it's not relevant to our point here, and mostly because I'm not an expert on Sphinx.

Sphinx provides three main command-line utilities: `searchd` is the actual search daemon that receives requests from the client (in this case, our web app) and returns the search results. `indexer` parses the set of documents and creates the search index. `search` is a debugging utility that will run simple queries against Sphinx.

There are two important settings: the source and the index. The source tells Sphinx where to read document information from. It has direct support for MySQL and PostgreSQL, as well as a more general XML format known as xmlpipe2. We're going

197

to use the last one. This not only will give us more flexibility with choosing Persistent backends, but will also demonstrate some more powerful Yesod concepts.

The second setting is the index. Sphinx can handle multiple indices simultaneously, which allows it to provide search for multiple services at once. Each index will have a source it pulls from.

In our case, we're going to provide a URL from our application (/search/xmlpipe) that provides the XML file required by Sphinx, and then pipe that through to the indexer. So we'll add the following to our Sphinx config file:

```
source searcher_src
{
    type = xmlpipe2
    xmlpipe_command = curl http://localhost:3000/search/xmlpipe
}

index searcher
{
    source = searcher_src
    path = /var/data/searcher
    docinfo = extern
    charset_type = utf-8
}
```

In order to build your search index, you would run `indexer searcher`. Obviously this won't work until you have your web app running. For a production site, it would make sense to run this command via a crontab script so the index is regularly updated.

Basic Yesod Setup

Let's get our basic Yesod setup going. We're going to have a single table in the database for holding documents, which consist of a title and content. We'll store this in a SQLite database, and provide routes for searching, adding documents, viewing documents, and providing the xmlpipe file to Sphinx.

```
share [mkPersist sqlSettings, mkMigrate "migrateAll"] [persist|
Doc
    title Text
    content Textarea
|]

data Searcher = Searcher ConnectionPool

mkYesod "Searcher" [parseRoutes|
/ RootR GET
/doc/#DocId DocR GET
/add-doc AddDocR POST
/search SearchR GET
/search/xmlpipe XmlpipeR GET
|]
```

```
instance Yesod Searcher

instance YesodPersist Searcher where
    type YesodPersistBackend Searcher = SqlPersist

    runDB action = do
        Searcher pool <- getYesod
        runSqlPool action pool

instance RenderMessage Searcher FormMessage where
    renderMessage _ _ = defaultFormMessage
```

Hopefully all of this looks pretty familiar by now. Next we'll define some forms: one for creating documents, and one for searching:

```
addDocForm :: Html -> MForm Searcher Searcher (FormResult Doc, Widget)
addDocForm = renderTable $ Doc
    <$> areq textField "Title" Nothing
    <*> areq textareaField "Contents" Nothing

searchForm :: Html -> MForm Searcher Searcher (FormResult Text, Widget)
searchForm = renderDivs $ areq (searchField True) "Query" Nothing
```

The True parameter to searchField makes the field auto-focus on page load. Finally, we have some standard handlers for the homepage (shows the add document form and the search form), the document display, and adding a document.

```
getRootR :: Handler RepHtml
getRootR = do
    docCount <- runDB $ count ([] :: [Filter Doc])
    ((_, docWidget), _) <- runFormPost addDocForm
    ((_, searchWidget), _) <- runFormGet searchForm
    let docs = if docCount == 1
                then "There is currently 1 document."
                else "There are currently " ++ show docCount ++ " documents."
    defaultLayout [whamlet|
<p>Welcome to the search application. #{docs}
<form method=post action=@{AddDocR}>
    <table>
        ^{docWidget}
        <tr>
            <td colspan=3>
                <input type=submit value="Add document">
<form method=get action=@{SearchR}>
    ^{searchWidget}
    <input type=submit value=Search>
|]

postAddDocR :: Handler RepHtml
postAddDocR = do
    ((res, docWidget), _) <- runFormPost addDocForm
    case res of
        FormSuccess doc -> do
            docid <- runDB $ insert doc
            setMessage "Document added"
            redirect $ DocR docid
```

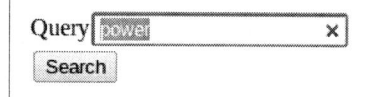

Figure 21-1. Search Result

```
        _ -> defaultLayout [whamlet|
<form method=post action=@{AddDocR}>
    <table>
        ^{docWidget}
        <tr>
            <td colspan=3>
                <input type=submit value="Add document">
|]

getDocR :: DocId -> Handler RepHtml
getDocR docid = do
    doc <- runDB $ get404 docid
    defaultLayout $
        [whamlet|
<h1>#{docTitle doc}
<div .content>#{docContent doc}
|]
```

Searching

Now that we've got the boring stuff out of the way, let's jump into the actual searching. We're going to need three pieces of information for displaying a result: the document ID it comes from, the title of that document, and the *excerpts*. Excerpts are the highlighted portions of the document which contain the search term.

So let's start off by defining a Result data type:

```
data Result = Result
    { resultId :: DocId
    , resultTitle :: Text
    , resultExcerpt :: Html
    }
```

Next we'll look at the search handler:

```
getSearchR :: Handler RepHtml
getSearchR = do
    ((formRes, searchWidget), _) <- runFormGet searchForm
    searchResults <-
        case formRes of
            FormSuccess qstring -> getResults qstring
            _ -> return []
    defaultLayout $ do
        addLucius [lucius|
.excerpt {
    color: green; font-style: italic
}
.match {
    background-color: yellow;
}
|]
        [whamlet|
<form method=get action=@{SearchR}>
    ^{searchWidget}
    <input type=submit value=Search>
$if not $ null searchResults
    <h1>Results
    $forall result <- searchResults
        <div .result>
            <a href=@{DocR $ resultId result}>#{resultTitle result}
            <div .excerpt>#{resultExcerpt result}
|]
```

Nothing magical here, we're just relying on the `searchForm` defined above, and the `getResults` function, which hasn't been defined yet. This function just takes a search string, and returns a list of results. This is where we first interact with the Sphinx API. We'll be using two functions: `query` will return a list of matches, and `buildExcerpts` will return the highlighted excerpts. Let's first look at query:

```
getResults :: Text -> Handler [Result]
getResults qstring = do
    sphinxRes' <- liftIO $ S.query config "searcher" (unpack qstring)
    case sphinxRes' of
        ST.Ok sphinxRes -> do
            let docids = map (Key . PersistInt64 . ST.documentId) $ ST.matches sphinxRes
            fmap catMaybes $ runDB $ forM docids $ \docid -> do
                mdoc <- get docid
                case mdoc of
                    Nothing -> return Nothing
                    Just doc -> liftIO $ Just <$> getResult docid doc qstring
        _ -> error $ show sphinxRes'
  where
    config = S.defaultConfig
        { S.port = 9312
        , S.mode = ST.Any
        }
```

query takes three parameters: the configuration options, the index to search against (searcher in this case), and the search string. It returns a list of document IDs that contain the search string. The tricky bit here is that those documents are returned as Int64 values, whereas we need DocIds. We're taking advantage of the fact that the SQL Persistent backends use a PersistInt64 constructor for their IDs, and simply wrap up the values appropriately.

> If you're dealing with a backend that has non-numeric IDs, like MongoDB, you'll need to work out something a bit more clever than this.

We then loop over the resulting IDs to get a [Maybe Result] value, and use catMaybes to turn it into a [Result]. In the where clause, we define our local settings, which override the default port and set up the search to work when *any* term matches the document.

Let's finally look at the getResult function:

```
getResult :: DocId -> Doc -> Text -> IO Result
getResult docid doc qstring = do
    excerpt' <- S.buildExcerpts
        excerptConfig
        [T.unpack $ escape $ docContent doc]
        "searcher"
        (unpack qstring)
    let excerpt =
            case excerpt' of
                ST.Ok bss -> preEscapedLazyText $ decodeUtf8With ignore $ L.concat bss
                _ -> ""
    return Result
        { resultId = docid
        , resultTitle = docTitle doc
        , resultExcerpt = excerpt
        }
  where
    excerptConfig = E.altConfig { E.port = 9312 }

escape :: Textarea -> Text
escape =
    T.concatMap escapeChar . unTextarea
  where
    escapeChar '<' = "&lt;"
    escapeChar '>' = "&gt;"
    escapeChar '&' = "&amp;"
    escapeChar c   = T.singleton c
```

buildExcerpts takes four parameters: the configuration options, the textual contents of the document, the search index, and the search term. The interesting bit is that we entity escape the text content. Sphinx won't automatically escape these for us, so we must do it explicitly.

Similarly, the result from Sphinx is a list of lazy ByteStrings. But of course, we'd rather have HTML. So we concat that list into a single lazy ByteString, decode it to a lazy text (ignoring invalid UTF-8 character sequences), and use preEscapedLazyText to make sure that the tags inserted for matches are not escaped. A sample of this HTML is:

```
&#8230; Departments.  The President shall have <span class='match'>Power</span> to
fill up all Vacancies
&#8230;  people. Amendment 11 The Judicial <span class='match'>power</span> of the
United States shall
&#8230; jurisdiction. 2. Congress shall have <span class='match'>power</span> to
enforce this article by
&#8230; 5. The Congress shall have <span class='match'>power</span> to enforce, by
appropriate legislation
&#8230;
```

Streaming xmlpipe Output

We've saved the best for last. For the majority of Yesod handlers, the recommended approach is to load up the database results into memory and then produce the output document based on that. It's simpler to work with, but more importantly it's more resilient to exceptions. If there's a problem loading the data from the database, the user will get a proper 500 response code.

> What do I mean by "proper 500 response code"? If you start streaming a response to a client, and encounter an exception halfway through, there's no way to change the status code; the user will see a 200 response that simply stops in the middle. Not only can this partial content be confusing, but it's an invalid usage of the HTTP spec.

However, generating the xmlpipe output is a perfect example of the alternative. There are potentially a huge number of documents (the yesodweb.com code handles tens of thousands of these), and documents could easily be several hundred kilobytes. If we take a non-streaming approach, this can lead to huge memory usage and slow response times.

So how exactly do we create a streaming response? As we cover in the WAI chapter, we have a `ResponseSource` constructor that uses a stream of blaze-builder `Builders`. From the Yesod side, we can avoid the normal Yesod response procedure and send a WAI response directly using the `sendWaiResponse` function. So there are at least two of the pieces of this puzzle.

Now we know we want to create a stream of `Builders` from some XML content. Fortunately, the `xml-conduit` package provides this interface directly. `xml-conduit` provides some high-level interfaces for dealing with documents as a whole, but in our case, we're going to need to use the low-level Event interface to ensure minimal memory impact. So the function we're interested in is:

```
renderBuilder :: Resource m => RenderSettings -> Conduit Event m Builder b
```

In plain English, that means renderBuilder takes some settings (we'll just use the defaults), and will then convert a stream of Events to a stream of Builders. This is looking pretty good, so all we need now is a stream of Events.

Speaking of which, what should our XML document actually look like? It's pretty simple: we have a `sphinx:docset` root element, a `sphinx:schema` element containing a single `sphinx:field` (which defines the content field), and then a `sphinx:document` for each document in our database. That last element will have an `id` attribute and a child content element.

Example 21-1. Sample xmlpipe document

```
<sphinx:docset xmlns:sphinx="http://sphinxsearch.com/">
    <sphinx:schema>
        <sphinx:field name="content"/>
    </sphinx:schema>
    <sphinx:document id="1">
        <content>bar</content>
    </sphinx:document>
    <sphinx:document id="2">
        <content>foo bar baz</content>
    </sphinx:document>
</sphinx:docset>
```

Every document is going to start off with the same events (start the docset, start the schema, etc) and end with the same event (end the docset). We'll start off by defining those:

```
toName :: Text -> X.Name
toName x = X.Name x (Just "http://sphinxsearch.com/") (Just "sphinx")

docset, schema, field, document, content :: X.Name
docset = toName "docset"
schema = toName "schema"
field = toName "field"
document = toName "document"
content = "content" -- no prefix

startEvents, endEvents :: [X.Event]
startEvents =
    [ X.EventBeginDocument
    , X.EventBeginElement docset []
    , X.EventBeginElement schema []
    , X.EventBeginElement field [("name", [X.ContentText "content"])]
    , X.EventEndElement field
    , X.EventEndElement schema
    ]

endEvents =
    [ X.EventEndElement docset
    ]
```

Now that we have the shell of our document, we need to get the `Events` for each individual document. This is actually a fairly simple function:

```
entityToEvents :: (Entity Doc) -> [X.Event]
entityToEvents (Entity docid doc) =
    [ X.EventBeginElement document [("id", [X.ContentText $ toPathPiece docid])]
    , X.EventBeginElement content []
    , X.EventContent $ X.ContentText $ unTextarea $ docContent doc
    , X.EventEndElement content
    , X.EventEndElement document
    ]
```

We start the document element with an `id` attribute, start the content, insert the content, and then close both elements. We use `toPathPiece` to convert a `DocId` into a `Text` value. Next, we need to be able to convert a stream of these entities into a stream of events. For this, we can use the built-in `concatMap` function from `Data.Conduit.List`: `CL.concatMap entityToEvents`.

But what we *really* want is to stream those events directly from the database. For most of this book, we've used the `selectList` function, but Persistent also provides the (more powerful) `selectSourceConn` function. So we end up with the function:

```
docSource :: Connection -> C.Source IO X.Event
docSource conn = selectSourceConn conn [] [] C.$= CL.concatMap entityToEvents
```

The `$=` operator joins together a source and a conduit into a new source. Now that we have our `Event` source, all we need to do is surround it with the document start and end events. With `Source`'s `Monoid` instance, this is a piece of cake:

```
fullDocSource :: Connection -> C.Source IO X.Event
fullDocSource conn = mconcat
    [ CL.sourceList startEvents
    , docSource conn
    , CL.sourceList endEvents
    ]
```

We're almost there. Now we just need to tie it together in `getXmlpipeR`. We need to get a database connection to be used. Normally, database connections are taken and returned automatically via the `runDB` function. In our case, we want to check out a connection and keep it available until the response body is completely sent. To do this, we use the `takeResource` function, which registers a cleanup action with the `ResourceT` monad.

> All WAI applications live in a `ResourceT` transformer. You can get more information on `ResourceT` in the conduit appendix.

By default, a resource will not be returned to the pool. This has to do with proper exception handling, but is not relevant for our use case. Therefore, we need to force the connection to be returned to the pool.

```
getXmlpipeR :: Handler RepXml
getXmlpipeR = do
    Searcher pool <- getYesod
    let headers = [("Content-Type", "text/xml")]
    managedConn <- lift $ takeResource pool
    let conn = mrValue managedConn
    lift $ mrReuse managedConn True let source = fullDocSource conn C.$= renderBuilder def
    sendWaiResponse $ ResponseSource status200 headers source
```

We get our connection pool from the foundation variable, then send a WAI response. We use the `ResponseSource` constructor, and provide it the status code, response headers, and body.

Full Code

```
{-# LANGUAGE OverloadedStrings, TypeFamilies, TemplateHaskell,
    QuasiQuotes, MultiParamTypeClasses, GADTs, FlexibleContexts
 #-}
import Yesod
import Data.Text (Text, unpack)
import Control.Applicative ((<$>), (<*>))
import Database.Persist.Sqlite
import Database.Persist.Query.GenericSql (selectSourceConn)
import Database.Persist.Store (PersistValue (PersistInt64))
import qualified Text.Search.Sphinx as S
import qualified Text.Search.Sphinx.Types as ST
import qualified Text.Search.Sphinx.ExcerptConfiguration as E
import qualified Data.ByteString.Lazy as L
import Data.Text.Lazy.Encoding (decodeUtf8With)
import Data.Text.Encoding.Error (ignore)
import Data.Maybe (catMaybes)
import Control.Monad (forM)
import qualified Data.Text as T
import Text.Blaze (preEscapedLazyText)
import qualified Data.Conduit as C
import qualified Data.Conduit.List as CL
import qualified Data.XML.Types as X
import Network.Wai (Response (ResponseSource))
import Network.HTTP.Types (status200)
import Text.XML.Stream.Render (renderBuilder, def)
import Data.Monoid (mconcat)
import Data.Conduit.Pool (takeResource, mrValue, mrReuse)

share [mkPersist sqlSettings, mkMigrate "migrateAll"] [persist|
Doc
    title Text
    content Textarea
|]

data Searcher = Searcher ConnectionPool

mkYesod "Searcher" [parseRoutes|
```

```
/ RootR GET
/doc/#DocId DocR GET
/add-doc AddDocR POST
/search SearchR GET
/search/xmlpipe XmlpipeR GET
|]

instance Yesod Searcher

instance YesodPersist Searcher where
    type YesodPersistBackend Searcher = SqlPersist

    runDB action = do
        Searcher pool <- getYesod
        runSqlPool action pool

instance RenderMessage Searcher FormMessage where
    renderMessage _ _ = defaultFormMessage

addDocForm :: Html -> MForm Searcher Searcher (FormResult Doc, Widget)
addDocForm = renderTable $ Doc
    <$> areq textField "Title" Nothing
    <*> areq textareaField "Contents" Nothing

searchForm :: Html -> MForm Searcher Searcher (FormResult Text, Widget)
searchForm = renderDivs $ areq (searchField True) "Query" Nothing

getRootR :: Handler RepHtml
getRootR = do
    docCount <- runDB $ count ([] :: [Filter Doc])
    ((_, docWidget), _) <- runFormPost addDocForm
    ((_, searchWidget), _) <- runFormGet searchForm
    let docs = if docCount == 1
                then "There is currently 1 document."
                else "There are currently " ++ show docCount ++ " documents."
    defaultLayout [whamlet|
<p>Welcome to the search application. #{docs}
<form method=post action=@{AddDocR}>
    <table>
        ^{docWidget}
        <tr>
            <td colspan=3>
                <input type=submit value="Add document">
<form method=get action=@{SearchR}>
    ^{searchWidget}
    <input type=submit value=Search>
|]

postAddDocR :: Handler RepHtml
postAddDocR = do
    ((res, docWidget), _) <- runFormPost addDocForm
    case res of
        FormSuccess doc -> do
            docid <- runDB $ insert doc
            setMessage "Document added"
```

```haskell
                    redirect $ DocR docid
            _ -> defaultLayout [whamlet|
<form method=post action=@{AddDocR}>
    <table>
        ^{docWidget}
        <tr>
            <td colspan=3>
                <input type=submit value="Add document">
|]

getDocR :: DocId -> Handler RepHtml
getDocR docid = do
    doc <- runDB $ get404 docid
    defaultLayout $
        [whamlet|
<h1>#{docTitle doc}
<div .content>#{docContent doc}
|]

data Result = Result
    { resultId :: DocId
    , resultTitle :: Text
    , resultExcerpt :: Html
    }

getResult :: DocId -> Doc -> Text -> IO Result
getResult docid doc qstring = do
    excerpt' <- S.buildExcerpts
        excerptConfig
        [T.unpack $ escape $ docContent doc]
        "searcher"
        (unpack qstring)
    let excerpt =
            case excerpt' of
                ST.Ok bss -> preEscapedLazyText $ decodeUtf8With ignore $ L.concat bss
                _ -> ""
    return Result
        { resultId = docid
        , resultTitle = docTitle doc
        , resultExcerpt = excerpt
        }
  where
    excerptConfig = E.altConfig { E.port = 9312 }

escape :: Textarea -> Text
escape =
    T.concatMap escapeChar . unTextarea
  where
    escapeChar '<' = "&lt;"
    escapeChar '>' = "&gt;"
    escapeChar '&' = "&amp;"
    escapeChar c   = T.singleton c

getResults :: Text -> Handler [Result]
getResults qstring = do
```

```haskell
        sphinxRes' <- liftIO $ S.query config "searcher" (unpack qstring)
        case sphinxRes' of
            ST.Ok sphinxRes -> do
                let docids = map (Key . PersistInt64 . ST.documentId) $ ST.matches sphinxRes
                fmap catMaybes $ runDB $ forM docids $ \docid -> do
                    mdoc <- get docid
                    case mdoc of
                        Nothing -> return Nothing
                        Just doc -> liftIO $ Just <$> getResult docid doc qstring
            _ -> error $ show sphinxRes'
  where
    config = S.defaultConfig
        { S.port = 9312
        , S.mode = ST.Any
        }

getSearchR :: Handler RepHtml
getSearchR = do
    ((formRes, searchWidget), _) <- runFormGet searchForm
    searchResults <-
        case formRes of
            FormSuccess qstring -> getResults qstring
            _ -> return []
    defaultLayout $ do
        addLucius [lucius|
.excerpt {
    color: green; font-style: italic
}
.match {
    background-color: yellow;
}
|]
        [whamlet|
<form method=get action=@{SearchR}>
    ^{searchWidget}
    <input type=submit value=Search>
$if not $ null searchResults
    <h1>Results
    $forall result <- searchResults
        <div .result>
            <a href=@{DocR $ resultId result}>#{resultTitle result}
            <div .excerpt>#{resultExcerpt result}
|]

getXmlpipeR :: Handler RepXml
getXmlpipeR = do
    Searcher pool <- getYesod
    let headers = [("Content-Type", "text/xml")]
    managedConn <- lift $ takeResource pool
    let conn = mrValue managedConn
    lift $ mrReuse managedConn True
    let source = fullDocSource conn C.$= renderBuilder def
        flushSource = fmap C.Chunk source
    sendWaiResponse $ ResponseSource status200 headers flushSource
```

```haskell
entityToEvents :: (Entity Doc) -> [X.Event]
entityToEvents (Entity docid doc) =
    [ X.EventBeginElement document [("id", [X.ContentText $ toPathPiece docid])]
    , X.EventBeginElement content []
    , X.EventContent $ X.ContentText $ unTextarea $ docContent doc
    , X.EventEndElement content
    , X.EventEndElement document
    ]

fullDocSource :: Connection -> C.Source IO X.Event
fullDocSource conn = mconcat
    [ CL.sourceList startEvents
    , docSource conn
    , CL.sourceList endEvents
    ]

docSource :: Connection -> C.Source IO X.Event
docSource conn = selectSourceConn conn [] [] C.$= CL.concatMap entityToEvents

toName :: Text -> X.Name
toName x = X.Name x (Just "http://sphinxsearch.com/") (Just "sphinx")

docset, schema, field, document, content :: X.Name
docset = toName "docset"
schema = toName "schema"
field = toName "field"
document = toName "document"
content = "content" -- no prefix

startEvents, endEvents :: [X.Event]
startEvents =
    [ X.EventBeginDocument
    , X.EventBeginElement docset []
    , X.EventBeginElement schema []
    , X.EventBeginElement field [("name", [X.ContentText "content"])]
    , X.EventEndElement field
    , X.EventEndElement schema
    ]

endEvents =
    [ X.EventEndElement docset
    ]

main :: IO ()
main = withSqlitePool "searcher.db3" 10 $ \pool -> do
    runSqlPool (runMigration migrateAll) pool
    warpDebug 3000 $ Searcher pool
```

PART IV
Appendices

APPENDIX A
monad-control

`monad-control` is used in a few places within Yesod, most notably to ensure proper exception handling within Persistent. It is a general purpose package to extend standard functionality in monad transformers.

Overview

One of the powerful, and sometimes confusing, features in Haskell is monad transformers. They allow you to take different pieces of functionality—such as mutable state, error handling, or logging—and compose them together easily. Though I swore I'd never write a monad tutorial, I'm going to employ a painful analogy here: monads are like onions. (Monads are not like cakes.) By that, I mean *layers*.

We have the core monad, also known as the innermost or bottom monad. On top of this core, we add layers, each adding a new feature and spreading outward/upward. As a motivating example, let's consider an Error monad stacked on top of the IO monad:

```
newtype ErrorT e m a = ErrorT { runErrorT :: m (Either e a) }
type MyStack = ErrorT MyError IO
```

Now pay close attention here: ErrorT is just a simple newtype around an Either wrapped in a monad. Getting rid of the newtype, we have:

```
type ErrorTUnwrapped e m a = m (Either e a)
```

At some point, we'll need to actually perform some IO inside our MyStack. If we went with the unwrapped approach, it would be trivial, since there would be no ErrorT constructor in the way. However, we need that newtype wrapper for a whole bunch of type reasons I won't go into here (this isn't a monad transformer tutorial, after all). So the solution is the MonadTrans typeclass:

```
class MonadTrans t where
    lift :: Monad m => m a -> t m a
```

I'll admit, the first time I saw that type signature, my response was stunned confusion, and incredulity that it actually meant anything. But looking at an instance helps a bit:

```
instance (Error e) => MonadTrans (ErrorT e) where
    lift m = ErrorT $ do
        a <- m
        return (Right a)
```

All we're doing is wrapping the inside of the IO with a Right value, and then applying our newtype wrapper. This allows us to take an action that lives in IO, and "lift" it to the outer/upper monad.

But now to the point at hand. This works very well for simple functions. For example:

```
sayHi :: IO ()
sayHi = putStrLn "Hello"

sayHiError :: ErrorT MyError IO ()
sayHiError = lift $ putStrLn "Hello"
```

But let's take something slightly more complicated, like a callback:

```
withMyFile :: (Handle -> IO a) -> IO a
withMyFile = withFile "test.txt" WriteMode

sayHi :: Handle -> IO ()
sayHi handle = hPutStrLn handle "Hi there"

useMyFile :: IO ()
useMyFile = withMyFile sayHi
```

So far so good, right? Now let's say that we need a version of sayHi that has access to the Error monad:

```
sayHiError :: Handle -> ErrorT MyError IO ()
sayHiError handle = do
    lift $ hPutStrLn handle "Hi there, error!"
    throwError MyError
```

We would like to write a function that combines withMyFile and sayHiError. Unfortunately, GHC doesn't like this very much:

```
useMyFileErrorBad :: ErrorT MyError IO ()
useMyFileErrorBad = withMyFile sayHiError

    Couldn't match expected type `ErrorT MyError IO ()'
           with actual type `IO ()'
```

Why does this happen, and how can we work around it?

Intuition

Let's try and develop an external intuition of what's happening here. The ErrorT monad transformer adds extra functionality to the IO monad. We've defined a way to "tack on" that extra functionality to normal IO actions: we add that Right constructor and wrap it all in ErrorT. Wrapping in Right is our way of saying "it went OK"; there wasn't anything wrong with this action.

Now this intuitively makes sense: since the IO monad doesn't have the concept of returning a MyError when something goes wrong, it will always succeed in the lifting phase. (Note: This has **nothing** to do with runtime exceptions, don't even think about them.) What we have is a guaranteed one-directional translation up the monad stack.

Let's take another example: the Reader monad. A Reader has access to some extra piece of data floating around. Whatever is running in the inner monad doesn't know about that extra piece of information. So how would you do a lift? You just ignore that extra information. The Writer monad? Don't write anything. State? Don't change anything. I'm seeing a pattern here.

But now let's try and go in the opposite direction: I have something in a Reader, and I'd like to run it in the base monad (e.g., IO). Well... that's not going to work, is it? I need that extra piece of information, I'm relying on it, and it's not there. There's simply no way to go in the opposite direction without providing that extra value.

Or is there? If you remember, we'd pointed out earlier that ErrorT is just a simple wrapper around the inner monad. In other words, if I have `errorValue :: ErrorT MyError IO MyValue`, I can apply `runErrorT` and get a value of type `IO (Either MyError MyValue)`. The looks quite a bit like bi-directional translation, doesn't it?

Well, not quite. We originally had an `ErrorT MyError IO` monad, with a value of type `MyValue`. Now we have a monad of type `IO` with a value of type `Either MyError MyValue`. So this process has in fact changed the value, while the lifting process leaves it the same.

But still, with a little fancy footwork we can unwrap the ErrorT, do some processing, and then wrap it back up again.

```
useMyFileError1 :: ErrorT MyError IO ()
useMyFileError1 =
    let unwrapped :: Handle -> IO (Either MyError ())
        unwrapped handle = runErrorT $ sayHiError handle
        applied :: IO (Either MyError ())
        applied = withMyFile unwrapped
        rewrapped :: ErrorT MyError IO ()
        rewrapped = ErrorT applied
    in rewrapped
```

This is the crucial point of this whole article, so look closely. We first unwrap our monad. This means that, to the outside world, it's now just a plain old IO value. Internally, we've stored all the information from our ErrorT transformer. Now that we have a plain old IO, we can easily pass it off to withMyFile. withMyFile takes in the internal state and passes it back out unchanged. Finally, we wrap everything back up into our original ErrorT.

This is the entire pattern of monad-control: we embed the extra features of our monad transformer inside the value. Once in the value, the type system ignores it and focuses on the inner monad. When we're done playing around with that inner monad, we can pull our state back out and reconstruct our original monad stack.

Types

I purposely started with the ErrorT transformer, as it is one of the simplest for this inversion mechanism. Unfortunately, others are a bit more complicated. Take for instance, ReaderT. It is defined as `newtype ReaderT r m a = ReaderT { runReaderT :: r -> m a }`. If we apply `runReaderT` to it, we get a function that returns a monadic value. So we're going to need some extra machinery to deal with all that stuff. And this is when we leave Kansas behind.

There are a few approaches to solving these problems. In the past, I implemented a solution using type families in the `neither` package. Anders Kaseorg implemented a much more straightforward solution in `monad-peel`. And for efficiency, in `monad-control`, Bas van Dijk uses CPS (continuation passing style) and existential types.

> The code taken from monad-control actually applies to version 0.2.0.3 changed things just a bit, by making the state explicit with an associated type, and generalizing `MonadControlIO` to `MonadBaseControl`, but the concepts are still the same.

The first type we're going to look at is:

```
type Run t = forall n o b. (Monad n, Monad o, Monad (t o)) => t n b -> n (t o b)
```

That's incredibly dense, so let's talk it out. The only "input" data type to this thing is t, a monad transformer. A Run is a function that will then work with **any** combination of types n, o, and b (that's what the forall means). n and o are both monads, while b is a simple value contained by them.

The lefthand side of the Run function, `t n b`, is our monad transformer wrapped around the n monad and holding a b value. So for example, that could be a `MyTrans FirstMonad MyValue`. It then returns a value with the transformer "popped" inside, with a brand new monad at its core. In other words, `FirstMonad (MyTrans NewMonad MyValue)`.

That might sound pretty scary at first, but it actually isn't as foreign as you'd think: this is essentially what we did with ErrorT. We started with ErrorT on the outside, wrapping around IO, and ended up with an IO by itself containing an Either. Well, guess what: another way to represent an Either is `ErrorT MyError Identity`. So essentially, we pulled the IO to the outside and plunked an Identity in its place. We're doing the same thing in a Run: pulling the FirstMonad outside and replacing it with a NewMonad.

> Now might be a good time to get a beer.

Alright, now we're getting somewhere. If we had access to one of those Run functions, we could use it to peel off the ErrorT on our sayHiError function and pass it to withMyFile. With the magic of undefined, we can play such a game:

```
errorRun :: Run (ErrorT MyError)
errorRun = undefined

useMyFileError2 :: IO (ErrorT MyError Identity ())
useMyFileError2 =
    let afterRun :: Handle -> IO (ErrorT MyError Identity ())
        afterRun handle = errorRun $ sayHiError handle
        applied :: IO (ErrorT MyError Identity ())
        applied = withMyFile afterRun
     in applied
```

This looks eerily similar to our previous example. In fact, errorRun is acting almost identically to runErrorT. However, we're still left with two problems: we don't know where to get that errorRun value from, and we still need to restructure the original ErrorT after we're done.

MonadTransControl

Obviously, in the specific case we have before us, we could use our knowledge of the ErrorT transformer to beat the types into submission and create our Run function manually. But what we *really* want is a general solution for many transformers. At this point, you know we need a typeclass.

So let's review what we need: access to a Run function, and some way to restructure our original transformer after the fact. And thus was born MonadTransControl, with its single method liftControl:

```
class MonadTrans t => MonadTransControl t where
    liftControl :: Monad m => (Run t -> m a) -> t m a
```

Let's look at this closely. liftControl takes a function (the one we'll be writing). That function is provided with a Run function, and must return a value in some monad (m). liftControl will then take the result of that function and reinstate the original transformer on top of everything.

```
useMyFileError3 :: Monad m => ErrorT MyError IO (ErrorT MyError m ())
useMyFileError3 =
    liftControl inside
  where
    inside :: Monad m => Run (ErrorT MyError) -> IO (ErrorT MyError m ())
    inside run = withMyFile $ helper run
```

```
helper :: Monad m
       => Run (ErrorT MyError) -> Handle -> IO (ErrorT MyError m ())
helper run handle = run (sayHiError handle :: ErrorT MyError IO ())
```

Close, but not exactly what I had in mind. What's up with the double monads? Well, let's start at the end: sayHiError handle returns a value of type `ErrorT MyError IO ()`. This we knew already, no surprises. What might be a little surprising (it got me, at least) is the next two steps.

First we apply run to that value. Like we'd discussed before, the result is that the IO inner monad is popped to the outside, to be replaced by some arbitrary monad (represented by m here). So we end up with an `IO (ErrorT MyError m ())`. OK...We then get the same result after applying withMyFile. Not surprising.

The last step took me a long time to understand correctly. Remember how we said that we reconstruct the original transformer? Well, so we do: by plopping it right on top of everything else we have. So our end result is the previous type `IO (ErrorT MyError m ())` - with a `ErrorT MyError` stuck on the front.

That seems just about utterly worthless, right? Well, almost. But don't forget, that "m" can be any monad, including IO. If we treat it that way, we get `ErrorT MyError IO (ErrorT MyError IO ())`. That looks a lot like `m (m a)`, and we want just plain old `m a`. Fortunately, now we're in luck:

```
useMyFileError4 :: ErrorT MyError IO ()
useMyFileError4 = join useMyFileError3
```

And it turns out that this usage is so common, that Bas had mercy on us and defined a helper function:

```
control :: (Monad m, Monad (t m), MonadTransControl t)
        => (Run t -> m (t m a)) -> t m a
control = join . liftControl
```

So all we need to write is:

```
useMyFileError5 :: ErrorT MyError IO ()
useMyFileError5 =
    control inside
  where
    inside :: Monad m => Run (ErrorT MyError) -> IO (ErrorT MyError m ())
    inside run = withMyFile $ helper run
    helper :: Monad m
           => Run (ErrorT MyError) -> Handle -> IO (ErrorT MyError m ())
    helper run handle = run (sayHiError handle :: ErrorT MyError IO ())
```

And just to make it a little shorter:

```
useMyFileError6 :: ErrorT MyError IO ()
useMyFileError6 = control $ \run -> withMyFile $ run . sayHiError
```

MonadControlIO

The MonadTrans class provides the lift method, which allows you to lift an action one level in the stack. There is also the MonadIO class that provides liftIO, which lifts an IO action as far in the stack as desired. We have the same breakdown in monad-control. But first, we need a corollary to Run:

```
type RunInBase m base = forall b. m b -> base (m b)
```

Instead of dealing with a transformer, we're dealing with two monads. base is the underlying monad, and m is a stack built on top of it. RunInBase is a function that takes a value of the entire stack, pops out that base, and puts in on the outside. Unlike in the Run type, we don't replace it with an arbitrary monad, but with the original one. To use some more concrete types:

```
RunInBase (ErrorT MyError IO) IO = forall b. ErrorT MyError IO b -> IO (ErrorT MyError IO b)
```

This should look fairly similar to what we've been looking at so far, the only difference is that we want to deal with a specific inner monad. Our MonadControlIO class is really just an extension of MonadControlTrans using this RunInBase.

```
class MonadIO m => MonadControlIO m where
    liftControlIO :: (RunInBase m IO -> IO a) -> m a
```

Simply put, liftControlIO takes a function, which receives a RunInBase. That RunInBase can be used to strip down our monad to just an IO, and then liftControlIO builds everything back up again. And like MonadControlTrans, it comes with a helper function:

```
controlIO :: MonadControlIO m => (RunInBase m IO -> IO (m a)) -> m a
controlIO = join . liftControlIO
```

We can easily rewrite our previous example with it:

```
useMyFileError7 :: ErrorT MyError IO ()
useMyFileError7 = controlIO $ \run -> withMyFile $ run . sayHiError
```

And as an advantage, it easily scales to multiple transformers:

```
sayHiCrazy :: Handle -> ReaderT Int (StateT Double (ErrorT MyError IO)) ()
sayHiCrazy handle = liftIO $ hPutStrLn handle "Madness!"

useMyFileCrazy :: ReaderT Int (StateT Double (ErrorT MyError IO)) ()
useMyFileCrazy = controlIO $ \run -> withMyFile $ run . sayHiCrazy
```

Real Life Examples

Let's solve some real-life problems with this code. Probably the biggest motivating use case is exception handling in a transformer stack. For example, let's say that we want to automatically run some cleanup code when an exception is thrown. If this were normal IO code, we'd use:

```
onException :: IO a -> IO b -> IO a
```

But if we're in the ErrorT monad, we can't pass in either the action or the cleanup. In comes controlIO to the rescue:

```
onExceptionError :: ErrorT MyError IO a
                 -> ErrorT MyError IO b
                 -> ErrorT MyError IO a
onExceptionError action after = controlIO $ \run ->
    run action `onException` run after
```

Let's say we need to allocate some memory to store a Double in. In the IO monad, we could just use the alloca function. Once again, our solution is simple:

```
allocaError :: (Ptr Double -> ErrorT MyError IO b)
            -> ErrorT MyError IO b
allocaError f = controlIO $ \run -> alloca $ run . f
```

Lost State

Let's rewind a bit to our onExceptionError. It uses onException under the surface, which has a type signature: IO a -> IO b -> IO a. Let me ask you something: what happened to the b in the output? Well, it was thoroughly ignored. But that seems to cause us a bit of a problem. After all, we store our transformer state information in the value of the inner monad. If we ignore it, we're essentially ignoring the monadic side effects as well!

And the answer is that, yes, this does happen with monad-control. Certain functions will drop some of the monadic side effects. This is put best by Bas, in the comments on the relevant functions:

> Note, any monadic side effects in m of the "release" computation will be discarded; it is run only for its side effects in IO.

In practice, monad-control will usually be doing the right thing for you, but you need to be aware that some side effects may disappear.

More Complicated Cases

In order to make our tricks work so far, we've needed to have functions that give us full access to play around with their values. Sometimes, this isn't the case. Take, for instance:

```
addMVarFinalizer :: MVar a -> IO () -> IO ()
```

In this case, we are required to have no value inside our finalizer function. Intuitively, the first thing we should notice is that there will be no way to capture our monadic side effects. So how do we get something like this to compile? Well, we need to explicitly tell it to drop all of its state-holding information:

```
addMVarFinalizerError :: MVar a -> ErrorT MyError IO () -> ErrorT MyError IO ()
addMVarFinalizerError mvar f = controlIO $ \run ->
    return $ liftIO $ addMVarFinalizer mvar (run f >> return ())
```

Another case from the same module is:

```
modifyMVar :: MVar a -> (a -> IO (a, b)) -> IO b
```

Here, we have a restriction on the return type in the second argument: it must be a tuple of the value passed to that function and the final return value. Unfortunately, I can't see a way of writing a little wrapper around modifyMVar to make it work for ErrorT. Instead, in this case, I copied the definition of modifyMVar and modified it:

```
modifyMVar :: MVar a
           -> (a -> ErrorT MyError IO (a, b))
           -> ErrorT MyError IO b
modifyMVar m io =
    Control.Exception.Control.mask $ \restore -> do
        a      <- liftIO $ takeMVar m
        (a',b) <- restore (io a) `onExceptionError` liftIO (putMVar m a)
        liftIO $ putMVar m a'
        return b
```

APPENDIX B
Conduit

Conduits are a solution to the streaming data problem. Oftentimes, laziness allows us to process large amounts of data without pulling all values into memory. However, doing so in the presence of I/O requires us to use *lazy I/O*. The main downside to lazy I/O is non-determinism: we have no guarantees of when our resource finalizers will be run. For small application, this may be acceptable, but for a high-load server, we could quickly run out of scarce resources, such as file handles.

Conduits allow us to process large streams of data while still retaining deterministic resource handling. They provide a unified interface for data streams, whether they come from files, sockets, or memory. And when combined with `ResourceT`, we can safely allocate resources, knowing that they will always be reclaimed—even in the presence of exceptions.

This appendix covers version 0.2 of the `conduit` package.

Conduits in Five Minutes

While a good understanding of the lower-level mechanics of conduits is advisable, you can get very far without it. Let's start off with some high-level examples. Don't worry if some of the details seem a bit magical right now. We'll cover everything in the course of this appendix. Let's start with the terminology, and then some sample code.

Source
: A producer of data. The data could be in a file, coming from a socket, or in memory as a list. To access this data, we *pull* from the source.

Sink
: A consumer of data. Basic examples would be a sum function (adding up a stream of numbers fed in), a file sink (which writes all incoming bytes to a file), or a socket. We *push* data into a sink. When the sink finishes processing (we'll explain that later), it returns some value.

Conduit
: A transformer of data. The simplest example is a map function, though there are many others. Like a sink, we *push* data into a conduit. But instead of returning a single value at the end, a conduit can return multiple outputs every time it is pushed to.

Fuse
: (Thanks to David Mazieres for the term.) A conduit can be *fused* with a source to produce a new, modified source (the $= operator). For example, you could have a source that reads bytes from a file, and a conduit that decodes bytes into text. If you fuse them together, you would now have a source that reads text from a file. Likewise, a conduit and a sink can fuse into a new sink (=$), and two conduits can fuse into a new conduit (=$=).

Connect
: You can connect a source to a sink using the $$ operator. Doing so will pull data from the source and push it to the sink, until either the source or sink signals that they are "done."

Let's see some examples of conduit code.

```
{-# LANGUAGE OverloadedStrings #-}
import Data.Conduit -- the core library
import qualified Data.Conduit.List as CL -- some list-like functions
import qualified Data.Conduit.Binary as CB -- bytes
import qualified Data.Conduit.Text as CT

import Data.ByteString (ByteString)
import Data.Text (Text)
import qualified Data.Text as T
import Control.Monad.ST (runST)

-- Let's start with the basics: connecting a source to a sink. We'll use the
-- built-in file functions to implementing efficient, constant-memory,
-- resource-friendly file copying.
--
-- Two things to note: we use $$ to connect our source to our sink, and then
-- use runResourceT.
copyFile :: FilePath -> FilePath -> IO ()
copyFile src dest = runResourceT $ CB.sourceFile src $$ CB.sinkFile dest


-- The Data.Conduit.List module provides a number of helper functions for
-- creating sources, sinks, and conduits. Let's look at a typical fold: summing
-- numbers.
sumSink :: Resource m => Sink Int m Int
sumSink = CL.fold (+) 0

-- If we want to go a little more low-level, we can code our sink with the
-- sinkState function. This function takes three parameters: an initial state,
-- a push function (receive some more data), and a close function.
sumSink2 :: Resource m => Sink Int m Int
sumSink2 = sinkState
```

```haskell
      0 -- initial value

    -- update the state with the new input and
    -- indicate that we want more input
    (\accum i -> return $ StateProcessing (accum + i))
    (\accum -> return accum) -- return the current accum value on close

-- Another common helper function is sourceList. Let's see how we can combine
-- that function with our sumSink to reimplement the built-in sum function.
sum' :: [Int] -> Int
sum' input = runST $ runResourceT $ CL.sourceList input $$ sumSink

-- Since this is Haskell, let's write a source to generate all of the
-- Fibonacci numbers. We'll use sourceState. The state will contain the next
-- two numbers in the sequence. We also need to provide a pull function, which
-- will return the next number and update the state.
fibs :: Resource m => Source m Int
fibs = sourceState
    (0, 1) -- initial state
    (\(x, y) -> return $ StateOpen (y, x + y) x)

-- Suppose we want to get the sum of the first 10 Fibonacci numbers. We can use
-- the isolate conduit to make sure the sum sink only consumes 10 values.
sumTenFibs :: Int
sumTenFibs =
      runST -- runs fine in pure code
    $ runResourceT
    $ fibs
    $= CL.isolate 10 -- fuse the source and conduit into a source
    $$ sumSink

-- We can also fuse the conduit into the sink instead, we just swap a few
-- operators.
sumTenFibs2 :: Int
sumTenFibs2 =
      runST
    $ runResourceT
    $ fibs
    $$ CL.isolate 10
    =$ sumSink

-- Alright, let's make some conduits. Let's turn our numbers into text. Sounds
-- like a job for a map...

intToText :: Int -> Text -- just a helper function
intToText = T.pack . show

textify :: Resource m => Conduit Int m Text
textify = CL.map intToText

-- Like previously, we can use a conduitState helper function. But here, we
-- don't even need state, so we provide a dummy state value.
textify2 :: Resource m => Conduit Int m Text
textify2 = conduitState
    ()
```

```
            (\() input -> return $ StateProducing () [intToText input])
            (\() -> return [])

    -- Let's make the unlines conduit, that puts a newline on the end of each piece
    -- of input. We'll just use CL.map; feel free to write it with conduitState as
    -- well for practice.
    unlines' :: Resource m => Conduit Text m Text
    unlines' = CL.map $ \t -> t `T.append` "\n"

    -- And let's write a function that prints the first N fibs to a file. We'll
    -- use UTF-8 encoding.
    writeFibs :: Int -> FilePath -> IO ()
    writeFibs count dest =
          runResourceT
        $ fibs
        $= CL.isolate count
        $= textify
        $= unlines'
        $= CT.encode CT.utf8
        $$ CB.sinkFile dest

    -- We used the $= operator to fuse the conduits into the sources, producing a
    -- single source. We can also do the opposite: fuse the conduits into the sink. We can
    -- even combine the two.
    writeFibs2 :: Int -> FilePath -> IO ()
    writeFibs2 count dest =
          runResourceT
        $ fibs
        $= CL.isolate count
        $= textify
        $$ unlines'
        =$ CT.encode CT.utf8
        =$ CB.sinkFile dest

    -- Or we could fuse all those inner conduits into a single conduit...
    someIntLines :: ResourceThrow m -- encoding can throw an exception
                 => Int
                 -> Conduit Int m ByteString
    someIntLines count =
          CL.isolate count
      =$= textify
      =$= unlines'
      =$= CT.encode CT.utf8

    -- and then use that conduit
    writeFibs3 :: Int -> FilePath -> IO ()
    writeFibs3 count dest =
          runResourceT
        $ fibs
        $= someIntLines count
        $$ CB.sinkFile dest

    main :: IO ()
    main = do
        putStrLn $ "First ten fibs: " ++ show sumTenFibs
```

```
writeFibs 20 "fibs.txt"
copyFile "fibs.txt" "fibs2.txt"
```

Structure of This Chapter

The remainder of this chapter covers five major topics in conduits:

- `ResourceT`, the underlying technique that allows us to have guaranteed resource deallocation
- Sources, our data producers
- Sinks, our data consumers
- Conduits, our data transformers
- Buffering, which allows us to avoid inversion of control

The Resource Monad Transformer

The Resource transformer (`ResourceT`) plays a vital role in proper resource management in the conduit project. It is included within the `conduit` package itself. We'll explain `ResourceT` as its own entity. While some of the design decisions clearly are biased toward conduits, `ResourceT` should remain a usable tool in its own right.

Goals

What's wrong with the following code?

```
import System.IO

main = do
    output <- openFile "output.txt" WriteMode
    input  <- openFile "input.txt"  ReadMode
    hGetContents input >>= hPutStr output
    hClose input
    hClose output
```

If the file *input.txt* does not exist, then an exception will be thrown when trying to open it. As a result, `hClose output` will never be called, and we'll have leaked a scarce resource (a file descriptor). In our tiny program, this isn't a big deal, but clearly we can't afford such waste in a long running, highly active server process.

Fortunately, solving the problem is easy:

```
import System.IO

main =
    withFile "output.txt" WriteMode $ \output ->
    withFile "input.txt" ReadMode $ \input ->
    hGetContents input >>= hPutStr output
```

withFile makes sure that the Handle is always closed, even in the presence of exceptions. It also handles asynchronous exceptions. Overall, it's a great approach to use...when you can use it. While often withFile is easy to use, sometimes it can require restructuring our programs. And this restructuring can range from mildly tedious to wildly inefficient.

Let's take enumerators for example. If you look in the documentation, there is an enumFile function (for reading contents from a file), but no iterFile (for writing contents to a file). That's because the flow of control in an iteratee doesn't allow proper allocation of the Handle. Instead, in order to write to a file, you need to allocate the Handle before entering the Iteratee, e.g.:

```
import System.IO
import Data.Enumerator
import Data.Enumerator.Binary

main =
    withFile "output.txt" WriteMode $ \output ->
    run_ $ enumFile "input.txt" $$ iterHandle output
```

This code works fine, but imagine that, instead of simply piping data directly to the file, there was a huge amount of computation that occurred before we need to use the output handle. We will have allocated a file descriptor long before we needed it, and thereby locked up a scarce resource in our application. Besides this, there are times when we *can't* allocate the file before hand, such as when we won't know which file to open until we've read from the input file.

One of the stated goals of conduits is to solve this problem, and it does so via ResourceT. As a result, the above program can be written in conduit as:

```
{-# LANGUAGE OverloadedStrings #-}
import Data.Conduit
import Data.Conduit.Binary

main = runResourceT $ sourceFile "input.txt" $$ sinkFile "output.txt"
```

How It Works

There are essentially three base functions on ResourceT, and then a bunch of conveniences thrown on top. The first function is:

```
register :: IO () -> ResourceT IO ReleaseKey
```

> This function, and the others below, are actually more polymorphic than implied here, allowing other monads besides IO. In fact, almost any transformer on top of IO, as well as any ST stacks, work. We'll cover the details of that later.

This function registers a piece of code that it asserts **must** be run. It gives back a `ReleaseKey`, which is used by the next function:

```
release :: ReleaseKey -> ResourceT IO ()
```

Calling `release` on a `ReleaseKey` immediately performs the action you previously registered. You may call `release` on the same `ReleaseKey` as many times as you like; the first time it is called, it *unregisters* the action. This means you can safely register an action like a memory free, and have no concerns that it will be called twice.

Eventually, we'll want to exit our special `ResourceT`. To do so, we use:

```
runResourceT :: ResourceT IO a -> IO a
```

This seemingly innocuous function is where all the magic happens. It runs through all of the registered cleanup actions and performs them. It is fully exception safe, meaning the cleanups will be performed in the presence of both synchronous and asynchronous exceptions. And as mentioned before, calling `release` will unregister an action, so there is no concern of double-freeing.

Finally, as a convenience, we provide one more function for the common case of allocating a resource and registering a release action:

```
with :: IO a -- ^ allocate
     -> (a -> IO ()) -- ^ free resource
     -> ResourceT IO (ReleaseKey, a)
```

So, to rework our first buggy example to use `ResourceT`, we would write:

```
import System.IO
import Control.Monad.Trans.Resource
import Control.Monad.Trans.Class (lift)

main = runResourceT $ do
    (release0, output) <- with (openFile "output.txt" WriteMode) hClose
    (releaseI, input)  <- with (openFile "input.txt"  ReadMode)  hClose
    lift $ hGetContents input >>= hPutStr output
    release releaseI
    release release0
```

Now there is no concern of any exceptions preventing the releasing of resources. We could skip the `release` calls if we want to, and in an example this small, it would not make any difference. But for larger applications, where we want processing to continue, this ensures that the `Handles` are freed as early as possible, keeping our scarce resource usage to a minimum.

Some Type Magic

As alluded to, there's a bit more to `ResourceT` than simply running in `IO`. Let's cover some of the things we need from this underlying `Monad`.

- Mutable references to keep track of the registered release actions. You might think we could just use a `StateT` transformer, but then our state wouldn't survive exceptions.
- We only want to register actions in the *base monad*. For example, if we have a `ResourceT (WriterT [Int] IO)` stack, we only want to register `IO` actions. This makes it easy to lift our stacks around (i.e., add an extra transformer to the middle of an existing stack), and avoids confusing issues about the threading of other monadic side effects.
- Some way to guarantee an action is performed, even in the presence of exceptions. This boils down to needing a `bracket`-like function.

For the first point, we define a new typeclass to represent monads that have mutable references:

```
class Monad m => HasRef m where
    type Ref m :: * -> *
    newRef' :: a -> m (Ref m a)
    readRef' :: Ref m a -> m a
    writeRef' :: Ref m a -> a -> m ()
    modifyRef' :: Ref m a -> (a -> (a, b)) -> m b
    mask :: ((forall a. m a -> m a) -> m b) -> m b
    mask_ :: m a -> m a
    try :: m a -> m (Either SomeException a)
```

We have an associated type to signify what the reference type should be. (For fans of fundeps, you'll see in the next section that this *has* to be an associated type.) Then we provide a number of basic reference operations. Finally, there are some functions to help with exceptions, which are needed to safely implement the functions described in the last section. The instance for IO is very straightforward:

```
instance HasRef IO where
    type Ref IO = I.IORef
    newRef' = I.newIORef
    modifyRef' = I.atomicModifyIORef
    readRef' = I.readIORef
    writeRef' = I.writeIORef
    mask = E.mask
    mask_ = E.mask_
    try = E.try
```

However, we have a problem when it comes to implementing the `ST` instance: there is no way to deal with exceptions in the `ST` monad. As a result, `mask`, `mask_` and `try` are given default implementations that do no exception checking. This gives rise to the first word of warning: **operations in the ST monad are not exception safe**. You should not be allocating scarce resources in ST when using `ResourceT`. You might be wondering why we would bother with `ResourceT` for `ST` at all. The answer is that there is a lot you can do with conduits without allocating scarce resources, and `ST` is a great method to do this in a pure way. But more on this later.

Now onto point 2: we need some way to deal with this base monad concept. Again, we use an associated type (again explained in the next section). Our solution looks something like:

```
class (HasRef (Base m), Monad m) => Resource m where
    type Base m :: * -> *

    resourceLiftBase :: Base m a -> m a
```

But we forgot about point 3: some **bracket**-like function. So we need one more method in this typeclass:

```
resourceBracket_ :: Base m a -> Base m b -> m c -> m c
```

The reason the first two arguments to `resourceBracket_` (allocation and cleanup) live in `Base m` instead of `m` is that, in `ResourceT`, all allocation and cleanup lives in the base monad.

So on top of our `HasRef` instance for `IO`, we now need a `Resource` instance as well. This is similarly straightforward:

```
instance Resource IO where
    type Base IO = IO
    resourceLiftBase = id
    resourceBracket_ = E.bracket_
```

We have similar `ST` instances, with `resourceBracket_` having no exception safety. The final step is dealing with monad transformers. We don't need to provide a `HasRef` instance, but we do need a `Resource` instance. The tricky part is providing a valid implementation of `resourceBracket_`. For this, we use some functions from monad-control:

```
instance (MonadTransControl t, Resource m, Monad (t m))
        => Resource (t m) where
    type Base (t m) = Base m

    resourceLiftBase = lift . resourceLiftBase
    resourceBracket_ a b c =
        control' $ \run -> resourceBracket_ a b (run c)
      where
        control' f = liftWith f >>= restoreT . return
```

For any transformer, its base is the base of its inner monad. Similarly, we lift to the base by lifting to the inner monad and then lifting to the base from there. The tricky part is the implementation of `resourceBracket_`. I will not go into a detailed explanation, as I would simply make a fool of myself.

Definition of ResourceT

We now have enough information to understand the definition of `ResourceT`:

```
newtype ReleaseKey = ReleaseKey Int
```

```
type RefCount = Int
type NextKey = Int

data ReleaseMap base =
    ReleaseMap !NextKey !RefCount !(IntMap (base ()))

newtype ResourceT m a =
    ResourceT (Ref (Base m) (ReleaseMap (Base m)) -> m a)
```

We see that `ReleaseKey` is simply an `Int`. If you skip a few lines down, this will make sense, since we're using an `IntMap` to keep track of the registered actions. We also define two type synonyms: `RefCount` and `NextKey`. `NextKey` keeps track of the most recently assigned value for a key, and is incremented each time `register` is called. We'll touch on `RefCount` later.

The `ReleaseMap` includes three pieces of information: the next key and the reference count, and then the map of all registered actions. Notice that `ReleaseMap` takes a type parameter `base`, which states which monad release actions must live in.

Finally, a `ResourceT` is essentially a `ReaderT` that keeps a mutable reference to a `ReleaseMap`. The reference type is determined by the base of the monad in question, as is the cleanup monad. This is why we need to use associated types.

The majority of the rest of the code in the `Control.Monad.Trans.Resource` module is just providing instances for the `ResourceT` type.

Other Typeclasses

There are three other typeclasses provided by the module:

ResourceUnsafeIO
: Any monad which can lift IO actions into it, but that this may be considered unsafe. The prime candidate here is `ST`. Care should be taken to only lift actions that do not acquire scarce resources and which don't "fire the missiles." In other words, all the normal warnings of `unsafeIOToST` apply.

ResourceThrow
: For actions that can throw exceptions. This automatically applies to all IO-based monads. For ST-based monads, you can use the supplied `ExceptionT` transformer to provide exception-throwing capabilities. Some functions in conduit, for example, will require this (e.g., text decoding).

ResourceIO
: A convenience class tying together a bunch of other classes, included the two mentioned above. This is purely for convenience; you could achieve the same effect without this type class, you'd just have to do a lot more typing.

Forking

It would seem that forking a thread would be inherently unsafe with `ResourceT`, since the parent thread may call `runResourceT` while the child thread is still accessing some of the allocated resources. This is indeed true, *if* you use the normal `forkIO` function.

> You can't actually use the standard `forkIO`, since it only operates in the IO monad, but you could use the `fork` function from `lifted-base`. In fact, due to this issue, the `regions` package does not provide a `MonadBaseControl` instance for its transformer (which is very similar to `ResourceT`). However, our goal in `ResourceT` is not to make it impossible for programmers to mess up, only to make it easier to do the right thing. Therefore, we still provide the instance, even though it could be abused.

In order to solve this, `ResourceT` includes reference counting. When you fork a new thread via `resourceForkIO`, the `RefCount` value of the `ReleaseMap` is incremented. Every time `runResourceT` is called, the value is decremented. Only when the value hits 0 are all the release actions called.

Convenience Exports

In addition to what's been listed so far, there are a few extra functions exported (mostly) for convenience.

- `newRef`, `writeRef`, and `readRef` wrap up the `HasRef` versions of the functions and allow them to run in any `ResourceT`.
- `withIO` is essentially a type-restricted version of `with`, but working around some of the nastiness with types you would otherwise run into. In general: you'll want to use `withIO` when writing IO code.
- `transResourceT` lets you modify which monad your ResourceT is running in, assuming it keeps the same base.

```
transResourceT :: (Base m ~ Base n)
               => (m a -> n a)
               -> ResourceT m a
               -> ResourceT n a
transResourceT f (ResourceT mx) = ResourceT (\r -> f (mx r))
```

Source

I think it's simplest to understand sources by looking at the types:

```
data SourceResult m a = Open (Source m a) a | Closed
data Source m a = Source
    { sourcePull :: ResourceT m (SourceResult m a)
```

```
, sourceClose :: ResourceT m ()
}
```

A source has just two operations on it: you can pull data from it, and you can close it (think of closing a file handle). When you pull, you either get some data and the a new Source (the source is still open), or nothing (the source is closed). Let's look at some of the simplest sources:

```
import Prelude hiding (repeat)
import Data.Conduit

-- | Never give any data
eof :: Monad m => Source m a
eof = Source
    { sourcePull = return Closed
    , sourceClose = return ()
    }

-- | Always give the same value
repeat :: Monad m => a -> Source m a
repeat a = Source
    { sourcePull = return $ Open (repeat a) a
    , sourceClose = return ()
    }
```

These sources are very straightforward, since they always return the same results. Additionally, their close records don't do anything. You might think that this is a bug: shouldn't a call to sourcePull return Closed after it's been closed? This isn't required, since one of the rules of sources is that they can never be reused. In other words:

- If a Source returns Open, it has provided you with a new Source, which you should use in place of the original one.
- If it returns Closed, then you cannot perform any more operations on it.

Don't worry too much about the invariant. In practice, you will almost never call sourcePull or sourceClose yourself. In fact, you hardly even write them yourself either (that's what sourceState and sourceIO are for). The point is that we can make some assumptions when we implement our sources.

State

There is something similar about the two sources mentioned above: they never change. They *always* return the same value. In other words, they have no state. For almost all serious sources, we'll need some kind of state.

> The state might actually be defined outside of our program. For example, if we write a source that reads data from a Handle, we don't need to manually specify any state, since the Handle itself already has.

The way we store state in a source is by updating the returned Source value in the Open constructor. This is best seen with an example.

```
import Data.Conduit
import Control.Monad.Trans.Resource

-- | Provide data from the list, one element at a time.
sourceList :: Resource m => [a] -> Source m a
sourceList list = Source
    { sourcePull =
        case list of
            [] -> return Closed -- no more data

            -- This is where we store our state: by returning a new
            -- Source with the rest of the list
            x:xs -> return $ Open (sourceList xs) x
    , sourceClose = return ()
    }
```

Each time we pull from the source, it checks the input list. If the list is empty, pulling returns Closed, which makes sense. If the list is not empty, pulling returns Open with both the next value in the list, and a new Source value containing the rest of the input list.

sourceState and sourceIO

In addition to being able to manually create Sources, we also have a few convenience functions that allow us to create most sources in a more high-level fashion. sourceState lets you write code similar to how you would use the State monad. You provide an initial state, your pull function is provided with the current state, and it returns a new state and a return value. Let's use this to reimplement sourceList.

```
import Data.Conduit
import Control.Monad.Trans.Resource

-- | Provide data from the list, one element at a time.
sourceList :: Resource m => [a] -> Source m a
sourceList state0 = sourceState
    state0
    pull
  where
    pull [] = return StateClosed
    pull (x:xs) = return $ StateOpen xs x
```

Notice the usage of the StateClosed and StateOpen constructors. These are very similar to Closed and Open, except that instead of specifying the next Source to be used, you provide the next state (here, the remainder of the list).

The other common activity is to perform some I/O allocation (like opening a file), registering some cleanup action (closing that file), and having a function for pulling data from that resource. conduit comes built-in with a sourceFile function that gives a stream of `ByteStrings`. Let's write a wildly inefficient alternative that returns a stream of characters.

```
import Data.Conduit
import Control.Monad.Trans.Resource
import System.IO
import Control.Monad.IO.Class (liftIO)

sourceFile :: ResourceIO m => FilePath -> Source m Char
sourceFile fp = sourceIO
    (openFile fp ReadMode)
    hClose
    (\h -> liftIO $ do
        eof <- hIsEOF h
        if eof
            then return IOClosed
            else fmap IOOpen $ hGetChar h)
```

Like `sourceState`, it uses a variant on the `Open` and `Closed` constructors. `sourceIO` does a number of things for us:

- It registers the cleanup function with the `ResourceT` transformer, ensuring it gets called even in the presence of exceptions.
- It sets up the `sourceClose` record to release the resource immediately.
- As soon as you return `IOClosed`, it will release the resource.

Sinks

A sink consumes a stream of data, and produces a result. A sink must always produce a result, and must always produce a single result. This is encoded in the types themselves.

There is a `Monad` instance for sink, making it simple to compose multiple sinks together into a larger sink. You can also use the built-in sink functions to perform most of your work. Like sources, you'll rarely need to dive into the inner workings. Let's start off with an example: getting lines from a stream of `Chars` (we'll assume Unix line endings for simplicity).

```
import Data.Conduit
import qualified Data.Conduit.List as CL

-- Get a single line from the stream.
sinkLine :: Resource m => Sink Char m String
sinkLine = sinkState
    id -- initial state, nothing at the beginning of the line
    push
    close
  where
    -- On a new line, return the contents up until here
    push front '\n' =
        return $ StateDone Nothing $ front []
```

```
        -- Just another character, add it to the front and keep going
        push front char =
            return $ StateProcessing $ front . (char:)

        -- Got an EOF before hitting a newline, just give what we have so far
        close front = return $ front []

    -- Get all the lines from the stream, until we hit a blank line or EOF.
    sinkLines :: Resource m => Sink Char m [String]
    sinkLines = do
        line <- sinkLine
        if null line
            then return []
            else do
                lines <- sinkLines
                return $ line : lines

    content :: String
    content = unlines
        [ "This is the first line."
        , "Here's the second."
        , ""
        , "After the blank."
        ]

    main :: IO ()
    main = do
        lines <- runResourceT $ CL.sourceList content $$ sinkLines
        mapM_ putStrLn lines
```

Running this sample produces the expected output:

```
This is the first line.
Here's the second.
```

sinkLine demonstrates usage of the sinkState function, which is very similar to the sourceState function we just saw. It takes three arguments: an initial state, a push function (takes the current state and next input, and returns a new state and result) and a close function (takes the current state and returns an output). As opposed to sourceState—which doesn't need a close function—a sink is required to always return a result.

Our push function has two clauses. When it gets a newline character, it indicates that processing is complete via StateDone. The Nothing indicates that there is no leftover input (we'll discuss that later). It also gives an output of all the characters it has received. The second clause simply appends the new character to the existing state and indicates that we are still working via StateProcessing. The close function returns all characters.

sinkLines shows how we can use the monadic interface to produce new sinks. If you replace sinkLine with getLine, this would look like standard code to pull lines from standard input. This familiar interface should make it easy to get up and running quickly.

Types

The types for sinks are just a bit more involved than sources. Let's have a look:

```
type SinkPush input m output = input -> ResourceT m (SinkResult input m output)
type SinkClose m output = ResourceT m output

data SinkResult input m output =
    Processing (SinkPush input m output) (SinkClose m output)
  | Done (Maybe input) output

data Sink input m output =
    SinkNoData output
  | SinkData
        { sinkPush :: SinkPush input m output
        , sinkClose :: SinkClose m output
        }
  | SinkLift (ResourceT m (Sink input m output))
```

Whenever a sink is pushed to, it can either say it needs more data (`Processing`) or say it's all done. When still processing, it must provide updated push and close functions; when done, it returns any leftover input and the output. Fairly straightforward.

The first real "gotcha" is the three constructors for `Sink`. Why do we need `SinkNoData`: aren't sinks all about consuming data? The answer is that we need it to efficiently implement our `Monad` instance. When we use `return`, we're giving back a value that requires no data in order to compute it. We could model this with the `SinkData` constructor, with something like:

```
myReturn a = SinkData (\input -> return (Done (Just input) a)) (return a)
```

But doing so would force reading in an extra bit of input that we don't need right now, and possibly will never need. (Have a look again at the `sinkLines` example.) So instead, we have an extra constructor to indicate that no input is required. Likewise, `SinkLift` is provided in order to implement an efficient `MonadTrans` instance.

Sinks: no helpers

Let's try to implement some sinks on the "bare metal," without any helper functions.

```
import Data.Conduit
import System.IO
import Control.Monad.Trans.Resource
import Control.Monad.IO.Class (liftIO)

-- Consume all input and discard it.
sinkNull :: Resource m => Sink a m ()
sinkNull =
    SinkData push close
  where
    push _ignored = return $ Processing push close
    close = return ()
```

```haskell
-- Let's stream characters to a file. Here we do need some kind of
-- initialization. We do this by initializing in a push function,
-- and then returning a different push function for subsequent
-- calls. By using withIO, we know that the handle will be closed even
-- if there's an exception.
sinkFile :: ResourceIO m => FilePath -> Sink Char m ()
sinkFile fp =
    SinkData pushInit closeInit
  where
    pushInit char = do
        (releaseKey, handle) <- withIO (openFile fp WriteMode) hClose
        push releaseKey handle char
    closeInit = do
        -- Never opened a file, so nothing to do here
        return ()

    push releaseKey handle char = do
        liftIO $ hPutChar handle char
        return $ Processing (push releaseKey handle) (close releaseKey handle)

    close releaseKey _ = do
        -- Close the file handle as soon as possible.
        return ()

-- And we'll count how many values were in the stream.
count :: Resource m => Sink a m Int
count =
    SinkData (push 0) (close 0)
  where
    push count _ignored =
        return $ Processing (push count') (close count')
      where
        count' = count + 1

    close count = return count
```

Nothing is particularly complicated to implement. You should notice a common pattern here: declaring your push and close functions in a `where` clause, and then using them twice: once for the initial `SinkData`, and once for the `Processing` constructor. This can become a bit tedious; that's why we have helper functions.

Sinks: with Helpers

Let's rewrite `sinkFile` and `count` to take advantage of the helper functions `sinkIO` and `sinkState`, respectively.

```haskell
import Data.Conduit
import System.IO
import Control.Monad.IO.Class (liftIO)

-- We never have to touch the release key directly; sinkIO automatically
-- releases our resource as soon as we return IODone from our push function,
```

```
-- or sinkClose is called.
sinkFile :: ResourceIO m => FilePath -> Sink Char m ()
sinkFile fp = sinkIO
    (openFile fp WriteMode)
    hClose
    -- push: notice that we are given the handle and the input
    (\handle char -> do
        liftIO $ hPutChar handle char
        return IOProcessing)
    -- close: we're also given the handle, but we don't use it
    (\_handle -> return ())

-- And we'll count how many values were in the stream.
count :: Resource m => Sink a m Int
count = sinkState
    0
    -- The push function gets both the current state and the next input...
    (\state _ignored ->
        -- and it returns the new state
        return $ StateProcessing $ state + 1)
    -- The close function gets the final state and returns the output.
    (\state -> return state)
```

Nothing dramatic, just slightly shorter, less error-prone code. Using these two helper functions is highly recommended, as it ensures proper resource management and state updating.

List Functions

As easy as it is to write your own sinks, you'll likely want to take advantage of the built-in sinks available in the `Data.Conduit.List` module. These provide analogues to common list functions, like folding. (The module also has some `Conduits`, like `map`.)

If you're looking for some way to practice with conduits, reimplementing the functions in the `List` module—both with and without the helper functions—would be a good start.

Let's look at some simple things we can make out of the built-in sinks.

```
import Data.Conduit
import qualified Data.Conduit.List as CL
import Control.Monad.IO.Class (liftIO)

-- A sum function.
sum' :: Resource m => Sink Int m Int
sum' = CL.fold (+) 0

-- Print every input value to standard output.
printer :: (Show a, ResourceIO m) => Sink a m ()
printer = CL.mapM_ (liftIO . print)

-- Sum up all the values in a stream after the first five.
sumSkipFive :: Resource m => Sink Int m Int
```

```
sumSkipFive = do
    CL.drop 5
    CL.fold (+) 0

-- Print each input number and sum the total
printSum :: ResourceIO m => Sink Int m Int
printSum = do
    total <- CL.foldM go 0
    liftIO $ putStrLn $ "Sum: " ++ show total
    return total
  where
    go accum int = do
        liftIO $ putStrLn $ "New input: " ++ show int
        return $ accum + int
```

Connecting

At the end of the day, we're actually going to want to use our sinks. While we could manually call `sinkPush` and `sinkClose`, it's tedious. For example:

```
main :: IO ()
main = runResourceT $ do
    res <-
        case printSum of
            SinkData push close -> loop [1..10] push close
            SinkNoData res -> return res
    liftIO $ putStrLn $ "Got a result: " ++ show res
  where
    start (SinkData push close) = loop [1..10] push close
    start (SinkNoData res) = return res
    start (SinkLift msink) = msink >>= start

    loop [] _push close = close
    loop (x:xs) push close = do
        mres <- push x
        case mres of
            Done _leftover res -> return res
            Processing push' close' -> loop xs push' close'
```

Instead, the recommended approach is to connect your sink to a source. Not only is this simpler, it's less error prone, and means you have a lot of flexibility in where your data is coming from. To rewrite the example above:

```
main :: IO ()
main = runResourceT $ do
    res <- CL.sourceList [1..10] $$ printSum
    liftIO $ putStrLn $ "Got a result: " ++ show res
```

Connecting takes care of testing for the sink constructor (`SinkData` versus `SinkNoData` versus `SinkLift`), pulling from the source, and pushing to/closing the sink.

However, there is one thing I wanted to point out from the long-winded example. On the second to last line, we ignore the leftover value of `Done`. This brings up the issue of *data loss*. This is an important topic that has had a lot of thought put into it.

Unfortunately, we can't fully cover it yet, as we haven't discussed the main culprit in the drama: Conduits (the type, not the package).

But as a quick note here, the leftover value from the Done constructor is not always ignored. The Monad instance, for example, uses it to pass data from one sink to the next in a binding. And in fact, the real connect operator *doesn't* always throw away the leftovers. When we cover resumable sources later, we'll see that the leftover value is put back on the buffer to allow later sinks reusing an existing source to pull the value.

Conduit

This section covers the final major data type in our package: conduits. While sources produce a stream of data and sinks consume a stream, conduits transform a stream.

Types

As we did previously, let's start off by looking at the types involved.

```
data ConduitResult input m output =
    Producing (Conduit input m output) [output]
  | Finished (Maybe input) [output]

data Conduit input m output = Conduit
    { conduitPush :: input -> ResourceT m (ConduitResult input m output)
    , conduitClose :: ResourceT m [output]
    }
```

This should look very similar to what we've seen with sinks. A conduit can be pushed to, in which case it returns a result. A result either indicates that it is still producing data, or that it is finished. When a conduit is closed, it returns some more output.

But let's examine the idiosyncrasies a bit. Like sinks, we can only push one piece of input at a time, and leftover data may be 0 or 1 pieces. However, there are a few changes:

- When producing (the equivalent of processing for a sink), we can return output. This is because a conduit will product a new stream of output instead of producing a single output value at the end of processing.
- A sink always returns a single output value, while a conduit returns 0 or more outputs (a list). To understand why, consider conduits such as concatMap (produces multiple outputs for one input) and filter (returns 0 or 1 output for each input).
- We have no special constructor like SinkNoData. That's because we provide no Monad instance for conduits. We'll see later how you can still use a familiar Monadic approach to creating conduits.

Overall conduits should seem very similar to what we've covered so far.

Simple Conduits

We'll start off by defining some simple conduits that don't have any state.

```
import Prelude hiding (map, concatMap)
import Data.Conduit

-- A simple conduit that just passes on the data as is.
passThrough :: Monad m => Conduit input m input
passThrough = Conduit
    { conduitPush = \input -> return $ Producing passThrough [input]
    , conduitClose = return []
    }

-- map values in a stream
map :: Monad m => (input -> output) -> Conduit input m output
map f = Conduit
    { conduitPush = \input -> return $ Producing (map f) [f input]
    , conduitClose = return []
    }

-- map and concatenate
concatMap :: Monad m => (input -> [output]) -> Conduit input m output
concatMap f = Conduit
    { conduitPush = \input -> return $ Producing (concatMap f) $ f input
    , conduitClose = return []
    }
```

Stateful Conduits

Of course, not all conduits can be declared without state. Doing so on the bare metal is not too difficult.

```
import Prelude hiding (reverse)
import qualified Data.List
import Data.Conduit
import Control.Monad.Trans.Resource

-- Reverse the elements in the stream. Note that this has the same downside as
-- the standard reverse function: you have to read the entire stream into
-- memory before producing any output.
reverse :: Resource m => Conduit input m input
reverse =
    mkConduit []
  where
    mkConduit state = Conduit (push state) (close state)
    push state input = return $ Producing (mkConduit $ input : state) []
    close state = return state

-- Same thing with sort: it will pull everything into memory
sort :: (Ord input, Resource m) => Conduit input m input
sort =
    mkConduit []
  where
```

```
mkConduit state = Conduit (push state) (close state)
push state input = return $ Producing (mkConduit $ input : state) []
close state = return $ Data.List.sort state
```

But we can do better. Just like `sourceState` and `sinkState`, we have `conduitState` to simplify things.

```
import Prelude hiding (reverse)
import qualified Data.List
import Data.Conduit

-- Reverse the elements in the stream. Note that this has the same downside as
-- the standard reverse function: you have to read the entire stream into
-- memory before producing any output.
reverse :: Resource m => Conduit input m input
reverse =
    conduitState [] push close
  where
    push state input = return $ StateProducing (input : state) []
    close state = return state

-- Same thing with sort: it will pull everything into memory
sort :: (Ord input, Resource m) => Conduit input m input
sort =
    conduitState [] push close
  where
    push state input = return $ StateProducing (input : state) []
    close state = return $ Data.List.sort state
```

Using Conduits

The way `Conduits` interact with the rest of the package is via *fusing*. A conduit can be fused into a source, producing a new source, fused into a sink to produce a new sink, or fused with another conduit to produce a new conduit. It's best to just look at the fusion operators.

```
-- Left fusion: source + conduit = source
($=) :: (Resource m, IsSource src) => src m a -> Conduit a m b -> Source m b

-- Right fusion: conduit + sink = sink
(=$) :: Resource m => Conduit a m b -> Sink b m c -> Sink a m c

-- Middle fusion: conduit + conduit = conduit
(=$=) :: Resource m => Conduit a m b -> Conduit b m c -> Conduit a m c
```

Using these operators is straightforward.

```
useConduits = do
    runResourceT
        $ CL.sourceList [1..10]
        $= reverse
        $= CL.map show
        $$ CL.consume
```

```
-- equivalent to
runResourceT
      $  CL.sourceList [1..10]
      $$ reverse
      =$ CL.map show
      =$ CL.consume

-- and equivalent to
runResourceT
      $  CL.sourceList [1..10]
      $$ (reverse =$= CL.map show)
      =$ CL.consume
```

There is in fact one last way of expressing the same idea. I'll leave it as an exercise to the reader to discover it.

It may seem like all these different approaches are redundant. While occasionally you can in fact choose whichever approach you feel like using, in many cases you will need a specific approach. For example:

- If you have a stream of numbers, and you want to apply a conduit (e.g., map show) to only some of the stream that will be passed to a specific sink, you'll want to use the right fusion operator.
- If you're reading a file, and want to parse the entire file as textual data, you'll want to use left fusion to convert the entire stream.
- If you want to create reusable conduits that combine together individual, smaller conduits, you'll use middle fusion.

Data Loss

Let's forget about conduits for a moment. Instead, suppose we want to write a program —using plain old lists—that will take a list of numbers, apply some kind of transformation to them, take the first five transformed values and do something with them, and then do something else with the remaining **non-transformed** values. For example, we want something like:

```
main = do
    let list = [1..10]
        transformed = map show list
        (begin, end) = splitAt 5 transformed
        untransformed = map read end
    mapM_ putStrLn begin
    print $ sum untransformed
```

But clearly this isn't a good general solution, since we don't want to have to transform and then untransform every element in the list. For one thing, we may not always have an inverse function. Another issue is efficiency. In this case, we can write something more efficient:

```
main = do
    let list = [1..10]
        (begin, end) = splitAt 5 list
        transformed = map show begin
    mapM_ putStrLn transformed
    print $ sum end
```

Note the change: we perform our split before transforming any elements. This works because, with `map`, we have a 1-to-1 correspondence between the input and output elements. So splitting at 5 before or after mapping `show` is the same thing. But what happens if we replace `map show` with something more devious?

```
deviousTransform =
    concatMap go
  where
    go 1 = [show 1]
    go 2 = [show 2, "two"]
    go 3 = replicate 5 "three"
    go x = [show x]
```

We no longer have the 1-to-1 correspondence. As a result, we can't use the second method. But it's even worse: we can't use the first method either, since there's no inverse of our `deviousTransform`.

There's only one solution to the problem that I'm aware of: transform elements one at a time. The final program looks like this:

```
deviousTransform 1 = [show 1]
deviousTransform 2 = [show 2, "two"]
deviousTransform 3 = replicate 5 "three"
deviousTransform x = [show x]

transform5 :: [Int] -> ([String], [Int])
transform5 list =
    go [] list
  where
    go output (x:xs)
        | newLen >= 5 = (take 5 output', xs)
        | otherwise = go output' xs
      where
        output' = output ++ deviousTransform x
        newLen = length output'

    -- Degenerate case: not enough input to make 5 outputs
    go output [] = (output, [])

main = do
    let list = [1..10]
        (begin, end) = transform5 list
    mapM_ putStrLn begin
    print $ sum end
```

The final output of this program is

```
1
2
```

```
two
three
three
49
```

What's important to note is that the number 3 is converted into five copies of the word "three," yet only two of them show up in the output. The rest are discarded in the take 5 call.

This whole exercise is just to demonstrate the issue of data loss in conduits. By forcing conduits to accept only one input at a time, we avoid the issue of transforming too many elements at once. That doesn't mean we don't lose *any* data: if a conduit produces too much output for the receiving sink to handle, some of it may be lost.

To put all this another way: conduits avoid chunking to get away from data loss. This is not an issue unique to conduits. If you look in the implementation of concatMapM for enumerator, you'll see that it forces elements to be handled one at a time. In conduits, we opted to force the issue at the type level.

SequencedSink

Suppose we want to be able to combine up existing conduits and sinks to produce a new, more powerful conduit. For example, we want to write a conduit that takes a stream of numbers and sums up every five. In other words, for the input [1..50], it should result in the sequence [15,40,65,90,115,140,165,190,215,240]. We can definitely do this with the low-level conduit interface.

```
sum5Raw :: Resource m => Conduit Int m Int
sum5Raw =
    conduitState (0, 0) push close
  where
    push (total, count) input
        | newCount == 5 = return $ StateProducing (0, 0) [newTotal]
        | otherwise     = return $ StateProducing (newTotal, newCount) []
      where
        newTotal = total + input
        newCount = count + 1
    close (total, count)
        | count == 0 = return []
        | otherwise  = return [total]
```

But this is frustrating, since we already have all the tools we need to do this at a high level! There's the fold sink for adding up the numbers, and the isolate conduit, which will only allow up to a certain number of elements to be passed to a sink. Can't we combine these somehow?

The answer is a SequencedSink. The idea is to create a normal Sink, except it returns a special output called a SequencedSinkResponse. This value can emit new output, stop processing data, or transfer control to a new conduit. (See the Haddocks for more information.) Then we can turn this into a Conduit using the sequenceSink function. This function also takes some state value that gets passed through to the sink.

So we can rewrite sum5Raw in a much more high-level manner.

```
sum5 :: Resource m => Conduit Int m Int
sum5 = sequenceSink () $ \() -> do
    nextSum <- CL.isolate 5 =$ CL.fold (+) 0
    return $ Emit () [nextSum]
```

All of the () in there are simply the unused state variable being passed around, and they can be ignored. Otherwise, we're doing exactly what we want. We fuse `isolate` to `fold` to get the sum of the next five elements from the stream. We then emit that value, and start all over again.

Let's say we want to modify this slightly. We want to get the first 8 sums, and then pass through the remaining values, multiplied by 2. We can keep track of how many values we've returned in our state, and then use the `StartConduit` constructor to pass control to the multiply-by-2 conduit next.

```
sum5Pass :: Resource m => Conduit Int m Int
sum5Pass = sequenceSink 0 $ \count -> do
    if count == 8
        then return $ StartConduit $ CL.map (* 2)
        else do
            nextSum <- CL.isolate 5 =$ CL.fold (+) 0
            return $ Emit (count + 1) [nextSum]
```

These are obviously very contrived examples, but I hope it makes clear the power and simplicity available from this approach.

Buffering

Buffering is one of the unique features of conduits. With buffering, conduits no longer need to control the flow of your application. In some cases, this can lead to simpler code.

Inversion of Control

Buffering was actually one of the main motivations in the creation of the conduit package. To see its importance, we need to consider the approach we've seen so far, which we'll call inversion of control, or IoC.

> Inversion of control can mean different things in different circles. If you object to its usage here, go ahead replace it with some other phrase like "warm, fuzzy thing." I won't be offended.

Suppose you want to count how many newline characters there are in a file. In the standard imperative approach, you would do something like:

1. Open the file.
2. Pull some data into a buffer.
3. Loop over the values in the buffer, incrementing a counter on each newline character.
4. Return to 2.
5. Close the file.

Notice that your code is explicitly calling out to other code, and that code is returning control back to your code. You have retained full control of the flow of execution of your program. The conduit approach we've seen so far does *not* work this way. Instead, you would:

1. Write a sink that counts newlines and adds the result to an accumulator.
2. Connect the sink to a source.

There's no doubt in my mind that this is an easier approach. You don't have to worry about opening and closing files or pulling data from the file. Instead, the data you need to process is simply presented to you. This is the advantage of IoC: you can focus on specifically your piece of the code.

We use this IoC approach all over Haskell: for example, instead of `readMVar` and `putMVar`, you can use `withMVar`. Don't bother with `openFile` and `closeFile`, just use `withFile` and pass in a function that uses the `Handle`. Even C has a version of this: why `malloc` and `free` when you could just `alloca`?

Actually, that last one is a huge red herring. Of course you can't just use `alloca` for everything. `alloca` only allocates memory locally on the stack, not dynamically on the heap. There's no way to return your allocated memory outside the current function.

But actually, the same restriction applies to the whole family of `with` functions: you can never return an allocated resource outside of the "block." Usually this works out just fine, but we need to recognize that this *is* a change in how we structure our programs. Oftentimes, with simple examples, this is a minor change. However, in larger settings this can become very difficult to manage, bordering on impossible at times.

A web server

Let's say we're going to write a web server. We're going to use the following low-level operations:

```
data Socket
recv    :: Socket -> Int -> IO ByteString -- returns empty when the socket is closed
sendAll :: Socket -> ByteString -> IO ()
```

We're up to the part where we need to implement the function `handleConn` that handles an individual connection. It will look something like this:

```
data Request  -- request headers, HTTP version, etc
data Response -- status code, response headers, response body
type Application = Request -> IO Response
handleConn :: Application -> Socket -> IO ()
```

What does our `handleConn` need to do? In broad strokes:

1. Parse the request line.
2. Parse the request headers.
3. Construct the `Request` value.
4. Pass `Request` to the `Application` and get back a `Response`.
5. Send the `Response` over the `Socket`.

We start off by writing steps 1 and 2 manually, without using conduits. We'll do this very simply and just assume three space-separated strings. We end up with something that looks like:

```
data RequestLine = RequestLine ByteString ByteString ByteString

parseRequestLine :: Socket -> IO RequestLine
parseRequestLine socket = do
    bs <- recv socket 4096
    let (method:path:version:ignored) = S8.words bs
    return $ RequestLine method path version
```

There are two issues here: it doesn't handle the case where there are fewer than three words in the chunk of data, and it throws away any extra data. We can definitely solve both of these issues manually, but it's very tedious. It's much easier to implement this in terms of conduits.

```
import Data.ByteString (ByteString)
import qualified Data.ByteString as S
import Data.Conduit
import qualified Data.Conduit.Binary as CB
import qualified Data.Conduit.List as CL

data RequestLine = RequestLine ByteString ByteString ByteString

parseRequestLine :: Sink ByteString IO RequestLine
parseRequestLine = do
    let space = toEnum $ fromEnum ' '
    let getWord = do
            CB.dropWhile (== space)
            bss <- CB.takeWhile (/= space) =$ CL.consume
            return $ S.concat bss

    method <- getWord
    path <- getWord
    version <- getWord
    return $ RequestLine method path version
```

This means that our code will automatically be supplied with more data as it comes in, and any extra data will automatically be buffered in the Source, ready for the next time it's used. Now we can easily structure our program together, demonstrating the power of the conduits approach:

```
import Data.ByteString (ByteString)
import Data.Conduit
import Data.Conduit.Network (sourceSocket)
import Control.Monad.IO.Class (liftIO)
import Network.Socket (Socket)

data RequestLine = RequestLine ByteString ByteString ByteString
type Headers = [(ByteString, ByteString)]
data Request = Request RequestLine Headers
data Response = Response
type Application = Request -> IO Response

parseRequestHeaders :: Sink ByteString IO Headers
parseRequestHeaders = undefined

parseRequestLine :: Sink ByteString IO RequestLine
parseRequestLine = undefined

sendResponse :: Socket -> Response -> IO ()
sendResponse = undefined

handleConn :: Application -> Socket -> IO ()
handleConn app socket = do
    req <- runResourceT $ sourceSocket socket $$ do
        requestLine <- parseRequestLine
        headers <- parseRequestHeaders
        return $ Request requestLine headers
    res <- liftIO $ app req
    liftIO $ sendResponse socket res
```

Whither the request body?

This is all great, until we realize *we can't read the request body*. The Application is simply given the Request, and lives in the IO monad. It has no access whatsoever to the incoming stream of data.

There's an easy fix for this actually: have the Application live in the Sink monad. This is the very approach we took with enumerator-based WAI 0.4. However, there are two problems:

- People find it confusing. What people *expect* is that the Request value would have a requestBody value of type Source.
- This makes certain kinds of usage incredibly difficult. For example, trying to write an HTTP proxy combining WAI and http-enumerator proved to be almost impossible.

This is the downside of inversion of control. Our code wants to be in control. It wants to be given something to pull from, something to push to, and run with it. We need some solution to the problem.

> If you think the situation I described with the proxy isn't so bad, it's because I've gone easy on the details. We also need to take into account streaming the response body, and the streaming needs to happen on both the client and server side.

The simplest solution would be to just create a new Source and pass that to the Application. Unfortunately, this will cause problems with our buffering. You see, when we connect our source to the parseRequestLine and parseRequestHeaders sinks, it made a call to recv. If the data it received was not enough to cover all of the headers, it would issue another call. When it had enough data, it would stop. However, odds are that it didn't stop *exactly* at the end of the headers. It likely consumed a bit of the request body as well.

If we just create a new source and pass that to the request, it will be missing the beginning of the request body. We need some way to pass that buffered data along.

BufferedSource

And so we finally get to introduce the last data type in conduits: BufferedSource. This is an abstract data type, but all it really does is keep a mutable reference to a buffer and an underlying Source. In order to create one of these, you use the bufferSource function.

```
bufferSource ::Resource m => Source m a -> ResourceT m (BufferedSource m a)
```

This one little change is what allows us to easily solve our web server dilemma. Instead of connecting a Source to our parsing Sinks, we use a BufferedSource. At the end of each connection, any leftover data is put back on the buffer. For our web server case, we can now create a BufferedSource, use that to read the request line and headers, and then pass that same BufferedSource to the application for reading the request body.

Typeclass

We want to be able to connect a buffered source to a sink, just like we would a regular source. We would also like to be able to fuse it to a conduit. In order to make this convenient, conduit has a typeclass, IsSource. There are instances provided for both Source and BufferedSource. Both the connect ($$) and left-fuse ($=) operators use this typeclass.

There's one "gotcha" in the BufferedSource instance of this typeclass, so let's explain it. Suppose we want to write a file copy function, without any buffering. This is a fairly standard usage of conduits:

```
sourceFile input $$ sinkFile output
```

When this line is run, both the input and output files are opened, the data is copied, and then both files are closed. Let's change this example slightly to use buffering:

```
bsrc <- bufferSource $ sourceFile input
bsrc $$ isolate 50 =$ sinkFile output1
bsrc $$ sinkFile output2
```

When is the input file opened and closed? The opening occurs on the first line, when buffering the source. And if we follow the normal rules from sources, the file should be closed after the second line. However, if we did that, we couldn't reuse `bsrc` for line 3!

So instead, $$ does *not* close the file. As a result, you can pass a buffered source to as many actions as you want, without concerns that the file handle has been closed out from under you.

> If you remember from earlier, the invariant of a source is that it cannot be pulled from after it returns a `Closed` response. In order to allow you to work more easily with a `BufferedSource`, this invariant is relaxed. It is the responsibility of the `BufferSource` implementation to ensure that after the underlying `Source` is closed, it is never used again.

This presents one caveat: when you're finished with a buffered source, you should manually call `bsourceClose` on it. However, as usual, this is merely an optimization, as the source will automatically be closed when `runResourceT` is called.

Recapping the Web Server

So what exactly does our web server look like now?

```
import Data.ByteString (ByteString)
import Data.Conduit
import Data.Conduit.Network (sourceSocket)
import Control.Monad.IO.Class (liftIO)
import Network.Socket (Socket)

data RequestLine = RequestLine ByteString ByteString ByteString
type Headers = [(ByteString, ByteString)]
data Request = Request RequestLine Headers (BufferedSource IO ByteString)
data Response = Response
type Application = Request -> ResourceT IO Response

parseRequestHeaders :: Sink ByteString IO Headers
parseRequestHeaders = undefined

parseRequestLine :: Sink ByteString IO RequestLine
parseRequestLine = undefined
```

```
sendResponse :: Socket -> Response -> IO ()
sendResponse = undefined

handleConn :: Application -> Socket -> IO ()
handleConn app socket = runResourceT $ do
    bsrc <- bufferSource $ sourceSocket socket
    requestLine <- bsrc $$ parseRequestLine
    headers <- bsrc $$ parseRequestHeaders
    let req = Request requestLine headers bsrc
    res <- app req
    liftIO $ sendResponse socket res
```

We've made a few minor changes. Firstly, the `Application` now lives in the `ResourceT` IO monad. This isn't strictly necessary, but it's very convenient: the application can now register cleanup actions that will only take place after the response has been fully sent to the client.

But the major changes are in the `handleConn` function. We now start off by buffering our source. This buffered source is then used twice in our function, and then passed off to the application.

APPENDIX C
Web Application Interface

It is a problem almost every language used for web development has dealt with: the low-level interface between the web server and the application. The earliest example of a solution is the venerable and battle-worn Common Gateway Interface (CGI), providing a language-agnostic interface using only standard input, standard output, and environment variables.

Back when Perl was becoming the de facto web programming language, a major shortcoming of CGI became apparent: the process needed to be started anew for each request. When dealing with an interpreted language and application requiring database connection, this overhead became unbearable. FastCGI (and later SCGI) arose as a successor to CGI, but it seems that much of the programming world went in a different direction.

Each language began creating its own standard for interfacing with servers: mod_perl, mod_python, mod_php, mod_ruby. Within the same language, multiple interfaces arose. In some cases, we even had interfaces on top of interfaces. And all of this led to much duplicated effort: a Python application designed to work with FastCGI wouldn't work with mod_python—mod_python only exists for certain web servers—and these programming language specific web server extensions need to be written for each programming language.

Haskell has its own history. We originally had the `cgi` package, which provided a monadic interface. The `fastcgi` package then provided the same interface. Meanwhile, it seemed that the majority of Haskell web development focused on the standalone server. The problem is that each server comes with its own interface, meaning that you need to target a specific backend. This means that it is impossible to share common features, like GZIP encoding, development servers, and testing frameworks.

WAI attempts to solve this, by providing a generic and efficient interface between web servers and applications. Any **handler** supporting the interface can serve any WAI application, while any application using the interface can run on any handler.

At the time of writing, there are various backends, including Warp, FastCGI, and development server. There are even more esoteric backends like `wai-handler-webkit` for creating desktop apps. `wai-extra` provides many common middleware components like GZIP, JSON-P, and virtual hosting. `wai-test` makes it easy to write unit tests, and `wai-handler-devel` lets you develop your applications without worrying about stopping to compile. Yesod targets WAI, and Happstack is in the process of converting over as well. It's also used by some applications that skip the framework entirely, including the new Hoogle.

> Yesod provides an alternate approach for a devel server, known as *yesod devel*. The difference from wai-handler-devel is that yesod devel actually compiles your code each time, respecting all settings in your cabal file. This is the recommended approach for general Yesod development.

The Interface

The interface itself is very straightforward: an application takes a request and returns a response. A response is an HTTP status, a list of headers and a response body. A request contains various information: the requested path, query string, request body, HTTP version, and so on.

Response Body

Haskell has a data type known as a lazy bytestring. By utilizing laziness, you can create large values without exhausting memory. Using lazy I/O, you can do such tricks as having a value which represents the entire contents of a file, yet only occupies a small memory footprint. In theory, a lazy bytestring is the only representation necessary for a response body.

In practice, while lazy byte strings are wonderful for generating "pure" values, the lazy I/O necessary to read a file introduces some non-determinism into our programs. When serving thousands of small files a second, the limiting factor is not memory, but file handles. Using lazy I/O, file handles may not be freed immediately, leading to resource exhaustion. To deal with this, WAI uses *conduits*.

> Versions of WAI before 1.0 used enumerators in place of conduits. While both conduits and enumerators solve the same basic problem, experience showed that enumerators were too constricting in their inversion of control approach, making it difficult to structure more complicated systems like a streaming proxy server. Conduits were designed with the express purpose of making a better WAI.

The data type relevant to us now is a *source*. A source produces a stream of data, producing a single chunk at a time. In the case of WAI, the request body would be a source passed to the application, and the response body would be a source returned from the application.

There are two further optimizations: many systems provide a sendfile system call, which sends a file directly to a socket, bypassing a lot of the memory copying inherent in more general I/O system calls. Additionally, there is a data type in Haskell called `Builder` which allows efficient copying of bytes into buffers.

The WAI response body therefore has three constructors: one for pure builders (`ResponseBuilder`), one for a source of builders (`ResponseSource`), and one for files (`ResponseFile`).

Request Body

In order to avoid the need to load the entire request body into memory, we use sources here as well. Since the purpose of these values are for reading (not writing), we use `ByteStrings` in place of `Builders`. There is a record inside `Request` called `requestBody`, with type `BufferedSource IO ByteString`. We can use all of the standard conduit functions to interact with this source.

The request body could in theory contain any type of data, but the most common are URL encoded and multipart form data. The `wai-extra` package contains built-in support for parsing these in a memory-efficient manner.

Hello World

To demonstrate the simplicity of WAI, let's look at a hello world example. In this example, we're going to use the OverloadedStrings language extension to avoid explicitly packing string values into bytestrings.

```
{-# LANGUAGE OverloadedStrings #-}
import Network.Wai
import Network.HTTP.Types (status200)
import Network.Wai.Handler.Warp (run)

application _ = return $
  responseLBS status200 [("Content-Type", "text/plain")] "Hello World"

main = run 3000 application
```

Lines 2 through 4 perform our imports. Warp is provided by the `warp` package, and is the premiere WAI backend. WAI is also built on top of the `http-types` package, which provides a number of data types and convenience values, including `status200`.

First we define our application. Since we don't care about the specific request parameters, we ignore the argument to the function. For any request, we are returning a response with status code 200 ("OK"), and text/plain content type and a body containing the words "Hello World." Pretty self-explanatory.

Middleware

In addition to allowing our applications to run on multiple backends without code changes, the WAI allows us another benefit: middleware. Middleware is essentially an *application transformer*, taking one application and returning another one.

Middleware components can be used to provide lots of services: cleaning up URLs, authentication, caching, JSON-P requests. But perhaps the most useful and most intuitive middleware is gzip compression. The middleware works very simply: it parses the request headers to determine if a client supports compression, and if so compresses the response body and adds the appropriate response header.

The great thing about middlewares is that they are unobtrusive. Let's see how we would apply the gzip middleware to our hello world application.

```
{-# LANGUAGE OverloadedStrings #-}
import Network.Wai
import Network.Wai.Handler.Warp (run)
import Network.Wai.Middleware.Gzip (gzip, def)
import Network.HTTP.Types (status200)

application _ = return $ responseLBS status200 [("Content-Type", "text/plain")]
                         "Hello World"

main = run 3000 $ gzip def application
```

We added an import line to actually have access to the middleware, and then simply applied gzip to our application. You can also *chain together* multiple middlewares: a line such as `gzip False $ jsonp $ othermiddleware $ myapplication` is perfectly valid. One word of warning: the order the middleware is applied can be important. For example, jsonp needs to work on uncompressed data, so if you apply it after you apply gzip, you'll have trouble.

APPENDIX D
Settings Types

Let's say you're writing a web server. You want the server to take a port to listen on, and an application to run. So you create the following function:

```
run :: Int -> Application -> IO ()
```

But suddenly you realize that some people will want to customize their timeout durations. So you modify your API:

```
run :: Int -> Int -> Application -> IO ()
```

So, which `Int` is the timeout, and which is the port? Well, you could create some type aliases, or comment your code. But there's another problem creeping into our code: this `run` function is getting unmanageable. Soon we'll need to take an extra parameter to indicate how exceptions should be handled, and then another one to control which host to bind to, and so on.

So a more extensible solution is to introduce a settings data type:

```
data Settings = Settings
    { settingsPort :: Int
    , settingsHost :: String
    , settingsTimeout :: Int
    }
```

And this makes the calling code almost self-documenting:

```
run Settings
    { settingsPort = 8080
    , settingsHost = "127.0.0.1"
    , settingsTimeout = 30
    } myApp
```

Great, couldn't be clearer, right? True, but what happens when you have 50 settings to your web server? Do you really want to have to specify all of those each time? Of course not. So instead, the web server should provide a set of defaults:

```
defaultSettings = Settings 3000 "127.0.0.1" 30
```

And now, instead of needing to write that long bit of code above, we can get away with:

```
run defaultSettings { settingsPort = 8080 } myApp -- (1)
```

This is great, except for one minor hitch. Let's say we now decide to add an extra record to `Settings`. Any code out in the wild looking like this:

```
run (Settings 8080 "127.0.0.1" 30) myApp -- (2)
```

will be broken, since the `Settings` constructor now takes 4 arguments. The proper thing to do would be to bump the major version number so that dependent packages don't get broken. But having to change major versions for every minor setting you add is a nuisance. The solution? Don't export the `Settings` constructor:

```
module MyServer
    ( Settings
    , settingsPort
    , settingsHost
    , settingsTimeout
    , run
    , defaultSettings
    ) where
```

With this approach, no one can write code like (2), so you can freely add new records without any fear of code breaking.

The one downside of this approach is that it's not immediately obvious from the Haddocks that you can actually change the settings via record syntax. That's the point of this chapter: to clarify what's going on in the libraries that use this technique.

I personally use this technique in a few places, feel free to have a look at the Haddocks to see what I mean.

- Warp: `Settings`
- http-conduit: `Request` and `ManagerSettings`
- xml-conduit
    - Parsing: `ParseSettings`
    - Rendering: `RenderSettings`

As a tangential issue, `http-conduit` and `xml-conduit` actually create instances of the `Default` typeclass instead of declaring a brand new identifier. This means you can just type `def` instead of `defaultParserSettings`.

APPENDIX E
http-conduit

Most of Yesod is about serving content over HTTP. But that's only half the story: someone has to receive it. And even when you're writing a web app, sometimes that someone will be you. If you want to consume content from other services or interact with RESTful APIs, you'll need to write client code. And the recommended approach for that is `http-conduit`.

This chapter is not directly connected to Yesod, and will be generally useful for anyone wanting to make HTTP requests.

Synopsis

```
{-# LANGUAGE OverloadedStrings #-}
import Network.HTTP.Conduit -- the main module

-- The streaming interface uses conduits
import Data.Conduit
import Data.Conduit.Binary (sinkFile)

import qualified Data.ByteString.Lazy as L
import Control.Monad.IO.Class (liftIO)

main :: IO ()
main = do
    -- Simplest query: just download the information from the given URL as a
    -- lazy ByteString.
    simpleHttp "http://www.example.com/foo.txt" >>= L.writeFile "foo.txt"

    -- Use the streaming interface instead. We need to run all of this inside a
    -- ResourceT, to ensure that all our connections get properly cleaned up in
    -- the case of an exception.
    runResourceT $ do
        -- We need a Manager, which keeps track of open connections. simpleHttp
        -- creates a new manager on each run (i.e., it never reuses
        -- connections).
        manager <- liftIO $ newManager def
```

```
-- A more efficient version of the simpleHttp query above. First we
-- parse the URL to a request.
req <- liftIO $ parseUrl "http://www.example.com/foo.txt"

-- Now get the response
res <- http req manager

-- And finally stream the value to a file
responseBody res $$ sinkFile "foo.txt"

-- Make it a POST request, don't follow redirects, and accept any
-- status code.
let req2 = req
        { method = "POST"
        , redirectCount = 0
        , checkStatus = \_ _ -> Nothing
        }
res2 <- http req2 manager
responseBody res2 $$ sinkFile "post-foo.txt"
```

Concepts

The simplest way to make a request in http-conduit is with the simpleHttp function. This function takes a String giving a URL and returns a ByteString with the contents of that URL. But under the surface, there are a few more steps:

- A new connection Manager is allocated.
- The URL is parsed to a Request. If the URL is invalid, then an exception is thrown.
- The HTTP request is made, following any redirects from the server.
- If the response has a status code outside the 200-range, an exception is thrown.
- The response body is read into memory and returned.
- runResourceT is called, which will free up any resources (e.g., the open socket to the server).

If you want more control of what's going on, then you can configure any of the steps above (plus a few more) by explicitly creating a Request value, allocating your Manager manually, and using the http and httpLbs functions.

Request

The easiest way to create a Request is with the parseUrl function. This function will return a value in any Failure monad, such as Maybe or IO. The last of those is the most commonly used, and results in a runtime exception whenever an invalid URL is provided. However, you can use a different monad if, for example, you want to validate user input.

```
import Network.HTTP.Conduit
import System.Environment (getArgs)
import qualified Data.ByteString.Lazy as L
import Control.Monad.IO.Class (liftIO)

main :: IO ()
main = do
    args <- getArgs
    case args of
        [urlString] ->
            case parseUrl urlString of
                Nothing -> putStrLn "Sorry, invalid URL"
                Just req -> withManager $ \manager -> do
                    Response _ _ lbs <- httpLbs req manager
                    liftIO $ L.putStr lbs
        _ -> putStrLn "Sorry, please provide exactly one URL"
```

The Request type is abstract so that http-conduit can add new settings in the future without breaking the API (see the Settings Type chapter for more information). In order to make changes to individual records, you use record notation. For example, a modification to our program that issues HEAD requests and prints the response headers would be:

```
{-# LANGUAGE OverloadedStrings #-}
import Network.HTTP.Conduit
import System.Environment (getArgs)
import qualified Data.ByteString.Lazy as L
import Control.Monad.IO.Class (liftIO)

main :: IO ()
main = do
    args <- getArgs
    case args of
        [urlString] ->
            case parseUrl urlString of
                Nothing -> putStrLn "Sorry, invalid URL"
                Just req -> withManager $ \manager -> do
                    let reqHead = req { method = "HEAD" }
                    Response status headers _ <- http reqHead manager
                    liftIO $ do
                        print status
                        mapM_ print headers
        _ -> putStrLn "Sorry, please provide exactly one URL"
```

There are a number of different configuration settings in the API. Some noteworthy ones are:

proxy
 Allows you to pass the request through the given proxy server.

redirectCount
 Indicate how many redirects to follow. Default is 10.

checkStatus
> Check the status code of the return value. By default, gives an exception for any non-2XX response.

requestBody
> The request body to be sent. Be sure to also update the `method`. For the common case of URL-encoded data, you can use the `urlEncodedBody` function.

Manager

The connection manager allows you to reuse connections. When making multiple queries to a single server (e.g., accessing Amazon S3), this can be critical for creating efficient code. A manager will keep track of multiple connections to a given server (taking into account port and SSL as well), automatically reaping unused connections as needed. When you make a request, `http-conduit` first tries to check out an existing connection. When you're finished with the connection (if the server allows keep-alive), the connection is returned to the manager. If anything goes wrong, the connection is closed.

To keep our code exception-safe, we use the `ResourceT` monad transformer. All this means for you is that your code needs to be wrapped inside a call to `runResourceT`, either implicitly or explicitly, and that code inside that block will need to `liftIO` to perform normal IO actions.

There are two ways you can get ahold of a manager. `newManager` will return a manager that will not be automatically closed (you can use `closeManager` to do so manually), while `withManager` will start a new `ResourceT` block, allow you to use the manager, and then automatically close the `ResourceT` when you're done. If you want to use a `ResourceT` for an entire application, and have no need to close it, you should probably use `newManager`.

One other thing to point out: you obviously don't want to create a new manager for each and every request; that would defeat the whole purpose. You should create your `Manager` early and then share it.

Response

The `Response` data type has three pieces of information: the status code, the response headers, and the response body. The first two are straightforward; let's discuss the body.

The `Response` type has a type variable to allow the response body to be of multiple types. If you want to use `http-conduit`'s streaming interface, you want this to be a `Source`. For the simple interface, it will be a lazy `ByteString`. One thing to note is that, even though we use a lazy `ByteString`, *the entire response is held in memory*. In other words, we perform no lazy I/O in this package.

> The `conduit` package does provide a lazy module which would allow you to read this value in lazily, but like any lazy I/O, it's a bit unsafe, and definitely non-deterministic. If you need it though, you can use it.

http and httpLbs

So let's tie it together. The `http` function gives you access to the streaming interface (i.e., it returns a `Response` using a `BufferedSource`) while `httpLbs` returns a lazy `ByteString`. Both of these return values in the `ResourceT` transformer so that they can access the `Manager` and have connections handled properly in the case of exceptions.

> If you want to ignore the remainder of a large response body, you can connect to the `sinkNull` sink. The underlying connection will automatically be closed, preventing you from having to read a large response body over the network.

APPENDIX F
xml-conduit

Many developers cringe at the thought of dealing with XML files. XML has the reputation of having a complicated data model, with obfuscated libraries and huge layers of complexity sitting between you and your goal. I'd like to posit that a lot of that pain is actually a language and library issue, not inherent to XML.

Once again, Haskell's type system allows us to easily break down the problem to its most basic form. The `xml-types` package neatly deconstructs the XML data model (both a streaming and DOM-based approach) into some simple ADTs. Haskell's standard immutable data structures make it easier to apply transforms to documents, and a simple set of functions makes parsing and rendering a breeze.

We're going to be covering the `xml-conduit` package. Under the surface, this package uses a lot of the approaches Yesod in general utilizes for high performance: `blaze-builder`, `text`, `conduit`, and `attoparsec`. But from a user perspective, it provides everything from the simplest APIs (`readFile`/`writeFile`) through full control of XML event streams.

In addition to `xml-conduit`, there are a few related packages that come into play, like `xml-hamlet` and `xml2html`. We'll cover both how to use all these packages, and when they should be used.

Synopsis

Example F-1. Input XML file

```
<document title="My Title">
    <para>This is a paragraph. It has <em>emphasized</em> and <strong>strong</strong> words.</para>
    <image href="myimage.png"/>
</document>
```

Example F-2. Haskell code

```haskell
{-# LANGUAGE QuasiQuotes #-}
{-# LANGUAGE OverloadedStrings #-}
import Prelude hiding (readFile, writeFile)
import Text.XML
import Text.Hamlet.XML

main :: IO ()
main = do
    -- readFile will throw any parse errors as runtime exceptions
    -- def uses the default settings
    Document prologue root epilogue <- readFile def "input.xml"

    -- root is the root element of the document, let's modify it
    let root' = transform root

    -- And now we write out. Let's indent our output
    writeFile def
        { rsPretty = True
        } "output.html" $ Document prologue root' epilogue

-- We'll turn out <document> into an XHTML document
transform :: Element -> Element
transform (Element _name attrs children) = Element "html" [] [xml|
<head>
    <title>
        $maybe title <- lookup "title" attrs
            \#{title}
        $nothing
            Untitled Document
<body>
    $forall child <- children
        ^{goNode child}
|]

goNode :: Node -> [Node]
goNode (NodeElement e) = [NodeElement $ goElem e]
goNode (NodeContent t) = [NodeContent t]
goNode (NodeComment _) = [] -- hide comments
goNode (NodeInstruction _) = [] -- and hide processing instructions too

-- convert each source element to its XHTML equivalent
goElem :: Element -> Element
goElem (Element "para" attrs children) =
    Element "p" attrs $ concatMap goNode children
goElem (Element "em" attrs children) =
    Element "i" attrs $ concatMap goNode children
goElem (Element "strong" attrs children) =
    Element "b" attrs $ concatMap goNode children
goElem (Element "image" attrs _children) =
    Element "img" (map fixAttr attrs) [] -- images can't have children
  where
    fixAttr ("href", value) = ("src", value)
    fixAttr x = x
goElem (Element name attrs children) =
```

```
    -- don't know what to do, just pass it through...
    Element name attrs $ concatMap goNode children
```

Example F-3. Output XHTML

```
<?xml version="1.0" encoding="UTF-8"?>
<html>
    <head>
        <title>
            My Title
        </title>
    </head>
    <body>
        <p>
            This is a paragraph. It has
            <i>
                emphasized
            </i>
            and
            <b>
                strong
            </b>
            words.
        </p>
        <img src="myimage.png"/>
    </body>
</html>
```

Types

Let's take a bottom-up approach to analyzing types. This section will also serve as a primer on the XML data model itself, so don't worry if you're not completely familiar with it.

I think the first place where Haskell really shows its strength is with the `Name` data type. Many languages (like Java) struggle with properly expressing names. The issue is that there are in fact three components to a name: its local name, its namespace (optional), and its prefix (also optional). Let's look at some XML to explain:

```
<no-namespace/>
<no-prefix xmlns="first-namespace" first-attr="value1"/>
<foo:with-prefix xmlns:foo="second-namespace" foo:second-attr="value2"/>
```

The first tag has a local name of `no-namespace`, and no namespace or prefix. The second tag (local name: `no-prefix`) *also* has no prefix, but it does have a namespace (`first-namespace`). `first-attr`, however, does *not* inherit that namespace: attribute namespaces must always be explicitly set with a prefix.

> Namespaces are almost always URIs of some sort, though there is nothing in any specification requiring that it be so.

The third tag has a local name of with-prefix, a prefix of foo and a namespace of second-namespace. Its attribute has a second-attr local name and the same prefix and namespace. The xmlns and xmlns:foo attributes are part of the namespace specification, and are not considered attributes of their respective elements.

So let's review what we need from a name: every name has a local name, and it can optionally have a prefix and namespace. Seems like a simple fit for a record type:

```
data Name = Name
    { nameLocalName :: Text
    , nameNamespace :: Maybe Text
    , namePrefix :: Maybe Text
    }
```

According the the XML namespace standard, two names are considered equivalent if they have the same localname and namespace. In other words, the prefix is not important. Therefore, xml-types defines Eq and Ord instances that ignore the prefix.

The last class instance worth mentioning is IsString. It would be very tedious to have to manually type out Name "p" Nothing Nothing every time we want a paragraph. If you turn on OverloadedStrings, "p" will resolve to that all by itself! In addition, the IsString instance recognizes something called Clark notation, which allows you to prefix the namespace surrounded in curly brackets. In other words:

```
"{namespace}element" == Name "element" (Just "namespace") Nothing
"element" == Name "element" Nothing Nothing
```

The Four Types of Nodes

XML documents are a tree of nested nodes. There are in fact four different types of nodes allowed: elements, content (i.e., text), comments, and processing instructions.

You may not be familiar with that last one, as it's less commonly used. It is marked up as: `<?target data?>` There are two surprising facts about processing instructions (PIs):

- PIs don't have attributes. While oftentimes you'll see processing instructions that appear to have attributes, there are in fact no rules about that data of an instruction.
- The `<?xml ...?>` stuff at the beginning of a document is not a processing instruction. It is simply the beginning of the document (known as the XML declaration), and happens to look an awful lot like a PI. The difference though is that the `<?xml ...?>` line will not appear in your parsed content.

Since processing instructions have two pieces of text associated with them (the target and the data), we have a simple data type:

```
data Instruction = Instruction
    { instructionTarget :: Text
    , instructionData :: Text
    }
```

Comments have no special data type since they are just text. But content is an interesting one: it could contain either plain text or unresolved entities (e.g., &copyright-statement;). xml-types keeps those unresolved entities in all the data types in order to completely match the spec. However, in practice, it can be very tedious to program against those data types. And in most use cases, an unresolved entity is going to end up as an error anyway.

So the `Text.XML` module defines its own set of data types for nodes, elements, and documents that removes all unresolved entities. If you need to deal with unresolved entities instead, you should use the `Text.XML.Unresolved` module. From now on, we'll be focusing only on the `Text.XML` data types, though they are almost identical to the `xml-types` versions.

Anyway, after that detour: content is just a piece of text, and therefore it too does not have a special data type. The last node type is an element, which contains three pieces of information: a name, a list of attributes and a list of children nodes. An attribute has two pieces of information: a name and a value. (In `xml-types`, this value could contain unresolved entities as well.) So our `Element` is defined as:

```
data Element = Element
    { elementName :: Name
    , elementAttributes :: [(Name, Text)]
    , elementNodes :: [Node]
    }
```

Which of course begs the question: what does a `Node` look like? This is where Haskell really shines: its sum types model the XML data model perfectly.

```
data Node
    = NodeElement Element
    | NodeInstruction Instruction
    | NodeContent Text
    | NodeComment Text
```

Documents

So now we have elements and nodes, but what about an entire document? Let's just lay out the data types:

```
data Document = Document
    { documentPrologue :: Prologue
    , documentRoot :: Element
    , documentEpilogue :: [Miscellaneous]
    }

data Prologue = Prologue
    { prologueBefore :: [Miscellaneous]
    , prologueDoctype :: Maybe Doctype
    , prologueAfter :: [Miscellaneous]
    }

data Miscellaneous
    = MiscInstruction Instruction
    | MiscComment Text

data Doctype = Doctype
    { doctypeName :: Text
    , doctypeID :: Maybe ExternalID
    }

data ExternalID
    = SystemID Text
    | PublicID Text Text
```

The XML spec says that a document has a single root element (documentRoot). It also has an optional doctype statement. Before and after both the doctype and the root element, you are allowed to have comments and processing instructions. (You can also have whitespace, but that is ignored in the parsing.)

So what's up with the doctype? Well, it specifies the root element of the document, and then optional public and system identifiers. These are used to refer to DTD files, which give more information about the file (e.g., validation rules, default attributes, entity resolution). Let's see some examples:

```
<!DOCTYPE root> <!-- no external identifier -->
<!DOCTYPE root SYSTEM "root.dtd"> <!-- a system identifier -->
<!DOCTYPE root PUBLIC "My Root Public Identifier" "root.dtd"> <!-- public identifiers
have a system ID as well -->
```

And that, my friends, is the entire XML data model. For many parsing purposes, you'll be able to simply ignore the entire `Document` data type and go immediately to the `documentRoot`.

Events

In addition to the document API, `xml-types` defines an `Event` data type. This can be used for constructing streaming tools, which can be much more memory efficient for certain kinds of processing (e.g., adding an extra attribute to all elements). We will not be covering the streaming API currently, though it should look very familiar after analyzingthe document API.

> You can see an example of the streaming API in the Sphinx case study.

Text.XML

The recommended entry point to xml-conduit is the `Text.XML` module. This module exports all of the data types you'll need to manipulate XML in a DOM fashion, as well as a number of different approaches for parsing and rendering XML content. Let's start with the simple ones:

```
readFile  :: ParseSettings  -> FilePath -> IO Document
writeFile :: RenderSettings -> FilePath -> Document -> IO ()
```

This introduces the `ParseSettings` and `RenderSettings` data types. You can use these to modify the behavior of the parser and renderer, such as adding character entities and turning on pretty (i.e., indented) output. Both these types are instances of the `Default` typeclass, so you can simply use `def` when these need to be supplied. That is how we will supply these values through the rest of the chapter; please see the API docs for more information.

It's worth pointing out that in addition to the file-based API, there is also a text- and bytestring-based API. The bytestring-powered functions all perform intelligent encoding detections, and support UTF-8, UTF-16, and UTF-32, in either big or little endian, with and without a Byte-Order Marker (BOM). All output is generated in UTF-8.

For complex data lookups, we recommend using the higher-level cursors API. The standard `Text.XML` API not only forms the basis for that higher level, but is also a great API for simple XML transformations and for XML generation. See the synopsis for an example.

A Note About File Paths

In the type signature above, we have a type `FilePath`. However, **this isn't `Prelude.FilePath`**. The standard `Prelude` defines a type synonym `type FilePath = [Char]`. Unfortunately, there are many limitations to using such an approach, including confusion of filename character encodings and differences in path separators.

Instead, `xml-conduit` uses the `system-filepath` package, which defines an abstract `FilePath` type. I've personally found this to be a much nicer approach to work with. The package is fairly easy to follow, so I won't go into details here. But I do want to give a few quick explanations of how to use it:

- Since a `FilePath` is an instance of `IsString`, you can type in regular strings and they will be treated properly, as long as the `OverloadedStrings` extension is enabled. (I highly recommend enabling it anyway, as it makes dealing with `Text` values much more pleasant.)
- If you need to explicitly convert to or from `Prelude`'s `FilePath`, you should use the `encodeString` and `decodeString`, respectively. This takes into account file path encodings.
- Instead of manually splicing together directory names and file names with extensions, use the operators in the `Filesystem.Path.CurrentOS` module, e.g., `myfolder </> filename <.> extension`.

Cursor

Suppose you want to pull the title out of an XHTML document. You could do so with the `Text.XML` interface we just described, using standard pattern matching on the children of elements. But that would get very tedious, very quickly. Probably the gold standard for these kinds of lookups is XPath, where you would be able to write /html/head/title. And that's exactly what inspired the design of the `Text.XML.Cursor` combinators.

A cursor is an XML node that knows its location in the tree; it's able to traverse upwards, sideways, and downwards. (Under the surface, this is achieved by tying the knot (*http://www.haskell.org/haskellwiki/Tying_the_Knot*).) There are two functions available for creating cursors from `Text.XML` types: `fromDocument` and `fromNode`.

We also have the concept of an *Axis*, defined as `type Axis = Cursor -> [Cursor]`. It's easiest to get started by looking at example axes: child returns zero or more cursors that are the child of the current one, parent returns the single parent cursor of the input, or an empty list if the input is the root element, and so on.

In addition, there are some axes that take predicates. `element` is a commonly used function that filters down to only elements that match the given name. For example, `element "title"` will return the input element if its name is "title," or an empty list otherwise.

Another common function which isn't quite an axis is `content :: Cursor -> [Text]`. For all content nodes, it returns the contained text; otherwise, it returns an empty list.

And thanks to the monad instance for lists, it's easy to string all of these together. For example, to do our title lookup, we would write the following program:

```
{-# LANGUAGE OverloadedStrings #-}
import Prelude hiding (readFile)
import Text.XML
import Text.XML.Cursor
import qualified Data.Text as T

main :: IO ()
main = do
    doc <- readFile def "test.xml"
    let cursor = fromDocument doc
    print $ T.concat $
            child cursor >>= element "head" >>= child
                         >>= element "title" >>= descendant >>= content
```

What this says is:

1. Get me all the child nodes of the root element.
2. Filter down to only the elements named "head."
3. Get all the children of all those head elements.
4. Filter down to only the elements named "title."
5. Get all the descendants of all those title elements. (A descendant is a child, or a descendant of a child. Yes, that was a recursive definition.)
6. Get only the text nodes.

So for the input document:

```
<html>
    <head>
        <title>My <b>Title</b></title>
    </head>
    <body>
        <p>Foo bar baz</p>
    </body>
</html>
```

We end up with the output `My Title`. This is all well and good, but it's much more verbose than the XPath solution. To combat this verbosity, Aristid Breitkreuz added a set of operators to the Cursor module to handle many common cases. So we can rewrite our example as:

```
{-# LANGUAGE OverloadedStrings #-}
import Prelude hiding (readFile)
import Text.XML
```

Cursor | 275

```
import Text.XML.Cursor
import qualified Data.Text as T

main :: IO ()
main = do
    doc <- readFile def "test.xml"
    let cursor = fromDocument doc
    print $ T.concat $
        cursor $/ element "head" &/ element "title" &// content
```

$/ says to apply the axis on the right to the children of the cursor on the left. &/ is almost identical, but is instead used to combine two axes together. This is a general rule in Text.XML.Cursor: operators beginning with $ directly apply an axis, while & will combine two together. &// is used for applying an axis to all descendants.

Let's go for a more complex, if more contrived, example. We have a document that looks like:

```
<html>
    <head>
        <title>Headings</title>
    </head>
    <body>
        <hgroup>
            <h1>Heading 1 foo</h1>
            <h2 class="foo">Heading 2 foo</h2>
        </hgroup>
        <hgroup>
            <h1>Heading 1 bar</h1>
            <h2 class="bar">Heading 2 bar</h2>
        </hgroup>
    </body>
</html>
```

We want to get the content of all the h1 tags which precede an h2 tag with a class attribute of "bar." To perform this convoluted lookup, we can write:

```
{-# LANGUAGE OverloadedStrings #-}
import Prelude hiding (readFile)
import Text.XML
import Text.XML.Cursor
import qualified Data.Text as T

main :: IO ()
main = do
    doc <- readFile def "test2.xml"
    let cursor = fromDocument doc
    print $ T.concat $
        cursor $// element "h2"
               >=> attributeIs "class" "bar"
               >=> precedingSibling
               >=> element "h1"
               &// content
```

Let's step through that. First we get all h2 elements in the document. ($// gets all descendants of the root element.) Then we filter out only those with class=bar. That >=> operator is actually the standard operator from Control.Monad; yet another advantage of the monad instance of lists. precedingSibling finds all nodes that come before our node **and** that share the same parent. (There is also a preceding axis which takes all elements earlier in the tree.) We then take just the h1 elements, and then grab their content.

> The equivalent XPath, for comparison, would be //h2[@class = 'bar']/preceding-sibling::h1//text().

While the cursor API isn't quite as succinct as XPath, it has the advantages of being standard Haskell code, and of type safety.

xml-hamlet

Thanks to the simplicity of Haskell's data type system, creating XML content with the Text.XML API is easy, if a bit verbose. The following code:

```
{-# LANGUAGE OverloadedStrings #-}
import Text.XML
import Prelude hiding (writeFile)

main :: IO ()
main =
    writeFile def "test3.xml" $ Document (Prologue [] Nothing []) root []
  where
    root = Element "html" []
        [ NodeElement $ Element "head" []
            [ NodeElement $ Element "title" []
                [ NodeContent "My "
                , NodeElement $ Element "b" []
                    [ NodeContent "Title"
                    ]
                ]
            ]
        , NodeElement $ Element "body" []
            [ NodeElement $ Element "p" []
                [ NodeContent "foo bar baz"
                ]
            ]
        ]
```

produces

```
<?xml version="1.0" encoding="UTF-8"?>
<html><head><title>My <b>Title</b></title></head><body><p>foo bar baz</p></body></html>
```

This is leaps and bounds easier than having to deal with an imperative, mutable-value-based API (cough, Java, cough), but it's far from pleasant, and obscures what we're really trying to achieve. To simplify things, we have the `xml-hamlet` package, which uses Quasi-Quotation to allow you to type in your XML in a natural syntax. For example, the above could be rewritten as:

```
{-# LANGUAGE OverloadedStrings #-}
{-# LANGUAGE QuasiQuotes #-}
import Text.XML
import Text.Hamlet.XML
import Prelude hiding (writeFile)

main :: IO ()
main =
    writeFile def "test3.xml" $ Document (Prologue [] Nothing []) root []
  where
    root = Element "html" [] [xml|
<head>
    <title>
        My #
        <b>Title
<body>
    <p>foo bar baz
|]
```

Let's make a few points:

- The syntax is almost identical to normal Hamlet, except URL-interpolation (@{...}) has been removed. As such:
    — No close tags.
    — Whitespace-sensitive.
    — If you want to have whitespace at the end of a line, use a # at the end. At the beginning, use a backslash.
- An xml interpolation will return a list of Nodes. So you still need to wrap up the output in all the normal Document and root Element constructs.
- There is no support for the special .class and #id attribute forms.

And like normal Hamlet, you can use variable interpolation and control structures. So a slightly more complex example would be:

```
{-# LANGUAGE OverloadedStrings #-}
{-# LANGUAGE QuasiQuotes #-}
import Text.XML
import Text.Hamlet.XML
import Prelude hiding (writeFile)
import Data.Text (Text, pack)

data Person = Person
    { personName :: Text
    , personAge :: Int
    }
```

```haskell
people :: [Person]
people =
    [ Person "Michael" 26
    , Person "Miriam" 25
    , Person "Eliezer" 3
    , Person "Gavriella" 1
    ]
main :: IO ()
main =
    writeFile def "people.xml" $ Document (Prologue [] Nothing []) root []
  where
    root = Element "html" [] [xml|
<head>
    <title>Some People
<body>
    <h1>Some People
    $if null people
        <p>There are no people.
    $else
        <dl>
            $forall person <- people
                ^{personNodes person}
|]

personNodes :: Person -> [Node]
personNodes person = [xml|
<dt>#{personName person}
<dd>#{pack $ show $ personAge person}
|]
```

A few more notes:

- The caret-interpolation (^{...}) takes a list of nodes, and so can easily embed other xml-quotations.

- Unlike Hamlet, hash-interpolations (#{...}) are not polymorphic, and can *only* accept Text values.

xml2html

So far in this chapter, our examples have revolved around XHTML. I've done that so far simply because it is likely to be the most familiar form of XML for most of our readers. But there's an ugly side to all this that we must acknowledge: not all XHTML will be correct HTML. The following discrepancies exist:

- There are some void tags (e.g., img, br) in HTML which do not need to have close tags, and in fact are not allowed to.

- HTML does not understand self-closing tags, so <script></script> and <script/> mean very different things.

- Combining the previous two points: you are free to self-close void tags, though to a browser it won't mean anything.
- In order to avoid quirks mode, you should start your HTML documents with a DOCTYPE statement.
- We do not want the XML declaration <?xml ...?> at the top of an HTML page.
- We do not want any namespaces used in HTML, while XHTML is fully namespaced.
- The contents of <style> and <script> tags should not be escaped.

That's where the xml2html package comes into play. It provides a ToHtml instance for Nodes, Documents, and Elements. In order to use it, just import the Text.XML.Xml2Html module.

```
{-# LANGUAGE OverloadedStrings, QuasiQuotes #-}
import Text.Blaze (toHtml)
import Text.Blaze.Renderer.String (renderHtml)
import Text.XML
import Text.Hamlet.XML
import Text.XML.Xml2Html ()

main :: IO ()
main = putStr $ renderHtml $ toHtml $ Document (Prologue [] Nothing []) root []

root :: Element
root = Element "html" [] [xml|
<head>
    <title>Test
    <script>if (5 < 6 || 8 > 9) alert("Hello World!");
    <style>body > h1 { color: red }
<body>
    <h1>Hello World!
|]
```

Outputs (whitespace added):

```
<!DOCTYPE HTML>
<html>
    <head>
        <title>Test</title>
        <script>if (5 < 6 || 8 > 9) alert("Hello World!");</script>
        <style>body > h1 { color: red }</style>
    </head>
    <body>
        <h1>Hello World!</h1>
    </body>
</html>
```

About the Author

Michael Snoyman, creator of Yesod, has been programming for about 15 years, using Haskell for the past five. He brings ten years of web development experience in a wide variety of environments as well as time spent creating documentation.

Have it your way.

O'Reilly eBooks

- Lifetime access to the book when you buy through oreilly.com
- Provided in up to four DRM-free file formats, for use on the devices of your choice: PDF, .epub, Kindle-compatible .mobi, and Android .apk
- Fully searchable, with copy-and-paste and print functionality
- Alerts when files are updated with corrections and additions

oreilly.com/ebooks/

Safari Books Online

- Access the contents and quickly search over 7000 books on technology, business, and certification guides
- Learn from expert video tutorials, and explore thousands of hours of video on technology and design topics
- Download whole books or chapters in PDF format, at no extra cost, to print or read on the go
- Get early access to books as they're being written
- Interact directly with authors of upcoming books
- Save up to 35% on O'Reilly print books

See the complete Safari Library at safari.oreilly.com

O'REILLY®

Spreading the knowledge of innovators.   oreilly.com

©2011 O'Reilly Media, Inc. O'Reilly logo is a registered trademark of O'Reilly Media, Inc. 00000

Get even more for your money.

Join the O'Reilly Community, and register the O'Reilly books you own. It's free, and you'll get:

- $4.99 ebook upgrade offer
- 40% upgrade offer on O'Reilly print books
- Membership discounts on books and events
- Free lifetime updates to ebooks and videos
- Multiple ebook formats, DRM FREE
- Participation in the O'Reilly community
- Newsletters
- Account management
- 100% Satisfaction Guarantee

Signing up is easy:

1. Go to: oreilly.com/go/register
2. Create an O'Reilly login.
3. Provide your address.
4. Register your books.

Note: English-language books only

To order books online:
oreilly.com/store

For questions about products or an order:
orders@oreilly.com

To sign up to get topic-specific email announcements and/or news about upcoming books, conferences, special offers, and new technologies:
elists@oreilly.com

For technical questions about book content:
booktech@oreilly.com

To submit new book proposals to our editors:
proposals@oreilly.com

O'Reilly books are available in multiple DRM-free ebook formats. For more information:
oreilly.com/ebooks

O'REILLY®

Spreading the knowledge of innovators

oreilly.com

©2010 O'Reilly Media, Inc. O'Reilly logo is a registered trademark of O'Reilly Media, Inc. 00000